A STUDY OF GR

A STUDY OF
GREGORY PALAMAS

JOHN MEYENDORFF

Translated by
GEORGE LAWRENCE

ST VLADIMIR'S SEMINARY PRESS
CRESTWOOD, NEW YORK 10707
1998

Library of Congress Cataloging-in-Publication Data

Meyendorff, John, 1926-1992
 [Introduction à l'étude de Grégoire Palamas. English]
 A study of Gregory Palamas / John Meyendorff; translated by George Lawrence.
   p.   cm.
 Originally published: 2nd ed. London: Faith Press, 1974, c1964.
 Includes bibliographical references and index.
 ISBN 0-913836-14-1 (alk. Paper)
 1. Gregory Palamas, Saint, 1296-1359.   I. Title.
BX395.P3M413   1998
281.9'092—dc21   98-36076
                                                              CIP

A STUDY OF GREGORY PALAMAS

First published in English in 1964
by
The Faith Press
Second edition 1974

This translation © George Lawrence, 1964

Translated from the French
Introduction à l'étude de Grégoire Palamas

Reprinted in 1998 by
ST VLADIMIR'S SEMINARY PRESS
575 Scarsdale Rd., Crestwood, NY 10707
1-800-204-2665

ISBN 0-913836-14-1

All Rights Reserved.

PRINTED IN THE UNITED STATES OF AMERICA

PREFACE

MEDIAEVAL Byzantine thought is still virgin land which has only just begun to be cleared. In contrast to the Western Middle Ages which developed steadily and without a break in the direction of our Modern World, the Byzantine East has had no direct heirs able to carry on that intellectual tradition, or even simply to edit the works of the past. Byzantine culture died a sudden death at the hands of the Turks in 1453. It is certainly to the great credit of the survivors of that catastrophe and their descendants, and to that of their Slav and Rumanian pupils, that they preserved the traditions of the past in their liturgy, in the spiritual life of the monasteries, and in some more or less clandestine schools. But they seldom possessed the material means or the education necessary to do so in a systematic and intellectually creative way. The Slavic countries, Russia in particular, might have been able to take the place of Byzantium, but they were often more strongly attracted towards the West of their own time than to their Byzantine past. . . . Especially in the seventeenth and eighteenth centuries, the time when the West was publishing the great editions of the Fathers which we still use to-day, the Christian East was in a particularly deplorable condition. Only a few isolated men of learning were in a position to revive the tradition. Peculiar respect is therefore due to Dositheos of Jerusalem, Nikodemos the Hagiorite and some others, although their works do not compare in extent or quality with that of their Western contemporaries.

Those are the essential reasons why so few Byzantine texts have been published in the East. In the West too only a few isolated individuals took any interest in the Greeks after the schism.

So to-day when we come to study such a personality as Gregory Palamas, who was responsible for a decisive step in the history of the Christian East, and whom the Orthodox Church ranks among its greatest doctors, we find that three-quarters of his works are unpublished. The manuscript sources which we need to study in order to follow the historic and doctrinal clashes in which he played so large a part, are too extensive to be digested completely, although detailed enough to undermine the bold hypotheses which the imagination of historians has sometimes substituted for lacking original sources.

My first task was therefore to list and briefly analyse Palamas's works. For the results of that work the interested reader must be referred to the Appendix to the French edition of this book, where also I have made due acknowledgment to those who preceded me in such labours.

Here I only wish to state the main conclusions, admittedly only provisional ones, to which I have come about matters of history and doctrine concerning Palamas.

Study of the details of Palamas's life, the written testimonies of contemporaries, and the attitude adopted towards him by the great men of that time, lead me to the conclusion that the great majority of his contemporaries did not regard him as an innovator, but rather as the spokesman of conservative Orthodoxy. It was purely political reasons which led to the condemnation under which he suffered for two years. If political circumstances had been different, the 'Palamite controversy' could not have lasted for more than a few months. That is a fact which, I think, impartial historians should understand. The doctrine which Palamas was defending, and which was attacked by only a very limited number of Byzantine theologians taking different points of view and without any unity among themselves, appears as a development of the teaching of the Greek Fathers. His teaching therefore should be judged by reference to them, and not to systems worked out afterwards. It must also be realized that Palamas formulated his views progressively as was required by his polemics against his adversaries. This progressive development, studied in detail in the second part of this book, helps one to understand the sometimes ambiguous formulas in which his teaching was expressed, and which are only important in so far as they help towards an understanding of his essential doctrine. To judge the great Byzantine theologian objectively, one must place him in the context of his own spiritual world. I feel sure that the present revival of patristic studies will aid the better understanding and appreciation in the West of a theologian who, in some respects, is more in tune than others with the preoccupations of modern thought.

If the doctrinal conclusions of the East and the West seem divergent, and if the distance separating Palamas and Thomas Aquinas seems hard to cross, it is nonetheless true that both branches of the separated Christian world go back to a common Patristic tradition and, ultimately, to a common Gospel. If a common and concerted return to the sources could determine our attitude to teachers of the later date, the clash between the latter would perhaps become less violent.

J. MEYENDORFF

FOREWORD TO THE ENGLISH EDITION

The original French edition of my study (*Introduction à l'étude de Grégoire Palamas*, Patristica, Sorbonensia, collection dirigée par H.-I. Marrou, No. 3, Editions du Seuil, Paris, 1959) contains more substantial footnotes and two important appendices with an analysis of Palamas writings—both published and unpublished—and of the major Byzantine sources related to his life and time. In the present English edition, I limited myself to the essential results of my research and to the most indispensable references. The English text, although it does not replace entirely the more documented French original, constitutes however a progress in my study of Palamas in as much as it gave me an opportunity to correct a few errors and to give consideration to several pertinent remarks of my critics.

To all those who thus contributed to the completion of my work I wish to express here my sincere gratitude.

J.M.

CONTENTS

PREFACE *page* 5

FOREWORD TO THE ENGLISH EDITION 7

PART ONE: THE MAN

I. THE IMMEDIATE FORERUNNERS 13

II. HIS EARLY YEARS 28

III. BARLAAM AND THE COUNCILS OF 1341 42

IV. THE TIME OF CIVIL WAR (1341–1347) 63

V. GREGORY PALAMAS: ARCHBISHOP IN THESSALONICA 86

VI. THE LAST YEARS 102

PART TWO: THE THOUGHT OF PALAMAS

I. OPPOSITION TO PROFANE HELLENISM: MAN DEPRIVED OF GRACE 116

II. THEOLOGICAL INTEGRATION OF HESYCHASM: THE LIFE IN CHRIST 134

III. CHRIST AND DEIFIED HUMANITY: REDEMPTION, DEIFICATION AND ECCLESIOLOGY 157

IV. A THEOLOGY OF HISTORY: SYMBOLS AND REALITIES 185

V. AN EXISTENTIAL THEOLOGY: ESSENCE AND ENERGY 202

VI. TWO PARTICULAR PROBLEMS: PROCESSION OF THE HOLY SPIRIT AND MARIOLOGY 228

CONCLUSION 237

BIBLIOGRAPHICAL NOTE 241

INDEX 242

PART ONE
THE MAN

CHAPTER I

THE IMMEDIATE FORERUNNERS

THE period before the theological disputes of the fourteenth century at Constantinople has as yet been little studied. It was a time of external crisis, internal conflict, and intellectual renaissance. This is not the place to deal with the matter at length, and we will only mention a few personalities who certainly had a direct influence on Palamas, and who all have played a prominent part in the religious and political life of their time.

Gregory of Cyprus

Gregory of Cyprus, Patriarch from 1283 to 1289, must come first, although his influence is more apparent in certain theological formulas than in spiritual life. No one has yet made a complete analysis of his theological thought, but many writers have seen the relation between his formulations and those of Palamas.[1] In principle he favoured the negotiations for religious union with the West, but he was disappointed with the way such union took shape at Lyons—simply by the will of the Emperor without any real theological dialogue—and, being raised to the patriarchate soon after the death of Michael VIII, he presided at the Council of Blakhernae which condemned the Byzantine 'Latinophrones.' Nevertheless Gregory was the only theologian who, after this triumph of Orthodox reaction, sought to find a real solution to that dialogue of the deaf, the thirteenth century controversy between Greeks and Latins about the procession of the Holy Spirit. Instead of simply repeating Photius's formulas about the 'eternal procession' of the Holy Spirit from the Father alone and the 'emission in time' by the Son, Gregory recognized the need to express the permanent relationship existing between the Son and the Holy Spirit as divine hypostases, and he spoke of an 'eternal manifestation' (ἔκφανσις ἀΐδιος) of the Spirit by the Son.

The Tome of 1285

This formula was not in fact an innovation in Byzantine theology; very similar terms can be found in the documents dealing with the negotia-

[1] For his doctrine see Troitski, *K istorii sporov po voprosu ob iskhozhdenii Sviatago Dukha*, in *Khristianskoe Chtenie*, LXIX, 1889, I, 338–77; II, 280–352, 520–70; cf. also M. Jugie, *Theologia Dogmatica Christianorum Orientalium*, II, pp. 358–66.

tions at Nymphaion, in 1234, under the Patriarch Germanos II. Gregory of Cyprus did no more than to develop this conception in several of his writings. We will confine ourselves to quoting the text of the *Tome* published by the Council of 1285, which Gennadios Scholarios [2] considered as equal in authority to an Oecumenical Council, and which was written by Gregory of Cyprus : 'It is recognized that the very Paraklete shines and manifests Itself eternally by the intermediary of the Son, as light shines from the sun by the intermediary of rays . . .; but that does not mean that It comes into being through the Son or from the Son.' [3] Gregory of Cyprus is here expressing himself in a different context to that in which Palamas's thought developed, but he certainly introduced the same distinction as did Palamas. We shall see that in one of his first works, the *Apodictic Treatises*, which deals in particular with the *Filioque* clause, Palamas takes up and develops Gregory of Cyprus's central conception without, however, referring to him explicitly. Later, the same terminology will be used in his polemics against Barlaam and Akindynos.

After the publication of his *Tome*, Gregory was violently attacked by some members of the Byzantine clergy, and Constantinople became the scene of passionate theological discussions. The circumstances and the side issues of these disputes have never been studied in detail, but they do, to a great extent, anticipate the Palamite controversy. All the antiuniate bishops appended their signatures at the bottom of the document.[4] However the argument began again when a monk named Mark, who belonged to the entourage of the Patriarch, published an 'authorized' commentary on the *Tome* in which he wanted to give a general meaning to the term 'procession' (ἐκπόρευσις), which corresponds to the Latin *processio* and is traditionally used to designate the hypostatic character of the Holy Spirit; according to Mark ἐκπόρευσις would be no more than a synonym for the other terms also used to designate the eternal manifestation of the Spirit (ἔλλαμψις, πρόοδος, ἔκφανσις, φανέρωσις, etc.).[5] Such a generalized use of the term clearly made it possible to give an inoffensive interpretation to certain texts of the Fathers which appeared to favour the Latins, but it was in danger of bringing into confusion the universally accepted doctrine of the Trinity, since it took away its primary sense from the term designating the relation between the Holy Spirit and the Father. Mark, whose commentary has not come down to us, sheltered under the Patriarch's authority; the latter found

[2] Ed. Petit-Jugie, III, Paris, 1930, pp. 85, 89, 173.
[3] Migne, *P.G.* 142, col. 240C; see also col. 250AC, 251B, 266C, 267B, etc.
[4] V. Laurent, *Les signataires du second concile des Blakhernes*, in *Echos d'Orient*, XXVI, 1927, pp. 129–49.
[5] *Letter of John Chilas to Andronicus II*, P. 6, 142, 245C.

himself compromised in the eyes of an important party among the bishops. Several of the bishops, John Chilas of Ephesus, Daniel of Cyzicus and Theoleptus of Philadelphia, gave up mentioning his name in the liturgy.[6] But there was no unity in this opposition: some blamed the Patriarch for the actual text of the *Tome* which they had themselves signed, but which seemed ambiguous to them after the interpretation given to it by Mark. They would not agree to the expression 'eternal manifestation' of the Spirit, and thus appear as direct precursors of Akindynos and Nicephorus Gregoras: 'procession through the Son' ($\pi\rho o\acute{\epsilon}\lambda\epsilon v\sigma\iota\varsigma$ $\delta\iota'$ $v\acute{\iota}o\hat{v}$) could only mean an emission *in time* of the Spirit, a created grace whereas the expression should designate the eternal procession of the divine Hypostasis itself.[7] This party, whose chief seems to have been John Chilas, Metropolitan of Ephesus, would not accept the thoughtful reconsideration which allowed Gregory of Cyprus to introduce a new traditional element into the *Filioque* controversy, so as to rescue it from the evident impasse into which it had been brought by the disputants' war of words. Another group, with Theoleptus of Philadelphia at its head, simply wanted Mark to be disowned, and only blamed the Patriarch for his support of him. When Gregory of Cyprus did publicly dissociate himself from Mark, Theoleptus and his followers willingly pronounced him orthodox, and opposed those who with John of Ephesus and Daniel of Cyzicus wanted to bring the Patriarch to judgment. The latter, moreover, agreed to draw back when he had had the moral satisfaction of having his orthodoxy publicly recognized.[8] But the adversaries of the doctrine enunciated in the *Tome* did not put down their arms. However, in the tempestuous meetings over which emperor Andronicus II presided in the palace, they did not succeed in having the text modified.[9] The *Tome* of 1285 in its original form expressing the relation between the Son and the Spirit as an 'eternal manifestation' of the Spirit by the Son, continued to be considered the official exposition of Orthodox doctrine about the procession.

From Gregory of Cyprus to Palamas

The connection between these thirteenth century events and the controversies of the fourteenth century becomes clear when one has understood the similarity between the thought of Gregory of Cyprus and of Palamas; his contemporaries too were aware of this. On the Palamite side patriarch Philotheus refers to Gregory and praises him because he

---

[6] Pachymeres, *De Andronico Paleologo*, II, 6, Bonn, II, 122.
[7] Gregory of Cyprus, *Apology*, P.G. 142, 266C, 267B.
[8] Pachymeres, ibid., II, 8–10, pp. 127–33.
[9] ibid., pp. 133–4.

had defended the doctrine concerning 'the Divinity, divine energy, holy illumination and participation.'[10] On the other hand Akindynos, who led the anti-Palamites between 1341 and 1347, in several very revealing passages tries to interpret the case of Gregory of Cyprus so as to favour his own views. He recognizes that Gregory's conceptions are the same as those of Palamas,[11] but he has his own peculiar account of what happened in 1289, and writes as follows: 'The Cypriot who had become Patriarch of the Oecumenical Church, having accepted, I do not know why, in his treatises against the Latins the doctrine according to which our Lord, by breathing upon the Apostles, granted them an eternal manifestation, different from the Spirit itself Creator of all things, was removed from his high position and deposed by the wise and great Emperor and by the synod of that time.'[12] In fact he favoured the Latins. 'If he had said that the most divine Spirit itself was given to the Apostles . . . or that a grace different from the divine Spirit, neither eternal nor uncreated, was in question . . . he would not have spoken in favour of the Latins, nor contradicted our dogmas.' Nevertheless, Akindynos recognizes, the Emperor and the synod treated him with 'a certain mildness': they were, in fact, anxious not to give the Latins the pleasure of seeing the Orthodox Patriarch fall so quickly into heresy. 'It would have been right for this dogma to be condemned by the synod, so that both it and its author should be publicly exposed. But they were content simply with the deposition of the man to blame, thinking that the dogma could be left to condemn itself by its own absurdity.'[13]

That very plainly shows how troublesome the text of the *Tome* of 1285 was for the adversaries of the Palamites in the fourteenth century, who were not specially recruited, as has often been thought and written, among the *Latinophrones* drawing their inspiration from Thomist thought, but were rather representatives of a frozen theology, of an oriental scholasticism which was content to manipulate Patristic formulas without regard to the real problems of the time. Akindynos was therefore bound to give his own interpretation to the Cypriot Patriarch's case, but he could not do so without falling into inconsistencies: if it was really the doctrine of 'eternal manifestation' and not the Patriarch's attitude to the monk Mark, which was the reason for his fall, why had the expression 'favouring the Latins' been preserved in the

---

[10] *Contra Gregoram,* VI, P.G. 151, col. 915CD. Another Palamite theologian, Joseph Calothetos, praises Gregory of Cyprus in similar terms (*Life of Athanasius,* in Θρακικά, XIII, 1940, p. 87).
[11] *Against Palamas* VII, Monac. gr. 223, *fol.* 355 2v.
[12] ibid., V, *fol.* 229v; VII, *fol.* 355v.
[13] ibid., *fol.* 229v–30v.

text of the *Tome*? Akindynos is also obliged to change Gregory's voluntary and conditional withdrawal, the text of which is given by Pachymeres,[14] into a formal deposition (καθαίρεσις).

In truth the theological discussions of the end of the thirteenth century, however wearisome they may appear, did prepare the way for the definite formulation of Palamas's doctrine. It is interesting to realize that the point of departure for this formulation was an attempt to enter into an understanding argument with Latin theology, and that the adversaries of Gregory, and thereafter of Palamas, belonged to that school of verbal polemics which, for too long unfortunately, carried on the *Filioque* controversy.

Theoleptus of Philadelphia

The most important personality after Gregory of Cyprus was Theoleptus of Philadelphia, to whom Palamas twice refers as one of the chief inspirers of the renewal of hesychasm and whose works were included later in the famous *Philocalia*. Gregory mentions him among those 'men who bore witness shortly before our time, and who are recognized to have possessed the power of the Holy Spirit,' and 'have passed on to us these things by word of mouth.'[15] The context shows that this refers to the well-known 'method' of prayer, which consisted in suggesting practical means to the monks to help them in 'vigilance' (νῆψις) of prayer: fixing their eyes on 'the middle of the body,' and control of breathing combined with 'the prayer of Jesus.' According to Philotheus, Palamas himself was initiated to this method by Theoleptus.[16] The latter, as we have already seen, played an important part in the discussions about the 'eternal manifestation,' and was generally active in the religious and political life of his time.[17] His authority remained greatly respected both by Palamites and by their opponents. Besides Palamas, Arsenius of Tyre mentions him with respect.[18] On the other hand Theoleptus counted among his spiritual daughters the princess Irene, daughter of Nicephorus Choumnos, who married the despot John Palaeologus, son of Andronicus II; when she became a widow she entered a convent under the name of Eulogia,[19] and from 1341 to 1347

---

[14] *De Andronico Paleologo*, II, 9, Bonn, II, 130–1.
[15] *Triads for the defence of the hesychasts*, I, 2, 12; cf. II, 2, 3 (the *Triads* will be later quoted as *Tr.*; the numbers refer to my edition, *Spicilegium Sacrum Lovaniense*, vol. 29–30, Louvain, 1959).
[16] *Encomion* of Palamas, P.G. CLI, 561A.
[17] cf. J. Gouillard, *Théolepte*, in *Dict. de théol. cath.*, XIV, 1 (1946), col. 339–41.
[18] *Vat. gr.* 1111, pars. IV, fol. 226–226v.
[19] V. Laurent, *Une princesse byzantine au cloître*, in *Echos d'Orient*, XXIX, 1930, pp. 29–60.

was one of Akindynos's firmest supporters. Theoleptus was long dead (before 1327) when Eulogia took such an active part in this great theological controversy, and it is not certain that he would have advised her to follow this course.

Theoleptus and hesychasm

Theoleptus's works are almost entirely unpublished, but we can form an impression about them from S. Salaville's interesting publications [20]: he considers Theoleptus a hesychast 'of good alloy' because there is nowhere in his works a description of the corporal 'method' of prayer. That 'method' was, in fact, only a secondary and inessential feature in the monastic spirituality of the time, and it was only the attacks launched against it by Barlaam of Calabria that brought it into prominence. Theoleptus may very well have advised some of his disciples to follow it without referring to it in his spiritual works: it is indeed certain that he did so, for Palamas would have had no reason to cite the bishop of Philadelphia if it had not been well known at the time that at Athos Theoleptos had been the disciple of Nicephorus the Hesychast, author of the treatise in which the method is described.[21]

We will come back later to the question of the integration of the method into Palamas's scheme of theological thought. Here it is enough to state that the practice of 'pure prayer,' whether or not accompanied by the corporal method, was common to Byzantine monks whose views, in other respects, were divergent. The spread of the practice does not date from the thirteenth century; already in the eleventh century Symeon the New Theologian had passed his whole life in cenobitic monasteries, while surrendering himself to a personal and intensive mystical devotion to the Name of Jesus. It is also certain that Symeon helped to prepare the fusion of the very different spiritual schools, both equally popular in the East, of St. John of the Ladder and St. Theodore the Studite. Whereas in early monasticism 'hesychia' necessarily implied a solitary life as far from men as possible, Symeon taught the practice thereof in the very centre of Constantinople, at the monastery of Stoudios. Theoleptus of Philadelphia conformed to the same hesychast-cenobite type: he was also well aware of the ancient tradition of anchorite hesychasm, but was not very favourable towards it.[22] The hesychasm which he

---

[20] *Formes de prière d'après un Byzantin du XIVe siècle*, in *Echos d'Orient*, XXXIX, 1940, pp. 1–25; cf. also Salaville's publications of texts in *Etudes byzantines*, II, 1944, pp. 119–25; V, 1947, pp. 101–36; in *Mélanges J. de Ghellinck*, II, 1951, pp. 877–87.

[21] cf. Palamas, *Tr.* II, 2, 3; also Nicephorus Choumnos, in Boissonade, *Anecdota graeca*, V, Paris 1833, pp. 201–3; Philotheus, *Encomion*, P. 6, CLI, 561A.

[22] Salaville, in *Etudes byzantines*, II, 1944, p. 120.

recommended is spiritual in nature: the concepts of ἡσυχία (quietude) and νῆψις (spiritual vigilance) come so close with him that they are almost synonyms, and in no way imply flight into the desert. 'Quietly in thy house,' he writes to Irene, 'entertain the memory of God: remove your spirit from everything, throw it towards God without words, and pour out before him all the dispositions of thy heart, clinging to him by love. For the memory of God is a contemplation of God, which draws the vision and the desire of the intelligence to him, and illuminates it with his own light.' [23]

'Suggestive synthesis of the ancient oriental mystical doctrines,' [24] the spirituality of Theoleptus is expressed in just the same terms as served Palamas to build his theological system. Moreover there is nothing original in this spirituality as compared with the earlier traditions, unless it be the simple and direct way in which Theoleptus explains it. What is particularly characteristic of the thought of the saintly bishop of Philadelphia is his sacramentalism and his sense of the Christian's responsibilities for the historic Church: these two traits make a marked distinction between him and spiritual writers of the Christian East who disinterest themselves, apparently at least, from all that does not concern the perfecting of the inner nature of the monk. The Bishop of Philadelphia, striving against the internal dissensions of the Byzantine Church—the case of Gregory of Cyprus and the Arsenite schism—shows an acute concern for local ecclesiastical unity and for the sacramental unity of the faithful. 'Once these people (the schismatics) are reunited with you, the Church grows, and the members come close together in one complete whole; the Church grows strong . . . our only head, Christ, then appears as the leader who holds us bound to him and bound to one another by the ties of the one faith, the one doctrine, and the one Church.' [25] 'The Son of God,' he continues, 'was made man for thee, and he led a life free from sin. By holy baptism and by his precious blood which he spilt upon the cross, he has re-created thee. . . . He has formed local churches, each a paradise, and assembled us therein; but he has established the Church, one in faith and doctrine. . . . The trees of this paradise are the orthodox pastors . . . who have been sent to churches appointed and charged with the

[23] *P.G.* CXLIII, 389A.
[24] Un moine de l'Eglise d'Orient, *La prière de Jésus*, Chevetogne, 1951, pp. 49–50.
[25] *Etudes byzantines*, V, 1947, p. 123. Theoleptus seems to have been one of the most radical adversaries of the Arsenites and opposed the measure of clemency taken in their favour in 1310 by patriarch Niphon I and maintained by John XIII (V. Laurent, *Les grandes crises religieuses à Byzance*, in *Académie Roumaine. Bulletin de la section hist.*, XXVI, 1945, pp. 61–89; *Les crises religieuses à Byzance*, in *Revue des études byzantines*, XVIII, 1960, pp. 45–54).

duty of instructing and governing Christians. . . . The bishop is the mediator between God and men. In the name of the people he constantly offers to God requests, supplications, prayers and thanksgivings. The act which is celebrated by orthodox priests and recognized in "the holy gifts," becomes the body and blood of Christ; such is the effect of the epiclesis of prayers and the descent of the Holy Spirit. . . . Not to participate in the salutary communion or to keep away from it . . . is that not to proclaim that Christ was no more than a man?' [26]

It is rare to find an Orthodox Byzantine express in such vivid words the sacramental essence which is the foundation of the hierarchic structure of the Church. Theoleptus certainly deserves credit for integrating the spiritual tradition—often a spiritualizing one—of the Oriental Christian mystics into an ecclesiological and Christocentric framework. He is the harbinger of the theological and sacramental revival associated with Palamas and Nicholas Cabasilas. The list which S. Salaville has made of his unpublished works, makes us hope that they will soon be published, and enable us better to understand the thought of this spiritual master mind, and the influence he exercised.

Athanasius I

Palamas mentions the name of the Patriarch of Constantinople, Athanasius I, beside that of Theoleptus in his list of the spiritual masters at the beginning of the fourteenth century who taught the psychotechnical method of prayer: 'That Athanasius who for many years lent lustre to the patriarchal throne, and whose tomb God honoured (by miracles).' [27] In a similar context Athanasius is mentioned by a marginal note in a manuscript containing Cantacuzene's antirrhetics against Prochoros Cydones: according to that note Athanasius was dialectician, prophet and miracle-worker, and Cantacuzene knew him personally in his youth.[28] Athanasius was admired both in the circle round Palamas, and by some of his adversaries. Nicephorus Gregoras in his 'History' is in general favourable both to the man and to his actions.

Athanasius was elevated to the patriarchate in 1289 to replace Gregory of Cyprus. He was deposed in 1293, but restored for a second time for six years (1303–9). Several writers have given an account of his activities,[29] but his own works—especially a very interesting cor-

[26] *Etudes byzantines,* ibid., pp. 123–9.
[27] *Tr.* I, 2, 12.
[28] *Paris gr.* 1347, *fol.* 93v; cf. *Paris gr.* 1341, *fol.* 31v–2.
[29] Two contemporaries have composed *Lives* of Athanasius: Joseph Calothetos, a known Palamite theologian (ed. by Athanasius in Θρακικά, XIII, 1940, pp. 59–107; repr. in Ἁγιορειτικὴ Βιβλιοθήκη, XV, 1950, pp. 107–41) and

respondence,[30] an important document for the religious and social history of Byzantium—remain largely unpublished.

His reforms

A simple monk who had lived in the monasteries of Asia Minor, Palestine and Mount Athos, having no secular education and ascetic in his private life, Athanasius set about reforming the morals of the clergy, of the Court and of Byzantine society, intervened in politics, where he was concerned to advance Christian principles and a strict loyalty to orthodoxy, and made himself the defender of the poor of the capital. All Athanasius's activity was dominated by a preoccupation for the living witness which, in his view, Christianity must bear in the context of historical reality. In common with several Byzantine prelates of his time —Arsenius, John Calecas and Philotheus—he conceived his duty as patriarch as including both a spiritual aspect and an obligation to play a political part in the Byzantine theocracy, a counterpart to the Emperor's authority in ecclesiastical matters. Thus Athanasius gave Andronicus II somewhat imperious advice, in the name of the interests of orthodoxy and morality, in such matters as the action he should take with regard to the notorious Catalan company of Roger de Flor, and about his matrimonial projects for his sons. The Patriarch was equally strict with the clergy: he suppressed the permanent synod of Constantinople which gave the bishops an excuse to abandon the care of their dioceses, and go and intrigue in the capital, and he re-established the ancient custom of an annual synod.[31] The wealth of some clerics roused his indignation: 'Their minds are always bent on criticizing and complaining about taxes and benevolences.' He was not afraid to castigate by name a certain bishop who drew an annual income of 800 pieces of gold from the property of the church, and another who possessed at Constantinople 'a vineyard, stables, a garden, workshops and benefices.'[32] He strove by all means to re-establish discipline in the monasteries, and to make the monks live in ascetic poverty. Monks, appointed by the Patriarch, were sent as visitors to inspect the convents and try to suppress all signs of material wealth there. 'He took the

Theoctistos the Studite (complete edition by A. Papadopoulos-Kerameus, in *Zapiski istoriko-filologicheskago fakul'teta* of the University of St. Petersburg, LXXVI, 1905, pp. 1–51; for the author, see A. Ehrhard, *Ueberlieferung und Bestand der hagiographischen und homiletischen Literatur der Byzantiner*, III, Berlin, 1952, p. 991).

[30] cf. R. Guilland, in *Mélanges Diehl*, I, 1930, pp. 121–40; M. Banescu, in *Académie roumaine. Bulletin de la section hist.*, XXIII, 1942, pp. 1–28.

[31] See text published in Gennadios, Ἱστορία τοῦ οἰκουμενικοῦ πατριαρχείου, Athens, 1953, p. 364, cf. Gregoras, *Hist.*, VI, 5, Bonn, I, 182.

[32] Guilland, op. cit., pp. 131–2.

money from the monasteries,' writes Pachymeres, 'confiscating it as temptation to sin, and hoping thus to extinguish the fire of passion.'[33] It was with that money that Athanasius was able to feed the needy in a great famine which ravaged Constantinople.[34] The Metropolitans, members of the Holy Synod, opposed these sequestrations, and Athanasius asked the Emperor to drive them out of the capital.[35]

Athanasius and monastic property

The Patriarch also, if we can trust a valuable hint of Pachymeres, created an important precedent by favouring the sequestration of ecclesiastical property to meet the urgent needs of the State. It is even possible that in this matter it was Athanasius who suggested the idea to Andronicus II with whom he was in constant personal touch, and who would not have dared, on his own, to adopt such a radical measure. Since Alexis Comnenus no emperor had in fact touched the goods of the church. Pachymeres relates that, 'it appeared most necessary, in view of the whole state of affairs, to take the only measure which remained possible; it was decided that property given in *pronoia* to the monasteries, churches and the Emperor's entourage, should be taken from their owners and given to the soldiers. . . . A branch of olive, with no letter, was sent by the Patriarch to the Emperor: he was therefore able to act as he thought best relying on his very great confidence in the Patriarch.'[36] It is true that it was a question of a local measure to prevent a speedy invasion of the Turks, and Pachymeres adds that this scheme of secularization remained a project only, as the imperial officers charged with its execution could not reach the spot in time.

His influence

The fact that Gregory Palamas and those in his circle had a particular veneration for Athanasius, merits our attention. The extreme complexity of politico-religious events in the fourteenth century is all too often simplified by explaining the hesychast success as due to a conjunction of the interests of the great feudal nobility and the property owning monasteries. It is true that the imperial government did try in that time to turn church land to its own use by giving it to the soldiers, and some monks did protest against these measures. But sequestrations of

---

[33] *De Andronico Pal.*, II, 16, Bonn, II, 149; cf. Gregoras, *Hist.*, VI, 5, Bonn, I, 182–3; Calothetos, *Life*, ed. cit., p. 94.
[34] Banescu, op. cit., pp. 25–7.
[35] *Letter to Andronicus II*, Paris. Suppl. gr. 516, pp. 141–141v.
[36] *De Andronico Pal.*, V, g, Bonn, p. 390; cf. interpretations of the text by P. Charanis, *The monastic properties and the State in the Byzantine Empire*, in *Dumbarton Oaks Papers*, 4, 1948, p. 111, and I. Ševčenko, *Nicholas Cabasilas' antizealot discourse*, in *Dumb. Oaks Papers*, 9, 1957, p. 157, n. 125.

monastic property equally took place when Cantacuzene, the great feudal lord and defender of the hesychasts, was in power as Great Domestic, and after he had proclaimed himself Emperor.[37] Never, so far as we know, did any of the leaders of the hesychast party protest against this policy whether pursued by Cantacuzene or by his adversaries. The only document which does seem to raise a vehement protest against the sequestration of monastic property is the 'Discourse' of Nicholas Cabasilas. Until I. Ševčenko's recent study of this document,[38] it might have appeared that it was exactly for that reason that the Zealots of Thessalonica fought the Palamite party; but it now seems that there is no document existing which says that the Zealots systematically sequestrated the property of monasteries. Nicholas Cabasilas was not writing about the Zealots, but, very probably, about the government of Constantinople with the *megas dux* Apocaucos and the Patriarch John Calecas at its head. Cabasilas was a young humanist, representative of the Byzantine aristocracy and a partisan of Cantacuzene, but it is not certain that, about 1342–6 which is the time when he wrote his 'Discourse,' he was a spokesman for Palamas. So there is no proof that the hesychasts shared his views about secularization. Moreover, even if it could be regarded as a Palamite manifesto, this 'Discourse' deals with the case of John Calecas exclusively, and may have been provoked by particular circumstances, notably persecutions directed at the monks for doctrinal reasons and the way in which the Patriarch used his power.

The question of ecclesiastical property played an important part throughout the fourteenth century. In 1367, for instance, the Emperor John V asked the Patriarch Philotheus, the principal disciple of Palamas, to surrender to him two villages belonging to St. Sophia. The Patriarch answered by a polite letter in which he stated the official canonical doctrine that the Patriarch and the bishops are not the owners, but only the guardians of the property belonging to the church, and as a result have no right to alienate it. The letter, however, ended in unexpected fashion: 'But if the sacred Emperor desires to take the villages on his own authority, let him do what he wishes, for it was he who gave them to the church, and if he himself desires to take them, let him do so; he has the authority to act in this sphere as he wishes. We ourselves will never do it, whatever may happen.'[39]

This answer of the Patriarch Philotheus is generally interpreted as a categorical refusal to comply with the Emperor's demand. But we

---

[37] cf. G. Ostrogorsky, *Pour l'histoire de la féodalité byzantine*, Bruxelles, 1954, p. 155; Soloviev-Moshin, *Grčke povelje Srpskich Vladara*, Belgrade, 1936, n. 21.
[38] *Dumbarton Oaks Papers*, 9, 1957.
[39] Miklosich-Müller, *Acta Patriarchatus C-ni*, I, 507–8.

think it is, in essentials, just the same as the branch of olive which Athanasius sent to Andronicus II sixty years before. By himself the Patriarch could not allow the sequestration of church property, of which in theory he was only the trustee, but he could quite well tolerate, and even approve, a unilateral act by the Emperor. This interpretation seems confirmed by the fact that four years later, in 1371, after the great Turkish victory of Marica, when the government took away half the monastic lands to distribute them to the soldiers by right of *pronoia*, this same Philotheus, who was still Patriarch, did not raise the slightest protest.[40]

Such facts are clearly insufficient to support an assertion that all the disciples of Palamas in the fourteenth century favoured the sequestration of ecclesiastical property in whatsoever circumstances and by whatsoever government. But it is important to remember that the hesychasts were traditionally at variance, especially at Athos, with the large cenobitic monasteries which were great landowners and constant beneficiaries of imperial favours. Palamas himself, in writing the life of St. Peter the Athonite, was to make out the case for a hermit's life. Likewise the many lives of saints written by his disciple, the Patriarch Philotheus, are all consecrated to the veneration of hesychasts living in small groups and working with their hands. They relate many stories about the latter, when placed at the head of large cenobitic monasteries, trying in vain to reform their life. That was especially the case with Gregory, when he was for a short time *hegoumenos* of Esphigmenou. So hesychasts are not normally inclined to defend monastic property. Their triumph in 1347 and 1351, and the power they acquired by having their representatives made patriarch and bishops of most of the sees, did not in any way hold up the process of secularization of church property. Promoting greater independence of the church towards the State, which was also the policy of Athanasius I, the Palamites may have opposed particular cases of sequestration, especially when faced by a government hostile to Orthodoxy, but, in general, they easily accepted it. In the case of Philotheus, the exceptional authorities which he was able to give to the office of Patriarch, certainly led him to wish to put some check on the process of secularization, just as he wished to control imperial policy in the name of the Church. That explains the nuances of his reply to John V. Finally, the influence of the hesychast movement was exercised in the same direction in the Slav countries, in Bulgaria, Serbia and especially Russia. The Russian hesychasts in particular were to be resolute supporters of monastic poverty and formally approved the policy of sequestration : the first thrust in that direction was to come

[40] G. Ostrogorsky, op. cit., p. 161.

from the Metropolitan Cyprian of Kiev (1390–1406) a former disciple of the Bulgarian hesychasts.

Nature of the hesychast revival

In dwelling at some length on the spiritual authorities to whom Palamas himself refers in defending his doctrine, I have been anxious to show that Byzantine hesychasm of the fourteenth century was far from being a movement of esoteric mysticism and unhealthy enthusiasm. It was a spiritual revival which touched every aspect of the Christian life, inner perfection as well as the sacramental life and social witness. Gregory of Cyprus in theology, Theoleptus in spirituality and ecclesiology, and Athanasius in practical affairs, breathed new life into the ancient and hardened arteries of Byzantine Christian society.

One also notes that, in a different cultural context and in very peculiar historical circumstances, Byzantine religious life at that time was following a course not very unlike that of the West: parallel with the progress of a profane humanism of more or less pagan tendency, a movement of spiritual revival putting the claims of Christianity at their highest is evident in monastic circles and exercises a great influence. It was that movement which finally triumphed in the East, and that triumph enabled Oriental Christianity to survive under the Turkish yoke, and long to remain a stranger to the great crisis of secularism which was brought on by the Renaissance in the West.

It has been said above that Palamas mentioned the names of Theoleptus and Athanasius in connection with the practice of the psycho-technical method of prayer. That method, in fact, appeared to most of their contemporaries as a normal element in monastic spirituality. Even men of action such as those two prelates recommended it. Whatever may have been its origin, the method was known very widely throughout the monasteries, and it was interpreted in a way that conformed completely with the spiritual tradition of the East: Barlaam of Calabria was practically the only man who attacked it; on that point he was disavowed by Akindynos and the later anti-Palamites.

The Mountain of St. Auxentius

Besides Theoleptus and Athanasius, Palamas mentions the names of several other monks of the same school, Nilus who came from Italy, Seliotes, Elias, Gabriel and Athanasius Lepentrinos.[41] Most of these names are known; they were monks of Mount Auxentius, a monastery on the eastern shore of the Bosphorus, not far from Chalcedon.[42]

[41] *Tr.* I, 2, 12; II, 2, 3.
[42] Theoctistos, *Life of Athanasius*, ed. cit., p. 9; cf. J. Pargroire, *Le Mont Saint-Auxence*, in *Revue de l'Orient chrétien*, 8, 1903, pp. 553–5; cf. our Introduction to the text of the *Triads*, pp. XLI–XLII.

Athanasius Lepentrinos was one of the leaders of the Arsenite party in 1284, and as such took part in the conferences at Adramyttium, where Andronicus II sought to re-establish ecclesiastical peace.[43] Nilus, 'the Italian,' may probably be identified with one of the teachers of Theoleptus of Philadelphia, to whom Nicephorus Choumnos refers,[44] and with the monk Nilus 'who came from Sicily,' mentioned by Pachymeres. According to Pachymeres, Nilus taught that charity should not be given to those who were already sufficiently rich. Pachymeres describes such teaching as an abomination preached by Nilus 'to the distress of the Roman Empire': Pachymeres's violent condemnation of such sensible teaching is explained by the context; in 1264 disciples of Nilus had been introduced to the Despot John Paleologus, 'who loved monks' and put some restraint on his largesses; a few lines farther down Pachymeres remarks that 'in the region of the Meander . . . there were some great monasteries under the patronage of the Despot.'[45] These observations of Pachymeres together with other things known about Nilus, in particular his relations at Mount Auxentius with Athanasius I, another man for whom Pachymeres felt a rather decided aversion, lead one to believe that the 'Italian' monk belonged to that circle which, when Athanasius became Patriarch, strove to enforce monastic poverty. Their rallying point was at Mount St. Auxentius, and it was there too that Nicodemus, a hesychast of Vatopedi, first began his life as a monk. Nicodemus was the first spiritual instructor whom Palamas found at Mount Athos.[46]

There are no documents to fill in the details of the spiritual atmosphere in which Palamas grew up. But there is no doubt that that monastic milieu with which he very soon identified himself was the most lively spiritual element in Byzantine society. This was the element which enabled the Church to win an ever greater influence over the Empire which was growing weaker and weaker from Turkish attacks and internal discords. It was this element which provided the Church with the best prelates of the time, and which enabled Byzantine Christianity in the Slavic lands, especially Bulgaria and Russia, to promote a far-reaching liturgical reform, and a revival of traditional spirituality. The Patriarch Euthymius of Trnovo, the Metropolitan Cyprian of Kiev, and the great *starets* Nilus of Sora were all disciples of Byzantine hesychasm.

---

[43] Pachymeres, *De Andr. Pal.* I, 21, Bonn, II, 59–64.
[44] Ed. Boissonade, *Anecdota graeca*, V, pp. 217–18.
[45] *De Michaele Pal.*, III, 21, Bonn, I, 218–19.
[46] Philotheus, *Encomion*, col. 566A.

Monks and humanists

As has often been stressed, Byzantine monasticism was, in general, traditionally opposed to purely profane studies. At the end of the thirteenth century the latter flourished at Constantinople, and a certain tension between monks and humanists was inevitable. Theodore Metochites, Great Logothete under Andronicus II and an eminent humanist, had re-established at Byzantium the tradition of Photius and Psellos. In spite of its aristocratic and somewhat artificial character reflected in the refined aestheticism and too studied Atticism of its literary productions, which are in contrast to the popular character of the monasteries, Byzantine humanism, if it had been free to develop, would probably have carried Byzantine culture in the same direction as that followed by Italian, and thereafter all Western European, culture. It was the fate of this humanism to nourish the Renaissance in Italy, but, at Byzantium itself, to run up against the fierce opposition of the monks.

The division between Palamites and anti-Palamites did not, it is true, coincide with that between humanists and anti-humanists. There are examples, and very eminent ones, of Palamites who were humanists (Nicholas Cabasilas), and of anti-Palamites with a monastic training (Gregory Akindynos). Moreover, Byzantine humanism was not completely drowned under the Palamite waves, and it was able to produce in the fifteenth century such an astonishing phenomenon as the neo-paganism of Gemisthos Plethon.

Nevertheless there were at stake principles already heralding the advent of the modern world in the dispute between Barlaam and Palamas, and, very often, it was those principles which divided the supporters of Palamas from his adversaries. The humanists, in fact, started from the assumption of a sort of autonomy for human reason, and its independence in relation to a God whom they conceived as some impenetrable and inaccessible Essence. The union of God and man, realized once for all in the person of Christ, and divine action, effective and real, among humanity regenerated by baptism, played no decisive part in their thought. Whereas the hesychasts were defending a conception of Christianity inherited from the Fathers, which left no form of human activity outside the sphere of God's action. The idea of a complete 'collaboration' (συνεργία) between these two activities was indeed the special message of Palamism. The Orthodox Church, by approving the Palamite doctrine in 1351 and recognizing Gregory Palamas as one of the Fathers, has solemnly condemned the secularism of modern times, opposing thereto a humanist ideal which is essentially Christian.

CHAPTER II

HIS EARLY YEARS

GREGORY PALAMAS belonged to an aristocratic family of Asia Minor which had emigrated to Constantinople at the end of the thirteenth century. His father, Constantine Palamas, was a senator and belonged to the immediate entourage of Andronicus II. The latter entrusted him with the education of his grandson, the future Emperor Andronicus III, and Philotheus emphasizes that Constantine was greatly respected by his pupil.[1] It would seem that the Palamas family were not involved in the quarrels which rent the House of Palaeologi at the beginning of the fourteenth century.

Gregory was born in 1296,[2] the first born of a large family. His biographer describes, in a stylized form but with essential probability, the atmosphere of extreme piety which prevailed in his family, a piety of monastic type, centred on 'pure prayer.' His father would even practise this during meetings of the Senate with such intensity that he did not hear words addressed to him by the Emperor. The pious Andronicus II had him in great esteem, and even allowed him to intervene in the affairs of the Imperial family. Thus when Constantine, the second son of Andronicus, maltreated the widow of a poor man, Gregory's father openly stood out against him.[3]

Gregory was exactly the same age as the grandson of the Emperor, the future Emperor Andronicus III, for whose education his father was responsible. When Constantine Palamas died in about 1303,[4] the Emperor took over the care of the small boy's education. Being at home in the palace,[5] Gregory must have had relations of friendship with the young prince who, later on, when he had ascended his grandfather's throne, gave him his support.

His studies

Philotheus also tells us something about the studies which Gregory pursued under the Emperor Andronicus II's patronage. 'Having

---
[1] Philotheus, *Encomion*, col. 553D–554D; cf. Cantacuzene, *Hist.* II, 39, Bonn, I, 545.
[2] D. Stanilooe, *Palamas*, p. 7; cf. K. I. Dyovouniotes, in Ἐπιστημονικὴ Ἐπετηρὶς τῆς θεολογικῆς σχολῆς τοῦ Ἀθήνεσι Πανεπιστημίου, I, 1924, p. 74.
[3] Philotheus, *Encomion*, col. 555B–556A.
[4] When Gregory was 7 years old, Philotheus, *Encomion*, col. 558C; Nilus, *Encomion*, col. 659A.
[5] Philotheus, *Encomion*, 559BC (quoting Palamas's *Refutation of the Patriarch of Antioch*, Coisl. 99, fol. 145); cf. Cantacuzene, *Hist.* II, 39, Bonn, I, p. 545.

attained great success both in grammar and in rhetoric, Gregory was admired by all, even by those who were then the instructors and masters of oratory.' He also studied 'physics, logics and all the science of Aristotle.'[6] Gregory probably pursued his studies at the Imperial University and the Emperor indeed intended him to fill high offices in the State. His principle instructor in profane learning was Theodore Metochites, the Great Logothete, who was in charge of the University.

The studies followed in that institution were not intended to prepare Gregory for a career in the Church. Recent researches have shown that the profane instruction provided at the University was traditionally kept distinct from the studies of future clerics in the Patriarchate's School.[7]

During the religious controversy in which Palamas was opposed to the humanists of his time, his adversaries cast doubt on the depth of the studies which the future doctor of hesychasm had followed. Barlaam insinuated that he was only 'an ignoramus without education'[8] and Gregoras treated him as an illiterate, and reproached him for giving up his studies before he was fifteen.[9] To refute Gregoras's assertion, Palamas mentions something that happened when he was seventeen years old, that is to say about 1313, in a work in which he refers to himself in the third person: 'Being once asked by the great Emperor Andronicus, the ancestor of the Emperors, to speak about Aristotle's logic, Palamas, who was then seventeen years old, showed such an understanding of philosophy that all the wise men who were then with the Emperor were delighted; as for the Great Logothete (Theodore Metochites), that universal sage, he was filled with admiration and said to the Emperor, "If Aristotle himself had been here in flesh and blood, he would have praised him." ' And he added, 'That is the natural aptitude which any one should have who wishes to understand the *Logic* of Aristotle.'[10]

This probably authentic story about Theodore Metochites does not tell us much about the actual programme of studies followed by Palamas at Constantinople. It is more revealing that neither Philotheus nor Palamas himself refer to Plato or the neo-Platonic writers as having formed part thereof. Platonic metaphysics generally came after the study of

[6] Philotheus, *Encomion*, col. 559D.
[7] F. Fuchs, *Die höheren Schulen*, S. 35–41, 54–62; L. Bréhier, *L'enseignement classique et l'enseignement religieux à Byzance*, in *Revue d'Hist. et de phil. rel.*, XXI, 1941, pp. 41, 56–9.
[8] *First Letter to Palamas*, ed. Schirò, *Barlaam epistole*, p. 253.
[9] *Hist. byz.*, XXX, 20, 22, Bonn, III, 282, 283; cf. also Akindynos, *Letter to an anonymous*, ed. Loenertz, Epeteris, 27, 1957, p. 106.
[10] *Against Gregoras*, I, Coisl. 100, *fol.* 236; quoted in Philotheus, *Encomion*, col. 559D–560A.

Aristotle in the programme of Byzantine universities. It is therefore highly probable that Gregory did not carry his studies on beyond the *trivium* and *quadrivium* (ἐγκύκλιος παίδευσις), or elementary and general course which every cultivated man, whether lay or cleric, followed at the school, and which did not include the study of Plato.[11]

This hypothesis is confirmed by Palamas's works themselves. Palamas in fact often asserts that the study of profane philosophy was only useful as a preparation for the 'true philosophy' of Christianity, and that it would be wrong to spend too long upon it.[12] In this he was conforming to a decision taken by the Synod in the eleventh century, when concerned with the case of Italos, which was inserted in the Synodikon of Orthodoxy.[13] When Nicephorus Gregoras referred to the example of Moses, who, according to Gregory of Nyssa, studied profane sciences with the Egyptians, Gregory readily admitted this, but said that Moses, 'only pursued profane studies up to the time of reaching adult manhood; Palamas too, at that age, roused general admiration by his proficiency in such studies.'[14] That was when he was seventeen; it is no accident that dates the anecdote concerning Metochites to that exact moment of his adolescence. Philotheus indeed tells us that he quitted the world 'having attained adult age'[15]; he wanted thereby to show that Palamas himself conformed to the principles he had several times advocated in his writings; having developed his natural faculties as far as was allowable, and having attracted the attention of Metochites, the undisputed leader of the fourteenth century Byzantine humanists—his future adversaries—Gregory renounced profane philosophy.

These secular studies, though interrupted rather early, nevertheless left their mark on Palamas's works. He thus preserved personal contact with the humanists; Akindynos mentions that he served as intermediary between himself and Gregoras in an exchange of books.[16] On occasion he quotes from some ancient authors, Homer, Plato and some neo-Platonists such as Diogenes Laertius, and Porphyry[17]; it is true that it is always to condemn them, or to be sarcastic at their expense. In his

---

[11] cf. Fuchs, op. cit., pp. 41–50.
[12] *Tr.* I, *1*, 4, 7, 8, 9, 12, 20; II, *1*, 16, 27; II, *3*, 3, 71, 75.
[13] The synodikon anathematizes those who practise 'Hellenic sciences' beyond a simple educational exercise, and who adopt the futile opinions of ancient philosophers (*Triodion*, Athens, 1930, p. 148).
[14] Gregory of Nyssa, *Vita Moysis*, I, 18, *P.G.* XLIV, 305A; Gregoras, *Hist.* XXX, 21,· Bonn, p. 283; Palamas, *Against Gregoras*, I, Coisl. 100, *fol.* 236, referring to Gregory of Nyssa, op. cit., II, 10, col. 329B.
[15] *Encomion*, col. 562A.
[16] Text in Gregoras, *Hist.*, Bonn, I, p. LXX (= *P.G.* CXLVIII, 69).
[17] *Tr.* I, *1*, 15; II, *3*, 4; *Letter I to Barlaam*, ed. Papamikhaïl, in Ἐκκλησιαστικὸς φάρος, XIII, 1914, pp. 45, 465, 470.

letters to Barlaam he shows a fairly deep knowledge of Aristotle's *Topics*. Although he says that he 'had given up literary research and ambition,' he freely recognizes having a 'natural disposition to speak pleasantly,' [18] and he sometimes has recourse to those scholastic clichés so dear to the Byzantines ('the Attic graces which adorn the meadow of discourse like flowers').[19]

But it must be said to Palamas's credit that he generally rejects artificial Atticism and the pure play of words which was in fashion among Byzantine humanists. His works as a whole are above all inspired by the ascetic and mystical literature of the Greek Fathers.

Monastic vocation

According to Palamas the monastic state is incompatible with profane occupations. He asserts very clearly: 'We do not prevent any one from being initiated into profane studies, if they so desire, provided they have not adopted the monastic life.' [20] 'How can the inner man become a monk,' he asks, 'in conformity with the unique higher life, if he does not transcend the created world and all human studies, and if he does not strive with all his powers towards God with complete and exclusive concentration?' And he immediately refutes an adversary's objection: 'The Lord has not expressly forbidden literary studies. But neither has he forbidden marriage, the eating of meat, or the cohabitation with married people. . . . Many things are done by ordinary Christians without incurring condemnation, although they are strictly forbidden to monks by reason of their particular way of life.' [21] Thus Palamas adopts towards profane studies the formal and strict attitude which was that of most Byzantine monks. This attitude in his case was not based on obscurantism in principle, but on the very highest view of what a monk stood for: the monk is not an ordinary Christian, but a prophet who announces, by his peculiar way of life, the presence here below of the Kingdom of God which transcends all the values of this world, even those most genuine.

Gregory's vocation to be a monk was prepared from infancy by the piety of his parents, who were in daily contact with monks, and entrusted their children to their spiritual direction from the time when they learnt to speak.[22] After the death of his father, who on his deathbed received the tonsure of a monk,[23] Gregory, though he devoted him-

[18] *Tr.* III, 1, 2.
[19] *Against Gregoras*, III, *Coisl.* 100, *fol.* 266.
[20] *Tr.* I, 1, 12.
[21] *Tr.* II, 1, 35.
[22] Philotheus, *Encomion*, 557A.
[23] ibid., 558A.

self to profane studies, continued to frequent his spiritual directors, and they decided his definite vocation. These were monks from Athos sojourning in Constantinople, and also the most renowned spiritual instructor of the day, Theoleptus, Metropolitan of Philadelphia; the latter iniated him in 'holy vigilance' and in 'intellectual prayer.'[24]

It was at the age of about twenty,[25] therefore about 1316, that Gregory definitely decided to leave the world. Having inherited his father's responsibilities and property, and being the eldest of a large family, he solved the difficulties of his departure in a way very characteristic of a pious Byzantine family: he persuaded all his nearest relations to follow his example. Thus his mother, Kale, who took the name of Kallone, and his two sisters, Epicharis and Theodote, together with the best of his servants, entered convents in Constantinople,[26] while his younger brothers, Macarius and Theodosius, decided to follow him to Athos. Andronicus II tried to retain Gregory in his service by promising him wealth and honours, but the young man's decision had been definitely taken.

Encounter with Messalianism

Leaving the capital in the autumn, the three brothers did not succeed in reaching the Holy Mountain before winter, and they stayed some months at Mount Papikion, half way between Constantinople and Salonica, on the borders of Thrace and Macedonia.[27] Mount Papikion had been celebrated since the eleventh century for the many monastic foundations there.[28] Philotheus tells an interesting story about the three brothers' stay on Mount Papikion; on a neighbouring mountain, so he says, were living men who for generations had been infected with 'Marcionite and Messalian' heresies [29]; they must certainly have been Bogomils, whom the Byzantines often described as 'Messalians.' We know from other sources that in the same region there were descendants of the 'Paulicians,' whom first the Iconoclast Emperors and then John Tzimisces had transported from Armenia to Thrace, and who had given much trouble to Alexis Comnenus.[30] These people came to the monastery where Palamas was living to discuss theological questions.

[24] ibid., 560B–561A.
[25] ibid., 562A.
[26] ibid., 558CD, 572CD.
[27] ibid., 562BC.
[28] Cinnamos, Bonn, p. 265; Nicetas Choniates, Bonn, 187, 557, 558–9, 704; the *Typikon* of Petritzos monastery, ed. Petit, in *Vizantiiskii Vremennik*, XI, 1904, *Prilozhenie*, No. 1, p. 10. Localization of Mount-Papikion in S. Kyriakides, Τὸ Παπίκιον ὄρος, in 'Αθηνᾶ, 35 (1923), pp. 219–25.
[29] Col. 562D.
[30] D. Obolensky, *The Bogomils*, Cambridge, 1948, pp. 258–9.

Taking his second brother, Theodosius, with him Gregory even visited them on their mountain and had discussions with them about prayer—the Bogomils would allow no other prayer but the 'Our Father'—and about the veneration of the Cross. The success of his argument exasperated the heretics who tried to poison him. He did however succeed in convincing their leader who, with several other Bogomils, came to Constantinople and was reconciled to the Church.[31]

Although it is difficult to check the historical accuracy of this story, it has a certain interest in itself: Palamas was to be accused of Messalianism by Barlaam of Calabria, and Philotheus certainly wanted to refute that calumny, at the beginning of his 'Eulogy' of St. Gregory, by insisting on his opposition to that sect. But it is possible that the story does record historic fact, and in that case we have an example of personal contacts between Bogomils and Orthodox monks: Bogomilism and hesychasm which, in the Balkans, were spreading in socially very similar circles, may have had traits of spirituality common to both of them. They only found themselves in basic opposition when it came to the traditional dogmas of the Church, to which the Orthodox hesychasts remained fiercely attached.

At Mount Athos

At the beginning of spring the three young men reached Mount Athos. Gregory put himself under the spiritual direction of a hesychast who lived not far from Vatopedi, Nicodemus, formerly a monk at Mount St. Auxentius.[32] The three years which Gregory passed under the direction of Nicodemus, 'in fasting, sleeplessness, spiritual vigilance and uninterrupted prayer' were troubled by nothing but the premature death of his younger brother, Theodosius.[33] When Nicodemus also died, the two remaining brothers chose to live at the Great Laura of St. Athanasius which thereafter became, *par excellence,* the 'mother-house' of Palamas. Cantacuzene tells us that Gregory and his brother Macarius submitted for eight years to the direction of another hesychast, but the details about Palamas's life at this time, which we gather from Philotheus, suggest that, if he did submit to the guidance of one director, that does not imply any permanent place of residence. Indeed we find that for three years Gregory lived in the *koinobion* of the Lavra, and was appointed cantor by the *hegoumenos*. Then he retired to the hermitage of Glossia which modern Athonite tradition places near Provata on

---

[31] Philotheus, *Encomion*, 563A–565D.
[32] ibid., col. 566A. Le *Paterikon* of Athos celebrates on July 11 the feast of 'Saint Nicodemus, master of Gregory Palamas.'
[33] Cantacuzene, *Hist.* II, 39, Bonn, I, 545.

the north-western slope of Athos, and put himself under the direction of one Gregory whom Philotheus calls 'Gregory the Great'; this Gregory came from Constantinople and enjoyed on Athos a great reputation as a master of hesychasm; he went back to die in the capital where his remains performed miracles. From Nicephorus Gregoras we know that he had the further name of Drimys (Δριμὺς).[34] These biographical details do not correspond with what we know of Gregory the Sinaite, with whom we might otherwise have been tempted to identify the teacher of Palamas.

Palamas's stay at Glossia lasted for two years. About 1325 Turkish incursions obliged a great number of hesychasts living outside the defences of the great monasteries to quit Athos. Among these was Gregory the Sinaite and his disciples who included Isidore and Callistos, the future Patriarchs, who were living at the *skite* of Magoula, not far from Glossia to the north-west. Palamas also left the holy mountain accompanied by eleven of his friends, and the groups of hesychasts came together at Thessalonica. They formed the common intention of going next to the East, to Jerusalem and Sinai. Only Gregory the Sinaite and Callistos, accompanied by one other monk, started two months later to put their idea into execution, but they reached no further than Constantinople. Palamas and Isidore remained at Thessalonica.[35]

At Thessalonica

While Palamas stayed in the town of which he was later to be bishop, he took part with his friends in a spiritual circle which included monks and also lay people, notably some ladies of the high society of Thessalonica. Isidore, though he had not yet received the monastic tonsure, seems to have been their leader. He remained nearly ten years at Thessalonica and preached renunciation and other monastic virtues to numerous disciples. His biographer, Philotheus, lays particular stress on the austerity of his preaching; Isidore loved to quote the words of scripture about the 'narrow door,' and the necessity of fleeing from Sodom and Gomorrah; 'let those who have wives,' he said to the Thessalonians, 'be like those that have not, for the face of this world passes away.'[36] *A priori*, it seems strange that such preaching should come from the mouth of a layman who was still young, and Philotheus

---

[34] Philotheus, *Encomion*, 567C–568B; Cantacuzene, ibid., 545–6; Gregoras, *Hist.* XIX, 1, Bonn, II, 919; cf. Stanilooe, op. cit., p. 12.

[35] Callistos, *Life of Gregory the Sinaite*, ed. I. Pamialovskii, in *Zapiski istoriko-filologicheskago Fakul'teta* of the University of St. Petersburg, XXXV, 1896, pp. 33–4; Philotheus, *Encomion*, col. 569C–570C; Philotheus, *Life of Isidore*, ed. A. Papadopoulus-Kerameus, in *Zapiski*, LXXVI, 1905, pp. 76–8.

[36] Philotheus, *Life of Isidore*, pp. 78–80; cf. Isidore, *Last Will*, Miklosich-Muller, *Acta*, I, 287–8.

explains that Isidore had received a special direction from his spiritual father, Gregory the Sinaite: he was to stay in the world and give an example to those who lived the world's life.[37] That again is a trait peculiar to the hesychasm of the thirteenth and fourteenth centuries, and Theoleptus of Philadelphia was one of those responsible for it: the monk's life was conceived as having a prophetic mission in and for the world, and not only as a means of individual salvation. However Isidore's activity at Thessalonica was criticized by certain anti-Palamites in terms very different from this eulogy, 'He did not learn the laws of obedience, nor live in a community: instead of that, in the middle of the city and mingling with the crowd, he undertook to instruct and educate children; it has happened, so it is said, that he has separated women from their husbands and children, once at Thessalonica and once at Byzantium: in the first case it was the daughter of Cydones, in the second that of Tzyrakes. Not to fill the air with blasphemies, we leave to those who have had to make a spiritual inquest into these matters, the responsibility of discovering the secret and foolish doctrines which, so it is said, he taught them in clandestine meetings. Indeed what useful instruction could be given by a man who was completely ignorant of periods of fasting, of abstinence from food and drink at prescribed times, and made no difference between the days after the manner of the barbarians . . .'[38] However, these severe judgments on Isidore's activity were not shared universally. We actually have the valuable witness of Demetrios Cydones, a friend of Cantacuzene, later a diplomat and a convert to the Roman Church, in favour of the future patriarch. Isidore was a sort of family tutor in the rich household of the Cydones, and that was the 'education' about which the anti-Palamites of 1347 reproached him. Demetrios, his old pupil, in a letter written to him in 1341, associates him closely with the best memories of his childhood and of his family.[39] The 'daughter of Cydones' whom Isidore led to adopt a religious life, was certainly a relative of Demetrios. So the hesychast circle in Thessalonica extended its influence to the intellectual élite of that great city.

New contacts with the Bogomils

We find an echo of the activities of this circle in other documents of the period, especially the correspondence of Akindynos, who associates Palamas with Isidore in accusing both of suspected contacts with the Messalians. We have seen that Palamas had had some dealings with

[37] ibid., p. 77.
[38] *Antipalamite declaration of July 1347*, P.G. CL, 881D–882A.
[39] *Correspondence*, ed. R.-J. Loenertz, I, *Studi e testi*, 186, Citta del Vaticano, 1956, No. 43, pp. 77–8; No. 86, lines 28–31.

the sect in his youth, and that certain traits of spirituality were common to hesychasts and Bogomils. Notably, it seems that the hesychasts, though they did not share the real iconoclasm of the Bogomils, had adopted a reserved attitude to certain contemporary forms of veneration of images. Akindynos, in a letter dating from about 1345 and addressed to James Koukounares, anti-Palamite Metropolitan of Monemvasia, writes that Messalianism, professing 'iconomachy,' had appeared at Athos, at Constantinople and at Thessalonica, and that its leader, George, had formerly lived in the same house as Isidore in the latter city, that he had been driven out, that he had recently been expelled from Mount Athos and branded on the forehead, and that among his disciples was a nun named Porine whom Isidore and Palamas venerated as a prophetess.[40]

These facts are confirmed from other sources, especially the Life of St. Theodosius of Trnovo, written by the Patriarch Callistos of Constantinople and Nicephorus Gregoras. Callistos affirms that Byzantine Bogomilism of the fourteenth century originated in Thessaly; a nun there called Irene, while pretending to be Orthodox, had initiated others therein; there were monks among her disciples and they contaminated Athos.[41] Nicephorus Gregoras is even more precise. Writing in 1347, that is to say almost at the same time as Akindynos's letter, he gives the names of the heretics on Athos; Joseph the Cretan, George of Larissa (probably the same as the George mentioned by Akindynos), Moses the Painter, David, Job and Isaac; all those were formally condemned by a *Tome* (τόμος ἔγγραφος) addressed by the Synod of Constantinople to the monks of Athos; iconoclasm is among the errors condemned by the *Tome*.[42] Without mentioning Isidore, Gregoras associates Palamas with the Athonite heretics but he does not assert that he was condemned with them, for he had left for Thessalonica before the heresy was discovered, and got lost in the polyglot crowd of the great city.[43] So, according to Gregoras, it was not to escape Turkish incursions, but to avoid a condemnation for Bogomilism, that Palamas left Athos. So in his anti-Palamite tract Gregoras, like Akindynos, wished to present Palamas as a direct disciple of Joseph of Crete and George of Larissa, known heretics formally condemned, but with some traits of spirituality and some attitudes which had a certain

[40] Ed. Loenertz, p. 91.
[41] *Life of Theodosius* (slavonic text), ed. V. N. Zlatarski, in *Sbornik za narodni umotvoreniya i knizhnina*, XX, Sofia, 1904, 14, pp. 19–20.
[42] *Antirrhetic Treatises against Palamas*, Gen. gr. 35, fol. 7v, written around 1347; the referred passage is also quoted by Gregoras in *Hist.*, XIV, 7, Bonn, II, 718–19.
[43] ibid., fol. 8 (a close but modified reference to this passage in *Hist.*, ibid., p. 720).

external resemblance to those of the hesychast; their preference for 'pure prayer' rather than the Psalm singing of the cenobitic monasteries; a certain detachment towards the traditional formalism about fasting; preaching that celibacy was preferable to the married state,[44] and also perhaps a certain austere contempt for the too rich decoration of churches, which led many hesychasts to be accused of iconomachy.[45]

All this information about the activities of Isidore and Palamas at Thessalonica about 1325 raises the whole question of the relations between Bogomilism and hesychasm in the fourteenth century. Gregoras certainly is writing in bad faith when he makes out that the leaders of the hesychasts were crypto-Bogomils; he does not even dare to assert that openly in his *History,* in the passages from his anti-Palamite Antirrhetics which he introduces therein. But the information he supplies, partly corroborated by Philotheus's *Life of Isidore,* allows us to form some impression of the youthful, perhaps daring, enthusiasm, of Palamas and Isidore at Thessalonica. But their later writings, and the respect they enjoyed, make it safe to reject any suspicion of Bogomilism. The hesychasts, just because they were active in the same circles as the heresy, were in a better position than others to fight against it. They answered the same need for a more intense spiritual life, but did so by putting forward a teaching about prayer and a form of spirituality which were authentic and traditional. It is certain that their final success in the Byzantine world helped to bring into the Church that popular movement of spiritual revival which the Bogomils were diverting into strange paths. The hesychasts were not afraid to keep in contact with those very circles in which Bogomilism was spreading, and the incidents at Thessalonica, echoed in our sources, prove that such contacts actually existed.[46]

At Beroea

Palamas did not stay long at Thessalonica. However, he was ordained priest there at his friends' insistence. He then retired, with ten other monks, to a hermitage on a mountain near Beroea. He was then thirty years old,[47] the canonical age for sacerdotal ordination in the Byzantine Church. The date is therefore 1326.

---

[44] ibid., *fol.* 10–10v.
[45] cf. similar accusation against Athanasius I (Calothetos, *Life,* ed. cit., pp. 102–3; Theoctistos, *Life,* ed. cit., pp. 37–8), against Palamas himself (Gregoras, *Hist.,* XXIV, 2, Bonn, II, 1146; *Antipalamite declaration, P.G.* CL, 882B).
[46] cf. other similar contacts between orthodox monks and Bogomils in Thessalonica in the same year 1325 in Miklosich-Muller, *Acta,* I, 140–3.
[47] Philotheus, *Encomion,* 571C.

At Beroea Gregory passed five days of the week in complete isolation, silence and 'prayer of the mind.' His health, still strong, allowed severe ascetic practices. On Saturday and Sunday he came out of his isolation to celebrate the Eucharist, and talk with the brothers in the hermitage: that was the type of life most strongly recommended by hesychast tradition from the beginning,[48] in that it was halfway between community life and that of a complete hermit, and so allowed a harmonious development of the spiritual life combining the advantages of both. Palamas's sojourn in his hermitage was only interrupted by the death of his mother, which took place at Constantinople. He went to the capital, and brought back to Beroea his two nun sisters whom he installed in a convent in that town. The eldest, Epicharis, was soon to die there.[49]

Philotheus also reports a story which is interesting for the history of hesychasm in the fourteenth century; a monk named Job, who lived not far from the hermitage and was a friend of Palamas, maintained in discussion that uninterrupted prayer was possible only for monks; Palamas on the contrary asserted that all Christians, without exception, had received the command to pray continually (1 Thess. 5: 17). Job was finally convinced by the appearance of an angel who confirmed Palamas's teaching.[50] In recounting this episode Philotheus certainly wanted to stress an important element in hesychasm of this period, that is to say, its concern for the whole Church. Palamas and his disciples did not mean to promote an esoteric method of spirituality intended only for a limited number of elect distinguished thereby from the mass of the faithful, but simply wished to express the real intimacy established by the incarnation between God and all Christians. Moreover the whole of Palamite theology is no more than a systematic working out of that essential basic proposition.

The hermitage of Sabbas

Palamas stayed five years in his hermitage, but had to quit it about 1331, when Serb incursions made the neighbourhood insecure.[51] He then returned to Athos and settled in the hermitage (ἡσυχαστήριον) of St. Sabbas, near the Lavra, to lead the same life there as he had led at Beroea; total isolation five days a week; liturgy and spiritual conversa-

---

[48] cf. for example John Moschos, *Pratum spiritale*, 4–5, P.G. LXXXVII, 2856BC.
[49] Philotheus, *Encomion*, 572B–573B.
[50] ibid., 573B–574B. Job appears also in Theoctistos, *Life of Athanasius* (ed. cit., p. 13) and in the *Life of Germanos the Hagorite* (ed. Joannou, in *Analecta Bollandiana*, 70, 1952, pp. 75–85). One may be tempted to identify him with the Job mentioned above and whom Gregoras considers as a Bogomil.
[51] Philotheus, ibid., 574BC.

tion with the brothers on Saturday and Sunday.[52] Gregory also took his turn officiating in the celebrations in the church of the Lavra and was in the monastery at all the most important times in the liturgical year. So it happened that, during the service on Holy Thursday, he was offended by the conversation of some of the monks during the singing of the hymns, and preferred to retreat into himself and give himself up to pure prayer. At another time, some years later, at Thessalonica, he had a vision of St. Anthony who forbade him to cut himself off from congregational prayer on the pretext that mental prayer is better than it. These episodes, both recounted by Philotheus,[53] are a true reflection of the attitude of fourteenth century hesychasts towards the communities of monks in their day. They often took notice of their spiritual decadence, but the sacramental and liturgical theology which they had set out to promote forbade them to oppose individual spirituality, based on the 'prayer of Jesus,' to the piety of church and community. For this reason at Thessalonica Palamas, following the example of Theoleptus of Philadelphia, preached a true liturgical renewal; his disciple, Philotheus, was also to be a codifier of the liturgy, and was to insist in all his *Lives* of the hesychast saints on their fidelity to the community life of the monasteries they inhabited.

At St. Sabbas Palamas began to be well known in the world of Athos, and about the year 1334, at the age of thirty-eight, he began to write. His first work was the *Life of Saint Peter the Athonite,* and his second the long *Treatise on the Presentation of the Virgin to the Temple* which was intended to refute those who denied the historic character of the event celebrated at that feast; it is possible that the man against whom his attack was directed was, even at that time, Nicephorus Gregoras.[54] So from the beginning of his literary activity, Palamas showed an extreme devotion to the Mother of God: Philotheus points that out, and we find the same throughout Palamas's works. We do not know what were the 'other' works which Palamas, still according to Philotheus, wrote at that time; perhaps the *Chapters on Prayer and Purity of Heart* and the *Answer to Paul Asen concerning the monastic tonsure.* Homily 40, on John the Baptist, was also delivered at Athos,[55] but perhaps during one of Palamas's later stays on the holy mountain. We can however confidently say that about 1336, and therefore at St. Sabbas's, Palamas wrote his *Apodictic Treatises* concerning the

[52] ibid., 574CD. Even to-day the monks of Lavra show the place where Palamas lived, on the abrupt side of the mountain above Lavra.
[53] 579BC, 594D-593A.
[54] Gregoras will be later excommunicated for his critical approach to the question (Miklosich-Muller, *Acta*, I, 490); for Palamas' intentions when writing the Treatise see Philotheus, *Encomion*, 581BC.
[55] *P.G.* CLI, 513B.

Procession of the Holy Spirit; the occasion was the new discussion of Union of the Churches, which two pontifical legates had come in 1333-4 to negotiate with the government of Andronicus III.

Thus while concentrating on a life of prayer in his hermitage on faraway Athos, Gregory continued to take a lively interest in external events. He seems to have enjoyed general respect, as is shown by one of his future adversaries, Gregory Akindynos, who, in 1340, advised Barlaam of Calabria against attacking so venerable a monk whom no one would wish to consider as a heretic.[56]

Akindynos at Athos

Akindynos himself was an old friend of Palamas. He had come to the Lavra as a novice and the hermit of St. Sabbas had exerted all his authority to have him definitely accepted in the brotherhood of the monastery; he moreover advised him to compose a Eulogy of the Lavra of St. Athanasius, and Akindynos delivered this before the chapter assembled in the presence of the abbot. The monks remained insensible to his eloquence, in spite of Palamas's support. Akindynos then went to the *skete* where lived Callistos, the future Patriarch, who gave him his support to enter the monastery of Iviron, or that of Philotheou or Petra, but those communities again rejected him, perhaps from jealousy of his talents as a humanist, as Callistos supposed at the time, though he came later to explain these rebuffs by a divine intervention destined to save Athos from Akindynos's heresies.[57] The old friendship between Palamas and Akindynos dated perhaps from the time when the former was living at Beroea; Akindynos had come to teach grammar there, having left his native town of Prilep in Macedonia, and having first studied at Pelagonia (the modern Bitolj), and then at Thessalonica under Thomas Magistros and Bryennios, and perhaps also under Barlaam. It is very probable that he then adopted Palamas as his spiritual father; the latter twice recalls that Akindynos had been his pupil, though he did not follow his course of instruction to the end.[58] Palamas also gives his own version of Akindynos's misadventures on Athos; Akindynos had come to St. Sabbas to practise pure prayer, but, after only a few drops, had claimed to see not only the divine light, but a human face, apparently that of Christ, appearing within himself. Palamas suggests that it was to punish him and save him from this demoniacal vision that he tried to have him received within the strict community of the Lavra; that

[56] *Scorial, gr.* Φ-III-11 (XIVs., autograph), *fol.* 234.
[57] The whole story is told in an unpublished homily of Callistos, *Patm.* 366, *fol.* 414v–415.
[58] cf. references to sources mainly manuscript in the French edition.

HIS EARLY YEARS

explanation enabled him to avoid the reproach, which some had made against him, of formerly according Akindynos his patronage.[59]

Hegoumenos of Esphigmenou

At some uncertain date, probably, about 1335 or 1336, Palamas was appointed Hegoumenos (or Abbot) of Esphigmenou,[60] on the northern side of the peninsula, by the Protos and the Central Council of Athos. That cenobitic monastery was then inhabited by two hundred monks. Philotheus mentions the sermons which Palamas preached there, and his particular care about the liturgical celebrations. But he does not seem to have come to a good understanding with the community, for he soon left the monastery followed by a certain number of disciples. The latter dispersed over Athos, while Palamas returned to St. Sabbas. The neighbourhood round the Lavra must then have been one of the principal centres of hesychasm on Athos, for we find that Gregory the Sinaite and his disciples, Callistos and Mark, were there at about the same time, but for only a few months.[61] No source however mentions the slightest contact between the Sinaite and Palamas. But the Sinaite's disciples became later the most active supporters of Palamite theology. Isidore Boukharis, in particular, received his monk's tonsure at Palamas's hands, and it was he who persuaded him to accept ordination as a deacon.[62]

It was at St. Sabbas that Palamas began to take notice of the activities of the 'Calabrian Philosopher,' Barlaam, at Thessalonica and in Constantinople.

---

[59] *Against Akindynos*, VII, 16, *Coisl.* 98, *fol.* 196.
[60] Philotheus, *Encomion*, 581D–583C.
[61] Callistos, *Life of Gregory the Sinaite*, p. 38.
[62] Philotheus, *Life of Isidore*, pp. 82–3.

CHAPTER III

BARLAAM AND THE COUNCILS OF 1341

As has often been observed, the whole history of Byzantine thought since the ninth century has been influenced by the opposition, at some times more and at some times less open, between the advocates of secular humanism and the monks. In the fourteenth century this opposition became more marked, as both these branches of Byzantine thought were developing with fresh strength. The spirit of the Renaissance and the traditional monastic spirituality became the two poles which attracted the finest intellectual forces and the most lively personalities in the Christian East. There were moreover on both sides moderate spirits who understood how, by following the tradition of the Fathers, to reconcile a true Greek humanism with Christianity and the sharp conflict which developed between the two tendencies might perhaps in other circumstances have been avoided. What made the clash inevitable was that some humanists carried their philosophical convictions into the theological sphere.

Barlaam
When he came to Constantinople about 1330, Barlaam, 'monk and philosopher,' from Seminaria in Calabria, a Greek by language and sentiment, but western educated and imbued with the spirit of the Italian Renaissance, sought above all a closer knowledge of ancient Hellas, the land of Plato and Aristotle. He was faithful to Orthodoxy as the religion of his Greek ancestors, and Palamas recognized that he had a sincere love of 'true piety.' [1] At Constantinople he found powerful support in the person of the Great Domestic, John Cantacuzene, under whose patronage he was chiefly engaged in commentaries on the Pseudo-Dionysius. His reputation seems to have grown quickly, and he very soon came to rank as a person of importance at Constantinople, and one who was consulted about such diverse matters at astronomy, philosophy, theology and diplomatic questions. His writings about these various subjects circulated in large numbers, and continued to be copied even after his troubles with the monks.

But the Calabrian philosopher never got on to good terms with his colleagues, the Byzantine humanists. Temperamentally flamboyant and

[1] *First Letter to Akindynos*, 4 (ed. Meyendorff, in *Theologia*, XXVI, 1955, p. 79).

ambitious, he treated them with disdain, which only increased their jealousy at his success. Palamites and anti-Palamites agree in ridiculing his pride. Nicephorus Gregoras, who had held public disputations with him on philosophic problems, represents him in his dialogue *Florentios* as a boaster whose only object was to discredit other philosophers. According to Akindynos Barlaam entered Thessalonica with a disdainful air, as if it was a place void of all culture.[2] Philotheus of Selymbria, a Palamite bishop, who also wrote a dialogue narrating the history of the controversy, represents him more as a man driven by ambition than as the leader of a heresy.[3] His character was probably more subtle, but there is no doubt that he had a capacity for rousing people against himself. Thus, about 1340, when George Lapithos, a learned Cypriot Maecenas, had put some questions to him about the relations between Plato and Aristotle, he answered in terms which outraged his correspondent and, despite Akindynos's advice, he made one enemy the more at a time when he badly needed all the support he could get. It was just when he had first come into conflict with the monks.[4]

His encounter with the monks

At the beginning there were two separate questions in dispute, doctrine and spirituality, but they very soon became confused. Palamas took the initiative in the purely doctrinal controversy. At Pentecost in 1337 he received at his hermitage at St. Sabbas some of the anti-Latin writings which Barlaam had published after his *pourparlers* with the Papal legates who came to Constantinople in 1333-4. Barlaam, on the basis of the apophatic theology of the Pseudo-Dionysius, used an original argument: God being unknowable, the Latins should give up their claim to *demonstrate* their doctrine of the Procession of the Holy Spirit. How could they demonstrate a reality which is outside all perception and all human reasoning? Latins and Greeks should be content to refer to the Fathers who had received a special illumination on the subject from God. But the Fathers themselves are not always perfectly clear; therefore the only thing to do is to relegate the doctrine of the Procession to the domain of private theological opinions which do not constitute an obstacle to the unity of the Church.[5] Thus Barlaam's theological agnosticism ended in dogmatic relativism.

[2] *Letter to Barlaam, Ambros. gr.* 290, *fol.* 67.
[3] *Patm. gr.* 366, *fol.* 370, 383v, etc.
[4] Barlaam, *Answers to Lapithos, Vatic. gr.* 1110, *fol.* 94; Akindynos, *Letters to Barlaam, Ambros. gr.* 190, *fol.* 67v.
[5] cf. our analysis of Barlaam's treatises, *Un mauvais théologien de l'unité*, in *L'Eglise et les Eglises* (Mélanges Beauduin Lambert), II, Chevetogne, 1955, pp. 47-64.

At the same period Palamas had written his two *Apodictic Treatises* against the Latin doctrine of the Procession [6]: the very title of these treatises suffices to show that his attitude to theological demonstration did not correspond with that of Barlaam. The Orthodox position seemed to him perfectly 'demonstrable,' and it coincided, in his view, with the opinions expressed fifty years earlier by the Patriarch Gregory of Cyprus. His friends at Thessalonica (which probably means Isidore and his circle) to whom he had sent his Treatises,[7] had been asking him, since 1336, whether there was not a contradiction between his views and those which the celebrated Barlaam, who in 1334 had been officially charged by the Emperor to negotiate with the legates, propounded in his numerous anti-Latin writings. Palamas then answered that he thought both positions were Orthodox.[8] But he began to have doubts on that point when he finally obtained a copy of Barlaam's anti-Latin writings which he had previously known only from hearsay. He then wrote to his friend and former disciple, Gregory Akindynos, who was then also at Thessalonica and had had a chance of meeting Barlaam. In this letter, expressed in terms of respect towards the Calabrian philosopher, he quotes long passages from his own *Apodictic Treatises,* contrasting them with Barlaam's views, and he expresses astonishment at the agnosticism of the latter who, while refuting the Latins, also undermines the Orthodox position. Did not the unknowable God of Dionysius reveal himself? If he revealed himself to the Fathers, why should he not reveal himself to-day to the Church through the theologians called to elucidate the mystery of the Trinity with the aid of the Holy Spirit? [9]

Akindynos as mediator

Akindynos and Barlaam both answered the hermit of St. Sabbas, having studied his objections together. Their answers were different in tone, but very similar in substance. Akindynos tried to play the part of a peacemaker, and continued to do so down to 1341. His letter to Palamas is very respectful, but reserved. Why argue about 'demonstration,' he writes, when one possesses such a divine blessing as friendship? Palamas had only read one of Barlaam's anti-Latin treatises, and so could not judge his work as a whole; Barlaam's sole aim was to confound the Latins, and he had no desire in any way to weaken the Greek position. As to the problem of demonstration, there was a misunderstanding; the word could have many meanings; demonstration in the technical,

---

[6] Edited in Constantinople in 1627 by Cyril Lukaris.
[7] *First Letter to Akindynos,* ed. Meyendorff, *Theologia* XXVI, 1955, p. 90.
[8] *First Letter to Barlaam,* ed. Papamikhail, in 'Εκκλησιαστικὸς Φάρος, XIII, 1914, p. 248.
[9] *First Letter to Akindynos,* ibid., pp 77–90.

purely logical and universally necessary sense should not be confounded with demonstration based on Scripture; the first is not applicable to theology, while the latter is in fact not a demonstration.[10]

But Barlaam, in spite of Akindynos's advice for moderation,[11] let his indignation burst right out against the man who had dared to criticize him : 'I will humiliate that man,' he declared.[12] His answer is full of sarcasm at Palamas who pretended to 'demonstrate' divine things. Like Akindynos, he distinguishes between the various meanings of the word 'demonstration,' but he specifically accepts the authority of pagan philosophers as providing, on a par with the Fathers of the Church, sure premises for 'dialectic' reasoning which, in matters concerning God, can never be 'apodictic.' Then, at the end of his letter, he promises to modify the text of his anti-Latin writings to avoid shocking Palamas.[13]

Palamas did not delay his answer; to Akindynos he replied that he could not place friendship above truth, and that his former pupil's complaisance towards Barlaam showed that he had been contaminated by profane Hellenism. And Barlaam received from the hermitage of St. Sabbas a long treatise against Aristotle, Plato and the Greek philosophers whose authority he had proclaimed.[14] The distinctions about the meanings of 'demonstration' had not convinced Palamas : it was not enough, in his view, to change the premises of a syllogism in order to transform its value and give it an apodictic sense; it is the process of human thought itself which must be basically transformed by the action of the Holy Spirit in order to receive a sure knowledge of God. Barlaam not only refused to accept that transformation, but preferred to consider the profane philosophers as 'enlightened by God,' that is to say to reduce grace to a natural gift and thus lessen its scope.

Without waiting for an answer to this letter from Barlaam, Palamas wrote another treatise, which has not been published, on the same subject,[15] and in it another cause of conflict already makes its appearance, namely the clash between Barlaam and the hesychasts of Thessalonica.

The hesychast method of prayer

At the same time as Palamas, Akindynos and Barlaam were corresponding about the latter's anti-Latin writings, Barlaam came to learn at Thessalonica about certain forms of monastic spirituality, in particular

[10] *Ambros. gr.* 290, *fol.* 75v–76v.
[11] *Letter to Barlaam, Ambros. gr.* 290, *fol.* 67v.
[12] Quoted by Akindynos, ibid.
[13] *Letter to Palamas*, in G. Schirò, *Barlaam Calabro Epistole*, Palermo, 1959, pp. 229-66.
[14] Both letters are edited by G. Papamikhail, in Ἐκκλησιαστικὸς Φάρος, XII–XIII, 1913–14.
[15] *Coisl.* 100, *fol.* 90–103.

a method of prayer described by several writers since the end of the thirteenth century (Nicephorus the Hesychast, the Pseudo-Symeon, Gregory of Sinai). The monks whom he met were poorly educated and could not satisfy, in the field of spirituality, the aspirations of an intellectual sceptic who had just denied, in his argument with Palamas, all effective action of grace over human reasoning. Barlaam's proud temperament and also his spiritualizing convictions, inspired by Platonic philosophy, roused him to the greatest indignation, when he was told that the human body could itself participate in prayer and feel the action of divine grace. He wrote some treatises for limited circulation; in these he referred to the monks as *omphalopsychoi* (men-with-their-souls-in-the-navel). In 1338 he went to Constantinople where he continued to inquire into that subject, came to the same conclusion, and finally lodged a complaint against them with the Patriarch and the Synod.[16] The Patriarch, John Calecas, formally dismissed it, and threatened him with sanctions if he did not leave the monks in peace.

Barlaam did not obey, but on his return to Thessalonica continued to attack the monks. On Isidore's initiative the latter took counsel and decided to call on Gregory Palamas to defend them against Barlaam's accusations.

Palamas then came to Thessalonica and lived for three years, down to 1341, near the hermitage presided over by his friend Isidore.[17] He met Barlaam several times, and tried to settle the quarrel with him amicably. When these efforts failed, he wrote the first of his *Triads*, a collection of three treatises defending the hesychasts ($\hyper\ \tau\hat{\omega}\nu\ \hier\hat{\omega}\varsigma\ \hsych azontwn$). The treatises take the form of answers to questions put to him by the monks; Barlaam is not once mentioned; Palamas had not yet seen the complete text of his treatises, and avoided starting an open argument with him.

Akindynos was then at Constantinople in the close *entourage* of the Patriarch, and his reactions to the dispute are very interesting. He still wants to play a moderating part; in the correspondence about 'demonstration' Palamas had attacked, and Akindynos defended, Barlaam. Now the opposite happened; he felt that the monks were the victims of Barlaam's aggressive spirit and gave them his support, which seems to have carried great weight; his continual representations to the Patriarch were the cause of Calecas's reaction against Barlaam.[18] But the latter remained intractable. He did tone down some phrases, in

---

[16] Palamas, *Coisl.* 100, *fol.* 100v; letters of Barlaam on the subject edited by Schirò, op. cit.

[17] Philotheus, *Encomion*, col. 592CD.

[18] He describes himself these efforts in his *Report* to Calecas, ed. Th. Uspenskii, *Sinodik v nedeliu Pravoslaviia*, Odessa, 1893, p. 86.

particular dropping the nickname *omphalopsychoi*. Basically he did not change his mind, and published his writings against the monks, answering the arguments which Palamas, without naming him, had used in his first *Triad*. In these he not only criticized the monks, but also expressed positive teaching 'on human perfection,' 'on prayer' and 'on knowledge.' [19]

Barlaam at Avignon

His rebuff by the Patriarch in the question of the monks does not seem to have appreciably diminished his prestige. Strong in the patronage of the Great Domestic, John Cantacuzene, Barlaam presented to the Synod a plan for the Union of the Churches, founded on just those relativist doctrines which Palamas had criticized.[20] This plan does not seem to have been formally rejected, for we find Barlaam leaving for Avignon in 1339 as Imperial Ambassador; it is clear however that he did not have a formal mandate from the Church. He propounded to the Pope the same views as he had advanced at Constantinople, but Benedict XII seems to have been as little inclined towards his dogmatic relativism as the Byzantine hesychasts had been, and his embassy produced no practical result.[21] On his return to Byzantium, an unpleasant surprise awaited him; Palamas had written a second *Triad* in which his ideas were sifted with no evasion. Barlaam was not the man to let a public refutation of his works pass unanswered. Akindynos tried to hold him back; dogmatic polemics with the qualified representatives of Byzantine monasticism was a risky matter, and Barlaam had little chance of coming out victorious. There are manuscripts preserved of four letters written to Barlaam by Gregory Akindynos in 1340-1, in all of which he counsels moderation and disapproves of his attacks against the monks. The first, in friendly terms, was written immediately after Barlaam's return. Akindynos did not yet know that he intended to answer Palamas; he slightly laughs at Barlaam for his pride in his embassy, regrets his continual attacks against the monks, against 'those pious folk without learning, those simple Christians who have no wealth or cares . . . who can say with the divine Paul . . . "we know nothing but Christ, Christ crucified."' Barlaam did not accept Akindynos's advice, and soon received another letter from him in which he writes that there was 'no strong disagreement between them on theological matters,' but that Barlaam made a tactical mistake in urging a charge of heresy against a

---

[19] Such were apparently the titles of his writings against the hesychasts, cf. our introduction to the text of Palamas's *Triads*, pp. XXVI-XXVII.
[20] Texts in C. Gianelli, *Un progetto di Barlaam per l'unione delle chiese*, in *Miscellanea G. Mercati*, III (= Studi e testi, 123) Vatican, 1946, pp. 185-201.
[21] J. Meyendorff, *Un mauvais théologien*, pp. 48-50.

man so worthy of respect as Palamas; for it was against canon law to treat a man as a heretic before he had been formally condemned. 'Therefore, be more moderate towards Palamas,' he repeated.[22]

Akindynos defends the monks

Barlaam continued to disregard this wise advice. Akindynos, growing more and more frightened at the scale on which the controversy was developing, repeated his former admonition, and reproached him for beginning the dispute, and for attacking practices long accepted by monastic tradition; it is completely unfair, he repeated, to reproach these forms of spirituality with Messalianism, there is no chance that the Church would approve such an accusation. Barlaam would be wiser to confine himself to attacking Palamas's definitions of nature and *energies*.[23] Akindynos is thus seen adopting the position which he took throughout the controversy; he criticizes Palamas only on theological grounds, but says nothing against the 'psychosomatic' method of prayer universally accepted in fourteenth century Byzantium both by the hesychasts and by the bitterest anti-Palamites.

Barlaam's answers to these letters of Akindynos do not seem to have been preserved. In any case he took these criticisms, like the former ones, very badly; he accused his correspondent of backing Palamas's errors from friendship for his former teacher, which gave Akindynos the chance of declaring his equal opposition to both the protagonists.[24]

Thus Akindynos's letters give us a vivid picture of the early adversaries of Palamism; around 1340 none of them was a *Latinophron*, still less a Byzantine Thomist. As we shall show later, they were recruited partly from the advocates of profane humanism, and partly from the defenders of a Byzantine neo-scholasticism; for the latter every living expression and every dynamic thought, even if it had a solid Patristic basis, was suspect of heresy. Barlaam and Akindynos were very characteristic representatives of these two attitudes.

The Hagioretic Tome

While Barlaam was still in Italy, or immediately after his return, Palamas went to Mount Athos and there obtained the approval of the principal monastic authorities for his famous *Hagioretic Tome*. This document, written by Palamas, is a solemn manifesto in which, without naming Barlaam, his ideas are irrevocably condemned. It is certain that its publication had the greatest effect on the issue of the controversy; the Barlaamites found themselves publicly excluded from the

[22] *Scorial gr.* Φ-III-11, *fol.* 232-4.
[23] ibid., *fol.* 230v–231.
[24] *Ambros. gr.* 290, *fol.* 71.

communio in sacris by the Bishop of Hierissos, Ordinary of Mount Athos, who thus gave ecclesiastical sanction to the monks' declaration. We find known signatures at the bottom of the *Tome*; that of the *protos* Isaac, who was later to support Palamas's case at Constantinople in 1342, that of Philotheus, *hieromonachos* at Lavra and future Patriarch, and those of the chief disciples of Gregory of Sinai, Isaias, Mark and Callistos, who were still at the Sinaite's *skite* at Magoula. On the original, besides the Greek signatures of the *hegoumenoi* of the Lavra, Vatopedi, Esphigmenou and Kutlumus, there is the Georgian signature of the *hegoumenos* Anthony of Iviron, and the Slavonic signature of the Serbian *hegoumenos* of Khilandari. A Syrian hesychast from Karyes also signed the document 'in his own language.'[25]

That was the solemn document with which Palamas returned to Thessalonica. He intended to go at once to Constantinople to combat Barlaam, but the latter reappeared at Thessalonica. The two protagonists had further meetings at which, according to Palamas, Barlaam adopted an evasive attitude, each time promising to drop the argument. One of these interviews even had a judicial character, for it took place in the presence of a *great diocetes* (a title then borne by Glabas who, at least up to 1337, was 'general judge of the Greeks') who was present especially to arbitrate the dispute. Before this important witness, Barlaam promised to modify his writings against the hesychasts, and to have the text approved by Palamas.[26] Palamas, therefore, did not so completely disapprove of the works of Barlaam as to demand their utter destruction: a possibility of understanding existed, in 1339-40, on the basis of a simple modification of Barlaam's works. However, despite the moderate advice of Akindynos, and despite the comparative goodwill of Palamas, he wrote his work *Against the Messalians,* in which for the first time he attacked Palamas by name, accusing him of espousing the heresy of Theodore, a priest of the church at Blakhernae, who had been condemned under Alexius Comnenus.[27]

'Against the Messalians'

In these circumstances, the affair took on yet larger dimensions. Anticipating Palamas's answer, Barlaam again tried to complain to the Patriarch John Calecas against the monks.

The situation in the capital is described in detail by Akindynos in a subsequent report to Calecas. The authorities at Constantinople had

[25] *P.G.* CL, 1236.
[26] Palamas, *Third Letter to Akindynos,* ed. Meyendorff, in *Theologia,* XXIV, 1953, p. 581; on Glabas, see P. Lemerle, *Le juge général des grecs,* in *Mémorial L. Petit,* Bucarest, 1948, p. 309.
[27] Palamas, *Tr.* III, 1, 7; III, 2, 3; III, 3, 4.

done all they could to prevent the controversy touching on dogmatic questions. They thought they could limit it to a personal matter, and then to a controversy about different forms of spirituality, while closing their eyes in fear before an inevitable choice which concerned dogma.

Barlaam presented his *Against the Messalians* to the Patriarch and members of the Synod, and also sought the support of Akindynos. The latter advised the Patriarch to dismiss the case once more : even if the monks and Palamas are in error, it is not for Barlaam to judge them, but for the Church. A council was then held; Akindynos criticized Barlaam's book, and praised Palamas in the presence of the Patriarch, the bishops and several monks; it was recognized that Barlaam had only attacked Palamas from quarrelsomeness.[28] The Patriarch himself spoke in support of Palamas.[29]

But Barlaam continued to go through the town demanding the condemnation of Palamas; he used an argument to which the Patriarch was sensible; the monks of Athos and Thessalonica had organized collective protests which infringed the authority of the Patriarch as guardian of dogma. He was alluding to the *Hagioretic Tome* and another *Tome* written by the monks at Thessalonica and addressed to Calecas, the contents of which decided, in anticipation, the issue of the dispute between Barlaam and Palamas without regard for a possible patriarchal ruling.[30] Palamas, for his part, was ready for any eventuality; in a letter written to Akindynos, he says he is soon coming to Constantinople : he will accompany thither the Emperor Andronicus III himself, who had passed the winter at Thessalonica, and was making ready to defend the friend of his childhood. In the same letter Palamas touched on some dogmatic points which shocked his correspondent, and which the latter was subsequently to refute. While waiting, Akindynos adopted a much more deferential attitude towards him than towards Barlaam at that time; he even expressed his admiration for his letter, while reserving his answer concerning the substance of it.[31]

Convocation of the Council

The Patriarch John Calecas sought to resolve the dispute at a simple session of the Patriarchal Court, as a matter of ecclesiastical discipline —he was to try later to interpret the *Tome* of 1341 in this sense—but he did not succeed. The Empress Anne of Savoy opposed this procedure,

---

[28] Akindynos, *Report*, ed. cit., p. 86.
[29] Palamas, *Letter to Philotheus*, Coisl. 99, fol. 172.
[30] ibid., p. 87; cf. also Palamas, *Refutation of Calecas*, Coisl. 99, fol. 128.
[31] Letter of Palamas in *Theologia*, XXIV, 1953; answer of Akindynos, Ambros. gr. 290, fol. 74; later refutation of Palamas by Akindynos, Monac. gr. 223, fol. 32–51.

and insisted on waiting for her husband's return.[32] Barlaam also demanded an imperial decision.[33] In the Emperor's absence he had gained the support of men of such influence that Palamas would be summoned before the Synod as a defendant. He was himself instructed to send an official letter, not to Palamas himself, but to the ecclesiastical authorities at Thessalonica, commanding them to send Palamas to answer before the Synod the accusations made against him. Akindynos, always anxious to limit the effect of the dispute, felt that this procedure really gave too much of an advantage to Barlaam: he wrote to Calecas, and then personally petitioned the Synod that a letter should be sent to Palamas himself: otherwise he would appear to be condemned in advance. The Patriarch again acquiesced; an attempt was made to hold back the first letter, but Barlaam had not waited for the Patriarch's hesitations before despatching it.[34] Akindynos then obtained a second letter, which he sent himself to Palamas—he was to write in his *Report* that it was such as Palamas himself would have desired—and accompanied it with a personal letter which has survived; 'I have not thought it necessary,' he writes, 'that thou shouldest be told by me what zeal I have shown for thy holiness before the bishops, and before thy persecutor. Many have already told thee of it, and many more will do so. The present document' [the Patriarch's second letter] 'is also a result of my zeal, for the Patriarch's former letter was, in my view, to be regretted...'[35]

Palamas immediately answered the summons. He came to the capital accompanied by three of his best friends, Mark, Isidore and Dorotheos.[36] Joseph Calothetos was also among the monks summoned by the Patriarch.[37] Passing through Adrianople, Gregory sent a letter to David Dishypatos, who was then in the wilderness of Paroria where Gregory of Sinai had established a hermitage,[38] asking him also to agree to come to Constantinople. David was to become one of the most eminent defenders of Palamism. He had been in contact with Barlaam at the time when he began to attack the monks of Thessalonica, and had tried

[32] Philotheus, *Encomion*, 596D.
[33] *Synodal Tome of 1341*, P.G. CLI, 681A.
[34] Akindynos, *Report*, p. 87.
[35] *Ambros. gr.* 73v–74.
[36] Philotheus, *Encomion*, col. 595CD; *Life of Isidore*, p. 86; Isidore, *Last Will*, in Miklosich-Muller, *Acta*, I, 288.
[37] Joseph Calothetos, *Against Gabras*, Angel gr. 66, fol. 120v; *Letter to Calecas*, ibid., fol. 132.
[38] Paroria was situated in the Strandja Mountains, between Adrianople and Sozopolis (B. Kiselkov, *Srednevekovna Paroriia i sinaitoviiat monastir*, in Sbornik v chest' na V. N. Zlatarski, Sofia, 1925, pp. 103–18) and was in the fourteenth century one of the main centres of hesychastic spirituality in the Balkans.

to restrain him. He was no longer at Paroria when Palamas's invitation arrived, for he had already received one from Akindynos,[39] and had started out, arriving at Constantinople three days after Palamas and his companions. Akindynos hoped that David would help him in his work of conciliation; it was a question of subduing Barlaam and moderating Palamas who gave the former too many openings, especially in his letter from Thessalonica; his own friends ought to persuade him to drop these dangerous expressions; he would listen to them more than to Akindynos who had already opposed him : for Palamas was obstinate (σφόδρα ἰσχυρογνώμων) and there was danger of arousing strife in the Church.

So when Gregory and his companions arrived, at the same time as the Emperor Andronicus, at Constantinople in the spring of 1341, the situation was not very good for them. Barlaam had arrived seven months before them,[40] and his campaign had produced results; he could count on a fairly large number of supporters, and a still larger number of notables, both civil and ecclesiastical, wished above all, as did Akindynos, to avoid a dispute about dogma. The Patriarch John Calecas was among the latter.

Attempts at conciliation

Philotheus states in his *Encomion* of Palamas that his *Triads* and his speeches before the Synod of Bishops convinced most of them, including Calecas.[41] Akindynos accompanied Palamas and openly supported him. Probably the presence at Constantinople of the spiritual leaders of the monks of Athos brought home to the Patriarch the importance of the forces they represented. Andronicus III, returned from his victorious campaign in the Balkans, tried by negotiation to make peace between the two parties. A late anti-Palamite source gives some details about the Emperor's efforts; in a preliminary meeting with the bishops and high officials, Andronicus III decided to forbid Barlaam to accuse Palamas of heresy, in order to avoid a controversy about dogma.[42]

Problems of evidence

Before discussing the actual events between June and August 1341 at Constantinople, we must find an answer to a question which has long

---

[39] Published by V. Laurent, *L'assaut avorté de la Horde d'Or contre l'Empire byzantin*, in *Revue des études byzantines*, XVIII, 1960, pp. 157–60.
[40] Palamas, *Theophanes*, P.G. CL, 913C.
[41] *Encomion*, 596AC.
[42] Arsenius of Tyre, *Project of Tome*, Vatic. gr. 2335, *fol.* 1; cf. Cantacuzene, *Hist.*, II, 39, Bonn, p. 550; Gregoras, *Hist.*, XI, 11, Bonn, I, 558.

puzzled historians; what is the precise authority and significance of the *Tome* which the Synod then published, and which is our principal source of information about these events.

Th. Uspenskii was the first to advance the hypothesis that the council did not constitute a real victory for Palamism; it was confined to condemning Barlaam, without specifically approving Palamas.[43] Many writers, M. Jugie in particular, have reasonably objected that 'too many things in the decree favoured the hesychast theologian for him to have resisted the temptation to raise a paean of victory.'[44] His contemporaries, whether supporters or adversaries of Palamas, also recognized the clearly Palamite character of the document. Akindynos and Arsenius of Tyre, in order to explain the presence of John Calecas's signature on the document, suggest that the Patriarch had not realized the heresy which it contained.[45] Calecas himself clearly refuses to admit such ignorance on his own part, and pleads the pressure brought to bear on him by Cantacuzene, after the death of Andronicus III, while at the same time trying to interpret the *Tome* to suit himself.[46] Finally, Nicephorus Gregoras is the most frank of the three; he states that the *Tome* is decidedly Palamite in content, and that Calecas simply repudiated his signature when fighting Palamas.[47]

Martin Jugie tries to show however that the document is not a faithful record of the debates, basing this view on Akindynos's account and the fact that the *Tome* was not published till two months after the council. There were actually two councils in 1341; one in June, the other in August. The one in June, according to Jugie, confined itself to condemning Barlaam, without much approving Palamas; but in August, after the death of Andronicus III, Cantacuzene imposed Palamism on the Patriarch and forced him to sign a cooked version of the debates of June.[48]

We must try to disentangle these contradictions. In the first place there seems no sufficient reason to suspect the *Tome* of giving a false account of the debates of June; only the vague expressions of Akindynos, whose interest in the matter is clear, support this hypothesis. On the other hand, the Patriarch John Calecas in his *Interpretation of the Tome,* unequivocably confirms its complete authenticity. He certainly speaks of the pressure brought to bear by Cantacuzene, but *that pressure*

---

[43] *Ocherki po istorii vizantiiskoi obrazovannosti,* pp. 334–40.
[44] *Palamas (Grégoire),* in *Dict. de théol. cath.,* XI, 2, col. 1739.
[45] Akindynos, *Report,* p. 90; Arsenius, quoted in G. Mercati, *Notizie di Procoro,* p. 204, n. 3.
[46] *Interpretation of the Tome,* P.G. CL, 901AB.
[47] *First Antirrhetics,* I, Geneva gr. 35, fol. 15.
[48] *Palamite (Controverse),* in *Dict. de Théol. cath.,* XI, 2, col. 1778–84.

concerns the publication of the document, and not its content, which Calecas approves, and for which he recognizes his responsibility.[49]

Attitude of the Patriarch

The many inconsistencies in the Patriarch's behaviour from 1338 onwards can be explained by his desire to avoid any dogmatic controversy; many times he shows a complete incapacity to make up his mind about the real point at issue between the Calabrian and the monks, and he longs to stop the argument without being forced to take part in it. When circumstances finally obliged him to preside over a Council, he did this while trying as far as possible to limit the strictly dogmatic element in his decision; for that reason he gladly accepted the imperial decision forbidding Barlaam from discussing any question of doctrine.

However, in fact, this tended to assure the triumph of the monks, since their adversary was prevented from contradicting them. As we shall see, purely political reasons were later to oblige him to deny this triumph which is unanimously attested by the Palamite sources. He was then to attempt to give an artificial interpretation of the debates of 1341; the Council was said indeed to have condemned Barlaam, but without entirely approving Palamas. However, he never denied the authenticity of the record of the debates, as it is found in the *Tome* of the month of August signed by himself, although he tried to overlook the fact that this record bore witness to the Palamite triumph. We can, therefore, trust this document as a perfectly authentic source for the Council's proceedings in June. The form of the *Tome* and the delay in its publication are explained by events which we will now briefly recapitulate.

The Council of June 1341

The meeting took place on June 10th in St. Sophia,[50] and lasted only one day. It was a true Council and not an ordinary session of the Synod; the hearings were public; Andronicus III presided in person, surrounded by senators and 'general judges' and those bishops then present in the capital, and several archimandrites and *hegoumenoi*.

The accuser was allowed to speak first, but Barlaam soon entered the forbidden sphere of argument about the energies. The Patriarch then ordered to be read the canons of former Councils which reserved the power of doctrinal instruction to bishops only. The canons read,

---

[49] *P.G.* CL, 901B; cf. his *Letter to the Athonites,* in Miklosich-Muller, *Acta,* I, 241.
[50] Cantacuzene, *Hist.* II, 40, Bonn, I, 557–60; Gregoras, *Hist.* XI, 11, Bonn, I, 559–60.

Barlaam's official complaint was put in evidence, and Palamas was allowed to defend himself. Then two points in Barlaam's *Against the Messalians* were examined, and thus the latter became the accused instead of accuser:

1. His teaching about the light on Mount Tabor, which he said was created (*Tome, P.G.* CLI, col. 682C–688C): thus in fact the session began to discuss theology, against the original will of the Patriarch....

2. His criticisms of the 'prayer of Jesus,' which, he asserted, introduced into the church practices of the Bogomils who also recognized only one prayer, the 'Our Father.' Barlaam had also found another way of attacking the form of the 'prayer of Jesus' then most commonly used ('Lord Jesus Christ, Son of God, have mercy on me'): according to him, it did not explicitly assert that Christ was God (ibid. col. 688D–691C)....

Identical procedure was used to examine both these questions: first some extracts from Barlaam's work were read; then the monks countered with quotations from the Fathers, and, finally, the Emperor stated the conclusions from the debate. In two places the *Tome* mentions, as self-evident, the distinction between the 'essence' and 'energy' of God; this occurs first in the preamble, where the accusation of ditheism brought against Palamas by Barlaam, and later to be repeated by Akindynos, is also refuted (680B), and then in the speech of Andronicus III (688C).

At the end of the day Barlaam saw that the atmosphere of the council was clearly unfavourable to him. He asked the advice of his protector, the Great Domestic, who sat by the side of Andronicus III. Cantacuzene advised him to confess his error, to which he agreed, and Palamas freely pardoned him. Palamite sources describe the conclusion of the Synod in terms of euphoria at regained peace.[51] Gregoras too praises Andronicus's speech in which he then celebrated the general reconciliation.[52]

This happy atmosphere did not last long. The Emperor suddenly fell ill on the day after the Council, and died on June 15th. Barlaam, supported by some disciples, started his attacks again; then, finally seeing that his ideas had no chance of triumphing at Constantinople, he left the Eastern Empire; Italy of the Renaissance and the Court of Avignon were in fact to prove much more open to his nominalistic humanism; there he taught Petrarch Greek, and was finally raised by the Pope to the bishopric of Gerace in the Greek Uniate Church.

[51] Cantacuzene, ibid., 555; Philotheus, *Encomion*, 599D; *Against Akindynos* II, *P.G.* CLI, 1157C.
[52] *Hist.* XI, 10, Bonn, 558–9.

So Gregory Palamas's victory had certainly been complete from June 10th, 1341. Immediately after the meeting, the Patriarch John published a circular letter denouncing 'what the monk Barlaam had said against the holy hesychasts,' and enjoining, on pain of excommunication, the inhabitants of Constantinople to deposit at the patriarchate any copies of Barlaam's works in their possession, and the inhabitants of other towns to bring them to the local ecclesiastical authorities to be publicly destroyed.[53]

Submission of Akindynos

But the adversaries of Palamism had not disarmed: apart from Barlaam himself, who recommenced his attacks for a short time, Akindynos began to object to certain expressions of Palamas. But Palamas considered that his theology had been approved as one whole, and he was right on this point; his *Third Triad* had, before the Council, clearly established the distinction between the divine 'essence' and 'energies': in that lay his essential argument against the accusation of Messalianism ('vision of the divine essence with corporal eyes') launched against him by Barlaam. No one, except Akindynos, had found any objection to raise, and even the latter had nonetheless agreed to support him before the authorities. Even if, as Akindynos asserts, they had a private agreement between them before the Council not to broach the problem that separated them,[54] that agreement was rendered void by Andronicus's speech at the Council, which had clearly mentioned the distinction between essence and grace.

Moreover it is clear that, in the purely theological field, there was no room for a *via media* between Palamas and Barlaam; it was Akindynos's sad fate to persist in wishing to find one, at whatever cost, by cleaving to the hesychasts in the field of spirituality, and to Barlaam in that of theology. But the two fields were inseparable, and Akindynos's thought, which was very weak on the theological side, and rather characteristic of medieval Byzantine scholasticism ended by continually vacillating between Barlaamite nominalism and a form of realism opposed both to Palamas and to all the tradition of the Greek Fathers, in that it asserted the possibility for man to share in the divine essence. He was sincerely convinced that Palamas was mistaken, especially because Palamas interpreted the patristic tradition in a living and creative way. In their discussion, two forms of conservatism came into conflict; the formal conservatism which consisted in verbal repetition of the formulas

---

[53] Miklosich-Muller, *Acta*, I, 201–2; the exact date of this document, which preceded the *Tome*, is indicated by Palamas, *Refutation of the Patriarch of Antioch*, Coisl. 99, fol. 150; *Refutation of Calecas*, Coisl. 99, fol. 157.
[54] Akindynos, *Report*, p. 88.

of the Fathers, and the truly traditional spirit which wished to share the living experience of the Fathers, always accessible in the catholic life of the Church, and not only the words they spoke. The first form of conservatism suited the Byzantine humanists well, for it allowed them freely to steep themselves in 'profane wisdom,' while remaining formally faithful to Orthodoxy, and avoiding all living confrontation with Christian truth. It is that which links the rather dim figure of Akindynos with such brilliant personalities as Nicephorus Gregoras and, later, Demetrios Cydones.

In personal talks with his new adversaries, in particular one which took place at the monastery of the Patriarch Athanasius I, Palamas must fairly easily have had the better of him; Akindynos was even obliged to confirm his agreement with him in writing,[55] but he retracted it soon afterwards. It was perhaps to account for this gesture out of keeping with the rest of his behaviour, that he talked of threats of assassination by the Palamites.[56]

The Council of August 1341

A second Council was convened in the galleries of St. Sophia [57] in the month of August 1341. Cantacuzene, who still performed the functions of Great Domestic and in fact ruled the Empire, was again present, as were all the participants in the Council of June, except the Emperor. The Patriarch summoned Akindynos as the accused, but at first sought, as always, to limit the discussion to simple questions of discipline. To this end he asked Theodore Dexios to read a passage of St. Basil about the impossibility of knowing God; that was the only act of the Patriarch which Akindynos considered favourable to the anti-Palamites.[58] For the rest he was ready to support Palamas right to the end; Palamite sources declare that he was frankly in favour of the monks,[59] whereas they might have represented him as dissimulating; that, anyhow, is how they described Akindynos's attitude before June 1341. Apart from the reading from St. Basil, Gregory Akindynos himself does not mention any motion in his favour by the Patriarch: on the other hand he does complain of the outrages to which he and his supporters were subjected, without mentioning any intervention by the

---

[55] The discussion is described by Joseph Calothetos, *Letter to Calecas*, Angel. gr. 66, *fol.* 134 2v; the written confession of Akindynos is mentioned in the *Tome of 1347* (Mikl., *Acta*, I, 246); its text is published in J. Meyendorff, *Le Tome synodal de 1347*, in *Zbornik Radova*, Belgrade, VIII, 1, 1963, p. 226.
[56] *Report*, p. 89.
[57] Calecas, *Interpretation of the Tome*, P.G. CL, 901A.
[58] Akindynos, *Report*, p. 89.
[59] Philotheus, *Encomion*, 596BC; Marc., *Appeal to Calecas*, Coisl. 288, *fol.* 305v.

Patriarch to protect him. Finally, in a letter of 1342 to George Lapithos, he mentions the anti-Palamism of Calecas as a *new* factor of the situation.[60] Moreover in his *Report* he omits any detailed description of what happened at the Synod in August, and for good reason for the Synod condemned him too, and made him sign a document in which he accepted the decision of the Synod against Barlaam and rejected his teaching about the light.[61] He did it not without reluctance, for the crowd attending the meeting did not disguise its disapproval of him.

This formal condemnation, naturally confirmed by all the Palamite sources, had important consequences at the time of civil war, between 1341 and 1347. The Empress Anne, who, at least at the beginning, raised no objection to the campaign he then launched against Palamas and his supporters, openly opposed his ordination as a deacon, on the ground that it was a formally anti-canonical proceeding, since the sentence against him had not previously been rescinded.

The condemnation of Akindynos is omitted by the *Tome,* which, in general, does not breathe a word about the second Council in August 1341, but only records the debates of June. The form thus given to the document allowed the anti-Palamites for some time to take no notice of the condemnation of Akindynos, and has allowed some modern historians to speak of a 'Palamite *conciliabulum* in the month of August.' [62] How can that silence be explained? An anonymous letter from a Palamite, dating from about 1342, attributes it to the desire of the monks to give Akindynos a chance to repent.[63] However political reasons were certainly decisive in shaping the *Tome* as we know it.

Political complications

After the death of Andronicus III power was disputed between two claimants to the regency, Cantacuzene and the Patriarch John Calecas. There is no indication that this political struggle coincided, from that moment, with the doctrinal convictions of the two main protagonists. As we have seen, Calecas does not appear very enthusiastic about supporting the anti-Palamites at that time. On the other hand he tells us himself that he refused to give an official character to the Council of August, and that for two reasons :

1. So as not to make a decision on dogma.

2. Not to give Cantacuzene the honour of presiding over a Council, that being an imperial prerogative.[64]

[60] *Marc. gr.* 155, *fol.* 54v.
[61] The document is in part quoted by Palamas, *Against Akindynos*, VI, 2, *Coisl.* 98. *fol.* 150v.
[62] M. Jugie, *Palamite (controverse)*, col. 1784.
[63] *Chalc. Panagh*, 157, *fol.* 287.
[64] *Interpretation of the Tome*, P.G. CL, 901B.

So Calecas agreed to publish a document confirming the victory of the monks, on condition that there was no mention of the Synod of August actually presided over by Cantacuzene.[65] Thus the Patriarch was powerful enough to stand up to the Great Domestic, imposing silence on him about a Synod at which he had acted as *de facto* emperor, and which might have proved a valuable precedent had his signature appeared on the *Tome*. That is exactly how such a Cantacuzenist as Philotheus interprets the events of August; 'The honoured Emperor,' he writes, referring to Cantacuzene, 'was present—although he was not then invested with power; or rather let us say that he possessed the power and directed the affairs of state, only the diadem and the name of "emperor" being still lacking—and he took the place of the honoured Emperor his brother (Andronicus III).'[66]

It was just that *de facto* position which the Patriarch would not recognize, and he succeeded in providing that the *Tome* said nothing about it. The document was edited as Calecas wished, which again proves that he could, had he so desired, have given it a less Palamite colouring. But, probably thinking that the controversy had been altogether closed by the triumph of the monks, he approved a text which Palamas himself may have edited, and he added a formal interdict against reopening the argument.[67] The monks could have wished for nothing better.

Moreover Calecas showered various favours on them, perhaps to win them to his side in his struggle of influence with Cantacuzene. Palamas tells us that the Patriarch offered him the bishopric of Monembasia and, on his refusal, had his great friend Isidore elected thereto, suggesting that Palamas should become Metropiltan of Thessalonica.[68] We shall see later that Palamas, still at Constantinople after the synods, played an important part in the unofficial political meetings accompanying the *coup d'état* of October 1341 : it is clear that his authority and influence were great, and that his victory in the religious field had been complete.

The Synodal Tome

The published text of the *Tome* does state in its title that *several* synods had pronounced on the case of Barlaam and Akindynos, but that same title also stresses the presence of Andronicus III, which alone gave full authority to its decisions. Several unpublished copies

---

[65] Akindynos, *Report*, p. 89; Calecas, *Interpretation*, 901B.
[66] *Encomion*, 601B; cf. *Tome of 1347*, ed. Meyendorff, in *Zbornik Radova*, 1963, p. 214.
[67] *P.G.* CLI, 692AB; cf. Akindynos, *Report*, p. 90.
[68] *Refutation of Calecas*, Coisl. 99, *fol.* 140v-141; cf. David Dishypatos, *Poems*, ed. R. Browning, in *Byzantion*, XXV-XXVII, 1955-7, fesc. 2, p. 726.

of the *Tome* have a longer title which makes the nature of the document even clearer; after the title found in the present published editions, one finds the following: 'the decision was taken in the presence of the Emperor, but the *Tome* was compiled after his death [he lived for one week after being ill] and signed in the month of August, ninth indiction, 1341.' [69] The editors of the document clearly felt that the 'decision' could only have been taken in the presence of Andronicus III, as the question of his successor had not been settled in August 1341. Therefore the Synod of August had not made a 'decision'; it had simply made the condemnation of June apply to Akindynos: 'should any one raise the same accusations as Barlaam had done against the monks . . . orally or in writing . . . he will fall within the scope of the same condemnation.' [70] That is why the contemporary writings of Palamas all tend to prove that Akindynos was a 'Barlaamite,' which is not quite correct.

The *Tome* was not however signed without some difficulties. Palamas and Joseph Calothetos say that the Akindynists did all they could to prevent the bishops following the example of the Patriarch who had signed first. However, as many as seven bishops, besides the Patriarch, did sign the document in August.[71] They were Gregory of Sardis, Gregory of Dyrrhacium, Nilus of Lacedemone, Isaac of Madyta, Malachy of Methymna, Macarius of Vidin and Athanasius of Cyzicus. Those names are found in two of the best copies of the *Tome*. The signature of Athanasius of Cyzicus was not obtained without difficulty; he had had annoyances at the Council of June; the assembly refused to read the documents he had brought; later, he had not been asked to take a share in editing the *Tome*, and he asked for delays before he would sign. Moreover he had been supplied with falsified ($παρακεχαραγ-μένα$) copies of Palamas's writings, which had given him a wrong idea of his opinions; it was only after he had seen the authentic version of Palamas's works that he would sign the *Tome*.[72]

The 'falsified writings'

What were these 'falsified writings' of Palamas, of which Athanasius of Cyzicus spoke? We find the answer to this question in Palamas's unpublished works which, throughout the controversy raging during the civil war from 1341 to 1347, accuse Akindynos of spreading false

[69] This long title is to be found for example in Patm. 423, s. XV (Sakellion, *Patmiake Bibliotheke*, p. 189).
[70] *P.G.* CLI, 691D–692A.
[71] Palamas, *Against Akindynos*, I, 8, *Coisl.* 98, *fol.* 39v; Calothetos, *Against Akindynos*, II, *Angel gr.* 66, *fol.* 26.
[72] *P.G.* CL, 692BD.

quotations from his writings. It would be impossible here to quote all the places where Palamas mentions this. We will just pick out a few at random. In his *Apology*, published at the end of 1341, Palamas already complains that Akindynos, now that Barlaam had left Byzantium, dragged certain phrases out of their context, suppressing some words and adding others, to falsify the sense.[73] Elsewhere he gives specific examples of this falsification, and the example recurring most frequently is Akindynos's treatment of a phrase in a letter from Palamas to himself from Thessalonica at the beginning of 1341: 'Deification is therefore a down-going divinity according to the divine theologians, as the great Dionysius says here,[74] for it is a gift of the transcendent essence of God. So Barlaam vainly accuses us of ditheism.'[75] As Palamas explains, Barlaam was already accusing him of ditheism, and had launched the phrase 'down-going divinity' ($\theta\epsilon\acute{o}\tau\eta s$ $\dot{v}\phi\epsilon\iota\mu\acute{e}\nu\eta$) to characterize the Palamite doctrine of grace; Palamas answers, quoting Dionysius, that the word 'down-going' is only admissible on condition of asserting that grace is *also* 'divinity,' for it is the life of the one God communicated to men. 'It is Barlaam, Palamas insists, who began to use this term.'[76] Now Akindynos, writing a *Refutation* of the letter of Palamas and quoting this passage, ends the quotation after 'transcendent' ($\dot{v}\pi\epsilon\rho\kappa\epsilon\iota\mu\acute{e}\nu\eta s$), which clearly makes that word depend on 'of divinity' ($\theta\epsilon\acute{o}\tau\eta\tau os$) understood [77] so Palamas seems to speak of two divinities, one transcendent ($\dot{v}\pi\epsilon\rho\kappa\epsilon\iota\mu\acute{e}\nu\eta$) and the other inferior ($\dot{v}\phi\epsilon\iota\mu\acute{e}\nu\eta$). That was to be the major accusation brought against him by his adversaries, and it is important to establish at once that that expression was not his, and he always indignantly denied its authorship.[78]

It is not necessary to suppose that, from the start, Akindynos had knowingly falsified Palamas's writings; he was only looking for passages which would confirm his personal interpretation of Palamism and, as often happens in such cases, quotations dragged out of context served to prove the opposite of what Palamas was really saying. ... We also know that collections of quotations of this sort compiled by anti-Palamites were circulating at Constantinople, and Athanasius of Cyzicus may have been deceived by one of them.[79]

Akindynos and a small group of his friends were really the only

---

[73] *Coisl.* 99, *fol.* 19.
[74] Reference to Dionysius, *Ep.* II, *P.G.* III, 1068–9.
[75] Ed. Meyendorff, in *Theologia*, XXIV, 1953, p. 577.
[76] *Against Barlaam and Akindynos*, Coisl. 99, *fol.* 36; *Against Akindynos*, II, 9, *Coisl.* 98, *fol.* 53.
[77] *Monac gr.* 223, *fol.* 35.
[78] *Letter to Daniel*, Coisl. 99, *fol.* 100; cf. *Theologia*, ibid., pp. 564–6.
[79] A collection of this sort is to be found in *Barber gr.* 291, *fol.* 216v–218.

people to oppose Palamite theology in 1341. Even Nicephorus Gregoras, in the funeral eulogy of Andronicus III which he delivered in the palace, mentions the speech of the late Emperor at the Council of June 10th condemning the perverse dogmas (διεφθορότα δόγματα) of Barlaam.[80] So the first reaction of the Byzantine Church as a whole was clearly favourable to Palamas, and his victory was by no means due to any alleged use of force by Cantacuzene; the Patriarch also gave him his approval, if not by conviction—Calecas changed his tactics so often that he does not seem ever to have had any—then from interest. Akindynos was thus reduced to the underhand circulation of anti-Palamite writings, whose comparative success was due largely to the misunderstanding of Palamas's thought which they aroused, misunderstandings which have lasted down to our day.

Circumstances purely political delayed the decisive triumph of Palamism, and caused the appearance of a number of polemical works, of which only a part really enrich the theological tradition of Byzantium. Palamas, as early as 1341, had propounded his doctrine with perfect clarity in his *Triads,* his essential life's work, and he could only go on constantly repeating the same arguments, whether in personal letters addressed to men of high standing, or in polemical writings in which he elaborated a more or less fixed theological terminology. However, to understand his thought aright, one should always turn back to his first works directed against Barlaam; in them he had fixed the lines of his theology, and his later writings, designed to refute the successors of that Calabrian philosopher, add nothing but greater precision.

---

[80] *Hist.* XI, 11, Bonn, I, 564; Philotheus quotes this passage to prove that Gregoras, in 1341, was 'in agreement with the Church of Christ' (*Against Gregoras,* VI, *P.G.* CLI, 920D–921A).

CHAPTER IV

THE TIME OF CIVIL WAR
(1341—1347)

The political situation

Dying on June 15th, 1341, Andronicus III Palaeologus left an heir only nine years old and a widow, the Empress Anne of Savoy, a Western princess ill prepared to steer her way through the shoals of Byzantine politics. From June 18th two claimants for the regency stood forward: the Patriarch John Calecas, supported by Alexis Apocaucos, and the Great Domestic Cantacuzene. The former relied on a document written by Andronicus and delivered to him and the members of the Synod at the time of his elevation to the patriarchate: the Emperor, according to the document, entrusted the Church with the guardianship of his wife and children in the event of political disturbance.[1] There was a Byzantine tradition which made the Patriarch of Constantinople the proper guardian of dynastic continuity. Claiming that authority Arsenius had opposed the usurpation of Michael VIII Palaeologus, and John Calecas explicitly cited that precedent, while promising to do better than he; to avoid having his hand forced, as had happened to Arsenius, Calecas took charge of all civil affairs jointly with the Empress Anne.[2] Thus the Patriarch claimed a regency similar to that of Nicholas the Mystikos in the tenth century.

Cantacuzene's claims were based mostly on the friendship expressed for him by Andronicus III, and the power he had actually wielded in the Emperor's lifetime. The ties between him and the dead Emperor were those of some spiritual fraternity, which enabled him to say throughout his reign, a reign contested at first but later universally recognized, that in proclaiming himself Emperor he was doing no violence to the legitimate succession, and that he was but clothing himself in a dignity which Andronicus himself had offered to him.[3]

Hence the political equilibrium could not be maintained after Andronicus's death, except by a *modus vivendi* between the two opposing forces. After numerous more or less stormy arguments, Cantacuzene and the Patriarch exchanged oaths of mutual fidelity, and Cantacuzene

---

[1] Gregoras, *Hist.* X, 7, Bonn, I, 496.
[2] ibid., XII, 3, Bonn, II, 579; the political ambitions of Calecas are rightly emphasized by D. Stanilooe, op. cit., pp. 120ff.
[3] Cantacuzene, *Hist.* II, 40, Bonn, 559; cf. F. Dolger, *Johannes VI Kantakuzenos als dynastischen Legitimist,* in *Annales de l'Institut Kondakov,* X, 1938, pp. 19–29.

left on a military campaign in the Balkans.[4] Apparently he had renounced any exclusive claim, for at the Patriarch's insistence he agreed that the Council of August should not be formally mentioned in the Synodal *Tome* of 1341. But in October Calecas and Apocaucos gained complete control of affairs by a sudden *coup d'état*.[5]

Palamas and the coup d'état

Gregory Palamas who was at Constantinople at the time of these events, did not remain insensible to them. At the *coup d'état* he sided openly against the Patriarch. His family connections, his spiritual authority and his recent victory over Barlaam gave him easy access to the high functionaries of the Empire; to them he became the advocate of 'unjustly abused' Cantacuzene, and he impressed on them the catastrophic consequences of a civil war which the *coup d'état* was bound to provoke.[6] In October 1341 Calecas had summoned him, communicated the project to him, and solicited his support. But Palamas urged peace between the opposing forces; the Patriarch then became so furious with Palamas that the *megas dux* Alexis Apocaucos had to intervene to protect him and bear witness to his good intentions.[7] Palamas's essential object was to preserve the *status quo* worked out with difficulty after Andronicus's death: in all his writings of this period he declares himself the defender of 'peace' and 'concord' between the two political clans who were tearing the Empire. 'What should we do,' he writes to the monks of Athos, 'when discord arises? Rouse our compatriots against each other, or make them understand that they are members of one body, and that they should not treat their compatriots as strangers? . . . Thus we have been designed by fate as ministers of peace.'[8]

Palamas was in the direct tradition of Athanasius I and of Theoleptos of Philadelphia when he thus took direct part in the political affairs of his time. His attitude cannot be explained by such a simplification as is suggested by O. Tafrali; 'Behind the hesychast question one must . . . see two parties face to face; the nobles and the rich on one side, the popular party on the other.'[9] Even if one adopts that view to explain the civil war between the government of Anne, supposed protector of the poor, and Cantacuzene, leader of the feudal nobility, it would still have to be proved that the hesychasts supported Cantacuzene

---

[4] Gregoras, *Hist.* XII, 6. Bonn, II, 595.
[5] cf. Ostrogorsky, *History*, Oxford, 1956, p. 455.
[6] *Tome of 1347*, ed. cit., p. 215; Philotheus, *Encomion*, 601D–602A.
[7] Palamas, *Letter to Philotheus*, Coisl. 99, *fol.* 169v.
[8] *Letter to the Athonites*, Coisl. 99, fol. 173v.
[9] *Thessalonique au XIVe siècle*, p. 203; for a more objective point of view, see now I. Ševčenko, *Alexios Makrembolites*, in *Srpska Akademija Nauka, Vizant. Institut, Zbornik Radova*, 6, 1960, p. 199.

THE TIME OF CIVIL WAR (1341-1347)

just because, in defending feudal privileges, he also protected monastic property. Now we have noted before that the hesychasts belonged to a Byzantine spiritual tradition generally opposed to the enrichment of the monks. Moreover we will show in the course of this chapter that all the supporters of Cantacuzene were not Palamites, and that, inversely, the government of Anne never completely accepted either the religious policy of the Patriarch John Calecas, or the theology of Akindynos.

What led Palamas to intervene in politics, was first the perfectly justified feeling that intestinal quarrels were the main cause of Byzantine decadence; in defending Cantacuzene he was also aware of another fact appreciated by the best modern historians; the Great Domestic was 'the only man able' to continue 'the work of rehabilitation' which Andronicus had begun with his collaboration.[10] Purely religious motives also determined the action of Gregory and his disciples, in that they had, with reason, more confidence in the Orthodoxy of Cantacuzene than in that of the other leading figures of Byzantium.

Anyhow Palamas did not intend to make a definite choice between the two opposing factions. In his writings he always showed the greatest respect not only for the Empress Anne of Savoy, but also for the *megas dux* Alexis Apocaucos, the chief enemy of Cantacuzene. In his stormy argument with the Patriarch, Alexis, as we saw, came to Palamas's defence against the Patriarch's wrath. Palamas mentions Apocaucos several times in writings dating from the civil war, and no mention is unfavourable. Palamas also indignantly dismissed allegations that he (Palamas) was in secret contact with Cantacuzene. As a defender of 'peace' he did not want to 'take part in politics,' but to combat the injustice and perjury of which the Patriarch had been guilty.

He did not change his mind when Cantacuzene had himself proclaimed Emperor at Didymotica. At Byzantium, as at Rome, there was no law of succession; family ties might indicate the man sent by providence and chosen by God, in Byzantine eyes, to be the Emperor; but the divine choice might be manifest in some other way, notably by what we should now call a usurpation. These two, juridically incompatible, doctrines (that of family legitimacy, and that of 'providential usurpation') have always coexisted in the Eastern Empire. In assuming the purple, Cantacuzene could appeal to many illustrious precedents; he was careful, however, to pay tribute to the doctrine of legitimacy by continuing to recognize the little John V as first Emperor.[11] The latter was crowned on November 19th, 1341, by Calecas as unique Emperor.[12]

[10] L. Bréhier, *Vie et Mort de Byzance*, pp. 434-5.
[11] cf. L. Bréhier, *Les institutions de l'Empire byzantin*, pp. 17-26.
[12] The homily pronounced by the patriarch at that occasion has been published by P. Joannou in *Orientalia Chr. Periodica*, XXVII, 1961, fosc. I, pp. 38-45.

Palamas at St. Michael of Sosthenion

Palamas himself gives a very detailed account of events in 1341-2. He tells how, after repeated unsuccessful attempts to reverse the political current at Constantinople, he decided to retire to the monastery of St. Michael of Sosthenion on the Bosphorus a few miles from Constantinople.[13] Away from the political intrigues of the capital, his authority was no less dangerous for the Patriarch who decided to get rid of this very formidable political adversary. In midwinter 1341-2 he gave Akindynos a certain licence to attack Palamas's theology,[14] without however allowing him to write. The idea of using Akindynos to strike at Palamas's moral authority had, therefore, come into Calecas's head, but he did not yet dare to rely openly on the monk condemned in August.

At the beginning of March 1342 a messenger from the Patriarch sought Palamas out in his monastery and made this proposal; if he would agree to come back to Constantinople to support the anti-Cantecuzenist party, Akindynos would again be prevented from harming him. Gregory was certainly not the man to be caught by that bait. He answered that he had no intention of modifying his political attitude which accorded with the true interests of the people and the Emperors; that as Akindynos had been formally condemned by the Synod, the Patriarch had only to do his duty in that matter; he agreed to come back to Constantinople, but only at the end of Lent.

At Constantinople

In fact he returned on Palm Sunday, March 24th. Meanwhile he had received news that a delegation of Athonite monks, with the *protos* Isaac at its head, was on its way to the capital to negotiate peace with the court of Anne of Savoy. He hurried to meet them, received them on their arrival on March 26th,[15] and brought them to his own quarters in the town, but he did not go with them to the palace. The delegation from Athos had gone to the capital at the express request of Cantacuzene, and it strengthened Palamas's position.[16] The *protos* was accompanied by several abbots, notably Macarius of Lavra and Lazarus of Philotheou, and by several well-known *hagiorites,* among whom Cantacuzene mentions Callistos, the future Patriarch of Constantinople and Sabbas of Vatopedi.

---

[13] *Letter to Philotheus, Coisl.* 99, *fol.* 169, 171, etc.; cf. R. Janin, *La géographie ecclésiastique,* pp. 359-62.

[14] Palamas, *Letter to Philotheus, Coisl.* 99, *fol.* 169; the greatest part of the historical information related below is also taken from this letter.

[15] Philotheus, *Life of Sabbas,* ed. cit., pp. 322-3.

[16] Cantacuzene, *Hist.* III, 34, Bonn, II, 209; Gregoras, *Hist.* XII, 14, Bonn, II, 620.

THE TIME OF CIVIL WAR (1341-1347)

During Easter week, in the first days of April, Palamas went alone to visit the Empress Anne; this audience did not last long, the Patriarch and high officials having insisted on attending the interview, which was again purely concerned with politics and led to nothing. Palamas writing to Philotheus sarcastically reports that the arguments of the principal dignitaries of the Court 'were not suitable for his ears'; they blamed him also for deciding their policies without knowing what was happening. The interview ended with polite phrases.

Palamas stayed another five weeks in the capital. After May 12th he went back to St. Michael's on the Bosphorus. The Patriarch sought some pretext to be rid of a weighty adversary, and Palamas preferred to avoid too violent a conflict. As was the practice of hesychasts, he did not live in the monastery; the place was not suited for repose, the sound of boatmen on the Bosphorus being constantly heard; he preferred to retreat to the hills, not far from the column of St. Daniel Stylites, where there were many hermitages.

Negotiations with the Patriarch

Between May 19th and 26th an official of the Patriarchate sought him at St. Michael's. Not finding him there, he returned to the capital. Palamas also went there, and heard through his friends that a Council had assembled to consider his case; some bishops, partisans of Calecas, took part in it, and some civil officials, mostly young and relations of Irene Choumnos, widow of the despot John Palaeologus, who, under the name of Eulogia, presided over a convent at Constantinople. These officials had brought along with them the condemned monk Akindynos and several of his supporters. The object of the meeting, quickly and secretly assembled, was to condemn Palamas, and to enforce sanctions against him. Nothing was decided in the absence of the accused, but it was clear that the Patriarch had found a pretext for getting rid of Palamas, who was going to be condemned for his theology. In the year which had passed since Barlaam's departure, Gregory had continued to write, refuting the teaching, mostly oral, of Akindynos: his *Dialogue between an Orthodox and a Barlaamite,* his *Apology* (a work composed of three treatises, a sort of *Triad* against Akindynos) date from this time: so perhaps does his other dialogue, the *Theophanes.* This polemical activity appeared perfectly legitimate to him, for he was simply developing his teaching about the distinction between the 'essence' and the *'energies,'* a doctrine already clearly stated in his third *Triad* against Barlaam, and explicitly approved by the *Tome* of August 1341. But Calecas was going to bring it under the paragraph which he had himself added to the *Tome,* and which forbade prolongation of the theological controversy.

Gregory remained for some time in the city, changing his residence rather often. One day, probably in June, he was at the monastery of St. John the Baptist at Petra, which had been chosen as the residence of the *protos* of Athos.[17] Two officials of the Patriarchate came there bringing him an order from the Empress to present himself immediately at the palace. Recognizing a ruse of the Patriarch, Palamas refused to follow them : it is not customary, he thought, for ecclesiastics to be bearers of imperial orders. The *protos* then sent Lazarus, *hegoumenos* of Philotheou, to ask for clarification : was it not a question of a new Council? In that case Palamas should not appear alone; the debates should be public, as in 1341, and all Christians, monks especially, should be summoned thither. Lazarus soon came back accompanied by the *nomophylax,* whom Palamas also calls 'judge of the Romans,' and the sacristan of the Great Church; through them Calacas informed the *protos* that there was no intention of summoning a new Council, the question having been decided by that of 1341 : but he did need Palamas in order to examine some of his writings. The Athonites then went all together, but without Palamas, and protested vigorously against Calecas's intentions. They reminded him that he had himself, in the presence of the *nomophylax* and, later, in that of the whole Council, praised Palamas and his theology. The *Tome* of the Synod bore witness to that. Neither Palamas nor they themselves wished to infringe the decisions of the Council. Calecas could not deny such plain facts, and changed the conversation : he alleged that letters of Palamas to Cantacuzene and his allies had been intercepted. Thus he revealed the political reason leading him to pursue Palamas. The monks denied the facts, called it a calumny, and demanded proofs of the accusation against their leader. Being unable to obtain them, they went back to the monastery, and advised Palamas to leave the town as quickly as possible. His presence in the capital really was dangerous for him. Calecas was seeking any pretext to persuade the government of Anne of Savoy to condemn him. For him theology was only a screen to hide his hatred of the 'defenders of peace.' [18]

At Heraclea

Palamas then retired to Heraclea 'so as not to provide a pretext for those who were seeking one.' [19] In his absence, a Synod presided over

[17] The text of the *Letter to Philotheus* (fol. 171v) is here confirmed by Palamas in his *Refutation of the Patriarch of Antioch,* Coisl. 99, fol. 148, and by Cantacuzene, *Hist.* III, 35, Bonn, II, 213; cf. R. Janin, *La géographie,* pp. 435–41.
[18] Besides Palamas, all his supporters emphasize the political motivation of Calecas' action; see for example, Joseph Calothetos, in *Vat. gr.* 704, *fol.* 159.
[19] *Letter to the Athonites,* fol. 174v.

THE TIME OF CIVIL WAR (1341-1347)

by Calecas ordered the destruction of his writings later than August 1341[20]; that was a sanction similar to the measure taken against Barlaam after the publication of the *Tome,* and Akindynos could consider both of them as equally heretical.[21] Isidore, as bishop elect of Monembasia, was also present at this Synod: he invoked the *Tome,* but his protests could not alter the issue of the debates.[22]

Arrest of Palamas

This first decision of the Synod was not enough to force the government of Anne to take measures against Palamas. Akindynos was not yet given complete licence. It was only four months later, at the end of September, and on a purely political charge,[23] that Palamas was arrested. An imperial official, Scoutariotes, came to Heraclea to make an inquiry into Palamas's activities; he made a search in his cell looking for letters from Cantacuzene, and interrogated the governor ($\kappa\epsilon\phi\alpha\lambda\dot\eta$) of Heraclea about his relations with Gregory. He discovered that Palamas had spent four months in complete isolation, and in his report mentioned no suspicious activity on his part. He then brought Gregory to Constantinople, and conducted him straight to a meeting at the palace over which the Empress presided. The civil officers, having heard Scoutariotes's report, declared him innocent, but Calecas, after they had gone, had him imprisoned in a monastery. Gregory protested to the *megas dux* Apocaucos who dismissed the soldiers sent by the Patriarch to guard him. Calecas then had him transferred to a monastery nearer his residence, and forbade him to communicate in any way with the outside world. One of these two monasteries, probably the second, is that of Christ Incomprehensible ($\tau o \tilde{v}$ $'A\kappa\alpha\tau\alpha\lambda\dot\eta\pi\tau o v$).[24] Palamas did not stay there long; thanks to personal friendships, which he still enjoyed at Court, he was able to go to St. Sophia and with sixteen of his disciples for two months claim the right of asylum there, while asking in vain that a new Council should be summoned.[25] The troubles resulting from their presence in the church occasioned an imperial decree ($\pi\rho\dot o\sigma\tau\alpha\gamma\mu\alpha$), dated March 1343, which confirmed the right of asylum in St. Sophia, but provided that the refugees should not live in the church itself, but should take up their quarters in the places

---

[20] Akindynos, *Report,* ed. cit., p. 91; *Letter to Lapithos, Marc. gr.* 155, *fol.* 54v.
[21] Anonymous letter, ibid., *fol.* 39.
[22] Akindynos, *Report,* ibid.
[23] Palamas, *Refutation of the Patriarch of Antioch, Coisl.* 99, *fol.* 148v–149; cf. Gregoras, *Hist.* XV, 7 Bonn, II, 768.
[24] Akindynos, *Report,* p. 91.
[25] Palamas, *Letter to the Athonites, Coisl.* 99, *fol.* 175v; *Refutation of the Patriarch of Antioch, fol.* 148v.

traditionally assigned to them.[26] It is difficult to tell whether this decree was meant to protect Palamas and his friends, or whether it served as a judicial pretext for expelling them. Anyhow we know that finally they were forced to leave St. Sophia, and that Gregory accused the Patriarch of responsibility for this violation of the privileges of the basilica.[27] Palamas's comparative security in the monasteries, and especially at St. Sophia, cut across Calecas's policies, and roused the indignation of Akindynos who, just at this moment, was allowed to present his *Report* to the Patriarch and Synod. That *Report,* from which we have often quoted, suggested to the Patriarch a version of the facts designed to make it easy for him to turn decisively against Palamas. In April or May 1343 the latter and his disciple Dorotheos were shut up in the palace prison,[28] where they found all the political adversaries of the government.[29] Palamas had not been condemned for his theology, and so Calecas took political sanctions against him, persuading the government to arrest him. But, as a political detainee, Palamas fell outside the direct jurisdiction of the Patriarch, and no one put any obstacles in his way to prevent him expounding his teaching and writing attacks against his adversaries with Dorotheos as his secretary. For Anne's government had nothing to do with the Patriarch's new-found taste for anti-Palamite theology.

Calecas and Akindynos

After Palamas's enforced return to Constantinople, Calecas risked making full use of Akindynos. In the autumn of 1342 he himself admitted to communion the monk who had been condemned in August 1341, and allowed him to write theological tracts against Palamas.[30] Akindynos rejoices therein in his letters, confirming that no activity had been possible for him before.[31] At Christmas 1342 Isidore should have been consecrated bishop of Monembasia, but Calecas subjected him to a public affront: he demanded a condemnation of Palamism in the confession of faith preceding the consecration. When the bishop-elect refused, he refused either to impose his hands or to accept him to communion.[32] The fact that Isidore, a professed Palamite, should so

[26] Miklosich, *Acta,* I, 232–3.
[27] *Letter to the Athonites,* ibid.
[28] All these events are related in Palamas's letters to the Athonites and his *Refutation of the Patriarch of Antioch* (*Coisl.* 99, *fol.* 148v–149v, 174v–175); cf. Philotheus, *Encomion,* 603AC.
[29] Gregoras, *Hist.* XV, 9, Bonn, II, 780; Cantacuzene, *Hist.* III, 100, Bonn, II, 611–13.
[30] Palamas, *Letter to the Athonites, fol.* 175.
[31] *Letter to Lapithos, Marc. gr.* 155, *fol.* 175.
[32] Akindynos, *Against Palamas,* VI, *Monac. gr.* 223, *fol.* 351v–352; cf. *Antipalamite declaration of 1347, P.G.* CL, 880C.

long have enjoyed the privileges of a bishop-elect is nevertheless further proof of the political, and not religious, nature of the persecution of Palamas.

It was also in the autumn of 1342 that the Athonite mission at Constantinople met a complete rebuff. Their attempts to re-establish peace, and the written memorandum they addressed to Anne to that end,[33] had no success. Calecas even succeeded in dividing the delegation: he appointed Macarius, *hegoumenos* of Lavra, Metropolitan of Thessalonica, and in that way turned him into an anti-Cantecuzenist. That was what he had tried in vain to do with Palamas and Isidore. Macarius was even sent as ambassador to Serbia, where he tried to persuade Cantacuzene to surrender.[34] But he was not, as some have stated, anti-Palamite; Palamite writers mention his name with respect, and Calecas, it seems, ended by deposing him in 1345 to replace him by an implacable Akindynist, Hyacinth.[35] The case of Macarius again illustrates the fundamentally political attitude of the Patriarch. The rest of the Athonite delegation left the capital, except Sabbas, the great ascetic of Vatopedi, who was sent to live at the monastery of Chora, and continued to support Cantacuzene.[36] On the other hand his position in the theological controversy was reserved: he refused to take sides with Palamas, and Akindynos wrote three letters congratulating him on that; according to the leader of the anti-Palamites, Sabbas' attitude made it possible for Anne and the members of her government finally to approve the condemnation of Palamas.[37] The *Life of Sabbas* subsequently written by Philotheus, presents him as a Palamite,[38] but the writer is clearly defending a view not shared by most of his readers, and he relates no definite fact to illustrate the Palamism of Sabbas who, as mentioned, was one of the Athonite delegation at Constantinople, and subsequently dwelt in the capital throughout the crucial period from 1342 to 1347. Moreover Philotheus himself, in his *Eulogy* of Palamas, states that the hesychast of Vatopedi, having been anti-Palamite, was miraculously converted to Orthodoxy.[39] In 1347 he was Cantacuzene's first choice for the patriarchate.

---

[33] Philotheus, *Life of Sabbas,* p. 324; Gregoras, *Hist.* XII, 14, Bonn, II, 620. 611–13.
[34] Cantacuzene, *Hist.* III, 35, 52, Bonn, II, 212, 306–9.
[35] cf. Philotheus, *Encomion,* 579C; Joseph Calothetos, *Against Calecas, Vat. gr.* 704, *fol.* 159v.
[36] Cantacuzene, ibid., 213.
[37] *Letter to Sabbas, Marc. gr.* 155, *fol.* 4–6.
[38] ed. cit., p. 335.
[39] *Encomion,* col. 610–13.

The activity of Akindynos

The unlimited support which the Patriarch John Calecas gave in the autumn of 1342 to Gregory Akindynos resulted in the renewal of the theological controversy which he wished to avoid. Differing in this from Calecas, Akindynos attached prime importance to doctrinal questions. Having at one time, up to June 1341, wished to arbitrate between Barlaam and Palamas, he acquired the unquestionably sincere conviction that the latter had strayed from the true faith. He therefore opposed him, while still claiming equally to reject Barlaamism. In fact, as we have seen, there was no fundamental disagreement between Barlaam and Akindynos. In December 1341 Akindynos could still write to George Lapithos who, in Cyprus, was asking for information about affairs at Constantinople, that Barlaam had not fallen so deeply into error as Palamas.[40] From that date, therefore, Akindynos did not claim any more to follow a *via media* between the hesychasts and the Calabrian, but clearly inclined to Barlaam's side. However his formal conservatism and the quotations from the Fathers with which he filled his interminable theological treatises, gave a false impression of doctrinal certainty and stilled the conscience of Calecas, who was preoccupied with political matters, and cared very little about those questions of doctrine whose solution was long to decide the fate of Byzantine Christianity.

As a theologian Akindynos was mediocre, but he had many friends at Constantinople. We have seen the important part he played, for that reason, in the preparations for the Council of June 1341. His correspondence gives us much information about his political influence between 1342 and 1346: not only was he on intimate terms with the Patriarch and in correspondence with many high ecclesiastics, but he could also appeal directly to the *megas dux* Apocaucos, and recommend his protegés to the *mystikos* Cinamos in order to secure places for them in the imperial secretariat. However his letters contain but few allusions to Cantacuzene, and are always intended to promote his purely doctrinal struggle with Palamas. His enemies also accuse him of extensive bribery, thanks to the funds put at his disposal by the very wealthy Eulogia Choumnos.[41]

His Report to the Patriarch

Having decided in the autumn of 1342 to support Akindynos openly, in March or April 1343 the Patriarch received a *Report* from him giving his interpretation of events since the beginning of 1341.

[40] Marc. gr. 155, fol. 69; cf. *Against Palamas*, Monac. gr. 223, fol. 36v, 114.
[41] Calothetos, *Against Akindynos*, II, Angel. gr. 66, fol. 32v.

THE TIME OF CIVIL WAR (1341–1347)

Obviously the Patriarch knew the facts himself, but he needed Akindynos to provide religious justification for political measures taken against Palamas. Akindynos skilfully supplied this; the *Report* stresses the justice of Barlaam's condemnation and Calecas's repugnance against all forms of dogmatic controversy: it ends with a traditional confession of faith; Akindynos omits all mention of the tributes paid to the hesychast leaders at the Council, and makes no reference to the political situation. The *Report* was adopted by Calecas as the official version of events, and Akindynos was entrusted by the Patriarch with the mission of refuting Palamite theology. This he fulfilled by publishing seven long treatises against Palamas between 1342 and 1344, all addressed to Calecas, and several of less importance, not to mention many letters to various important people on the same subject. At this same time the Patriarch appointed a friend of Akindynos, Hyacinth, Archbishop of Cos, as Metropolitan of Corinth.[42]

Palamas, on his side, was not inactive in his prison. Up to 1344 Anne's government did not support the Patriarch in his attempts to present Palamas as a heretic. Such a well-known Palamite as Isidore continued to take his place in the Synod as bishop-elect of Monembasia and, though Calecas succeeded in delaying his consecration, he continued to concern himself with the affairs of his diocese.[43] The decision to burn Palamas's works does not seem to have had much result; he never wrote more than in those two years from 1342 to 1344. Besides letters written to various people at Constantinople and in the provinces, he wrote seven treatises *Against Akindynos*, which answered his adversary's seven *Antirrhetics*.

Excommunication of Palamas

New developments took place at the end of 1344. After the failure of *pourparlers* with Cantacuzene in September,[44] the government at Constantinople took a harsher line against its opponents. In November known opponents of Cantacuzene were generously rewarded. On the 4th of that month Calecas made the Synod announce the deposition of Isidore [45] and the excommunication of Palamas. In the latter's case, religious reasons were invoked: Palamas and his supporters were said to give a false interpretation to the *Tome* of 1341, and ceased to men-

---

[42] Miklosich, *Acta*, I, 235; on Hyacinth, see Mercati, *Notizie di Procoro*, p. 233.
[43] His presence in the synod is mentioned in 1342 and 1343 (Miklosich, *Acta*, I, 227, 230, 237).
[44] Cantacuzene, *Hist.* III, 72, Bonn, II, 437–46; L. Bréhier, *Vie et mort*, p. 437.
[45] Dated title of the decree in G. Mercati, *Notizie*, p. 202–3.

tion the Patriarch's name in the liturgy.[46] Palamas was already in prison for political reasons, so there was no need to refer to his support of Cantacuzene. As to the condemnation of Isidore, who could be seen still taking his place in the Synod, its motives were as much political as disciplinary: Isidore governed his diocese without being a bishop, he interpreted the *Tome* as Palamas did, but, especially, 'he felt no true goodwill towards the Imperial Majesty, and supported the Apostate and Tyrant.'[47] There can, therefore, be no doubt about the mixed religious and political character of the measures against Palamas and Isidore in 1344. To give more authority to these measures, Calecas had them countersigned by two Eastern patriarchs, both closely dependent on him, the Patriarchs of Jerusalem [48] and Antioch. Ignatius of Antioch was himself present at the Synod with other bishops from his patriarchate,[49] and published a declaration against Palamas and another against Isidore. He was even more under obligations to Calecas than was his colleague of Jerusalem; an Armenian convert to Orthodoxy, he had come to the capital in the summer of 1344 to have his Patriarchal dignity confirmed by Constantinople.[50] The signatures of these Eastern prelates, entirely dependent upon the Oecumenical Patriarch, did not carry much weight. The imperial support finally given to the measures of the Synod was more important for Calecas. If we trust Palamite sources, the Patriarch was then at the height of his religious and political power. Living in the palace rather than at the patriarchate, he conducted the affairs of the Empire as seemed good to him. In this way he got Anne's government officially to support his religious policy.[51] But Calecas's actions were not devoid of prudence; be it noted that he avoided sending the text of the excommunication of Palamas to Athos, and he merely filed the letter which he had obtained from Ignatius of Antioch condemning Palamas, so that the latter only found

[46] *P.G.* CL, 863D–864A; an addition to the text in G. Mercati, op. cit., p. 195 (for the date, see our French edition, p. 110, note 68).

[47] The text of Isidore's condemnation is lost; the substance of it is however quoted in a declaration of the Patriarch of Antioch (Mercati, op. cit., pp. 199–200) and in Calecas's *Exegesis of the Tome* (*P.G.* CL, 903AB).

[48] The patriarchal throne of Jerusalem was then in dispute between Lazarus, a Cantacuzenist, and Gerasimos, appointed by Calecas. The condemnation of Palamas was obviously issued by the letter; cf. P. Wirth, *Die Patriarchate des Gerasimos und des Lazaros von Jerusalem*, in Byzantinische Zeitschrift, 54, 1961, pp. 319–23.

[49] Akindynos, *Letter to Matthew*, ed. Loenertz, in *Epeteris*, XXVII, 1957, p. 100.

[50] Palamas, *Refutation of the Patriarch of Antioch*, Coisl. 99, fol. 147; Calothetos, *Against Calecas*, Vat. gr. 704, fol. 158v.

[51] *Appeal of Bishops*, *P.G.* CLI, 769A; cf. Palamas, *Second Letter to Macarius*, Coisl. 99, fol. 180; Calecas, *Encyclica*, *P.G.* CL, 893A; Gregoras, *Hist.* XV, 7, Bonn, II, 768; *Tome of 1347*, ed. cit., p. 216.

out about it later and clandestinely.[52] As to the monks of Athos who had written both to Anne and to the Patriarch in defence of Palamas, their suit was in both cases dismissed.[53] Palamas himself at this time wrote a series of letters to Athos deploring and explaining the uselessness of their intervention (*Letter to Philotheus, Letter to the Athonites,* and *First Letter to Macarius*).

Ordination of Akindynos

His momentary success encouraged Calecas to go even further in asserting his position. In 1341 he had himself proclaimed that only bishops, endowed with the authority of the Apostles, had the right to teach the dogmas of the Church. Now circumstances obliged him to rely, in his struggle with Palamas, on a simple monk theologian, Akindynos. The latter, in his polemical works, several times recognizes this weak point in his position: sometimes he even denounced the decision of 1341, asserting that laymen could discuss theological questions[54]; perhaps he was thus insinuating that his ordination might help the good cause. Calecas then decided to raise him to the episcopate.[55]

Conflict between the Patriarch and Anne of Savoy

The Empress Anne and the whole Court resolutely opposed this act: the Patriarch might behave as he liked in the administration of the Church, but he should not infringe a decision taken under Andronicus III by disregarding the formal condemnation of Akindynos.[56] As in 1342 Alexis Apocaucos openly defended Palamas and vigorously opposed the Patriarch. A real conflict arose between Patriarch and Court; the Empress refused to recognize the ordination as deacon of the anti-Palamite theologian by the Patriarch, which she had three times forbidden him to perform.[57] Akindynos was even arrested.[58] The rumour circulated that the Patriarch had been deposed for ordaining a heretic.[59]

But John Calecas was strong enough to defy the Empress. Akindynos

---

[52] Palamas, *Second Letter to Macarius,* Coisl. 99, fol. 179; *Refutation of the Patriarch of Antioch,* Coisl. 99, fol. 144v.
[53] Palamas, *Second Letter to Macarius,* Coisl. 99, fol. 178v.
[54] *To Hierotheus,* Marc. gr. 155, fol. 87; *Against Palamas* VII, Monac. gr. 223, fol. 349v; cf. Palamas, *Letter to Philotheus,* Coisl. 99, fol. 168.
[55] Palamas, *Second Letter to Macarius,* Coisl. 99, fol. 179; *Arsenius of Tyre,* Project of *Tome* in Mercati, *Notizie,* p. 205; *Tome of 1347,* ed. cit., p. 216; Calothetos, *Letter to Sabbas,* Angel gr. 66, fol. 157v.
[56] Calothetos, ibid., fol. 158; *Tome of 1347* (quoting the *Refutation of Calecas* by Palamas), ibid.
[57] Calothetos, ibid., fol. 158–159v.
[58] *Tome of 1347* (quoting Palamas), ibid.
[59] Akindynos, *Letter to Matthew,* ed. Loenertz, p. 100.

escaped from Anne's wrath and was finally ordained priest. Several anti-Palamites were consecrated as bishops in 1344 and 1345. The most startling appointment was that of James Koukounares as Metropolitan of Monembasia, intended to root out Isidore's influence from the Peloponnese. James was entrusted with this mission as a reward for his zeal as an anti-Palamite.[60] Apparently Akindynos became all powerful; it was he who recommended candidates for the episcopate to the Patriarch,[61] who demanded and obtained disciplinary sanctions against the monk Mark, because that disciple of Gregory of Sinai had dared, from his retreat on Chios, to undertake the defence of Palamas in stirring letters to John V and to the Patriarch.[62]

Faced by the discontent aroused by these religious measures, Calecas published a series of documents to justify his attitude:

1. A letter to the monks of Athos who had often intervened in Palamas's favour by writing to Anne, to high officials at Constantinople, and to the Patriarch. This letter is dated November 1344, and seems to have followed immediately on the condemnation of Palamas and Isidore; it asks the Athonites to secure Palamas's submission. In fact, if Palamas is to be believed, the Patriarch did not immediately announce to the monks of Athos the excommunication of their spokesman. So the letter was not sent to its destination until some time later, perhaps to justify the ordination of Akindynos.[63]

2. An Encyclical in which he announced and justified the excommunication of Palamas.[64]

3. An *Exegesis of the Tome of 1341*, a sort of communiqué giving the official intepretation of that controversial document.[65]

The Patriarch's position was simple; according to him the *Tome* confined itself to condemning Barlaam on two points: his teaching about the light on Tabor, and his attacks against the prayer. 'We do not desire and will not admit the hearing of anything beyond these two chapters,' he proclaimed.[66] Palamas, by continuing to write and to interpret the *Tome* in ways favourable to his theology, infringed the interdict, pronounced by the *Tome*, against continuing to argue about

[60] Akindynos, *Letter to James*, ed. Loenertz, p. 90; cf. V. Laurent, *La Liste épiscopale du Synodicon de Monembasie*, in Echos d'Orient, XXXII, 1933, p. 150; D. A. Zakynthinos, *Le despotat grec de Morée*, II, 277.
[61] Anonymous Palamite, *Vat. gr.* 321, *fol.* 259v.
[62] Texts in *Coisl.* 288; cf. Akindynos, *Letter to Calecas*, ed. Th. Uspenskii *Sinodik v nedeliu Pravoslaviia*, p. 81; Palamas, *Refutation of the Patriarch of Antioch*, Coisl. 99, fol. 147.
[63] Miklosich, *Acta*, I, 238–42.
[64] P.G. CL, 891–4.
[65] ibid., 900–3.
[66] *Exegesis*, 902C; *Letter to the Athonites*, p. 240; *Encyclica*, 892B.

dogmatic problems. When he, Calecas, tried to persuade him to moderate his conduct, he fled to Heraclea. This argument of the Patriarch tends to justify the ordination of Akindynos by disregarding his condemnation in August 1341, and by concealing the political context of the excommunication of Palamas. We have already shown how far that interpretation was from reality. Gregory Palamas, in his *Refutation of Calecas* and in letters addressed to his friends at Athos in 1345, has little difficulty in reasserting the facts. It is also worth noting, as an extra argument in favour of the Palamite thesis, that Calecas waited till 1344 before formally condemning Palamas, and presenting a tendentious version of events preceding the ordination of Akindynos; it was only by stages that he came to adopt that version, and fully to support the position of the anti-Palamite theologian. But the Empress Anne never entirely adopted that position, and there was clear disagreement between her and the Patriarch from November 1344.

This disagreement came into the open again at the end of 1345, when Calecas, against the Empress's opposition, and taking the opportunity of the Zealot revolt at Thessalonica, deposed Macarius (the former abbot of Lavra) from the metropolitan see of that town, and appointed there an extreme Akindynist, the Cypriot Hyacinth, a monk from the monastery of Hodighitria. Akindynos announced the arrival shortly of the new bishop to the notables of Thessalonica, and revealed that the object of his nomination was to root out Palamism. Hyacinth turned zealously to that task; the Palamites remembered the persecutions which he launched against them, and which were perhaps an episode of the zealot reaction at Thessalonica.[67]

This policy of force, certainly applied at other places besides Thessalonica, did Calecas no good. Moreover no one was convinced by his explanation of the *Tome* of 1341, to which he claimed to be faithful.[68] So the supporters of the government of Apocaucos and Calecas had no alternative to adopting an official anti-Palamism, and those of them who considered Palamism and the *Tome* of 1341 as in conformity with Orthodoxy, joined Cantacuzene's camp in ever increasing numbers. The latter had a series of successes in 1345 and, especially after the death of Apocaucos on June 11th, his victory became certain.

Palamite reaction
During the year 1346 the different groups forming the anti-Can-

[67] On Hyacinth, see French edition, p. 116, note 97.
[68] Gregoras himself frankly admits that Calecas nullified the *Tome, Hist* XV, 7, Bonn, II, 768.

tacuzenist coalition at Constantinople sought to withdraw their stakes in the game. The Empress Anne became conscious of the mistake she had made in allowing the Patriarch to use the anti-Palamism of Akindynos for political ends. In January of that year the Athonites addressed two *Dogmatic Treatises*, written by Philotheus Kokkinos to her to prove that 'the priest of God, Gregory, does not worship several Gods as his accuser affirms.'[69] Anne even tried to study the facts of the theological argument in progress. She received a complete anti-Palamite *dossier* from the Patriarch.[70] At her request, Palamas himself addressed a *Report* to her in which he refuted the accusations of his adversaries, calling on the memory of Andronicus III who had supported him in 1341, and trying to confirm the anti-Akindynist convictions of the Empress.[71] The Empress also asked a learned monk, David Dishypatos, a disciple of Gregory of Sinai at Paroria, to explain to her the history of the controversy between Barlaam and Palamas, and the part which Akindynos took therein. David fulfilled her request, and accompanied his account with an anthology of passages from the Fathers favourable to Palamism.[72] Anne also turned to Nicephorus Gregoras who had stayed out of the controversy in spite of Akindynos's appeals. But that philosopher said he was opposed to Palamas, and at the end of the year began to write against his theology.[73]

But nothing could now arrest the course of events. On May 21st the Patriarch Lazarus of Jerusalem solemnly crowned Cantacuzene at Adrianople. A Council of Thracian Bishops and of those Metropolitans who had fled from Constantinople, assembled in that town for the coronation and pronounced the deposition of John Calecas on the ground that he had ordained condemned heretics.[74] Hence Calecas was no longer considered as legitimate Patriarch in the rebel camp, and Lazarus of Jerusalem was invested by Cantacuzene with a sort of *ad interim* authority. Another severe blow struck the anti-Palamite party just at that moment, the premature death of Hyacinth of Thessalonica.

Changed tactics of Calecas

Seeing that he had been on a false trail in condemning the Palamites, John Calecas tried to effect a reconciliation with them. Two letters

---

[69] *Marc. gr.* 582, *fol.* 139.
[70] *Tome of 1347*, ed. cit., p. 217.
[71] Text in Gregoras, *Hist.*, Bonn, II, 1282-3 (*P.G.* CXLVIII, 1010-12, footnote).
[72] Ed. M. Candal, *Origen ideologico del palamismo*, in *Orientalia Chr. Per.* XV, 1949, pp. 85-124.
[73] *Hist.* XV, 7, Bonn, II, 769-70.
[74] *Tome of 1347*, ed. cit., p. 217; Cantacuzene, *Decree*, *P.G.* CL, 771D; *Hist.* III, 92, Bonn, II, 564-5; Gregoras, *Hist.* XV, 5, Bonn, 762.

addressed by Akindynos to him make it clear that Calecas in his last extremity turned away from him in 1346, and the anti-Palamite leader allows all his indignation to burst out at this ingratitude.[75] Thus, a few months before his fall, the Patriarch again showed how little value he attached to his own commitments where his political interests were at stake. This last minute manoeuvre however served no purpose. Anne had definitely decided to rely on the Palamites. The agents of Cantacuzene opposed any rehabilitation of the Patriarch, and Palamas and his supporters clearly had no interest in defending so compromised a personality as Calecas. The Patriarch saw the number of his supporters rapidly melting away. Six bishops, among them Matthew of Ephesus and Athanasius of Cyzicus, whom Calecas kept away from any activity in September, addressed a letter to the Empress Anne asking that the Patriarch should be brought to judgment; they accused him of simony, sacrilege and heresy, while also confirming the accusation brought against him at the Council of Adrianople, that Calecas had ordained condemned heretics as priests.[76]

His deposition

In January 1347 the Empress decided to summon a Council to depose Calecas. She hoped by that means to strengthen her position *vis-à-vis* Cantacuzene who by then was under the walls of the capital. Only anti-Cantacuzenite bishops took part in this Council, while Palamas and the declared supporters of Cantacuzene were still under arrest. Before the meeting, Calecas received an order not to move from his apartments in the palace.[77] The assembly took place, in his absence, on February 2nd; the Empress and John V presided; there were present some bishops, the *protos* of Athos, and many monks and civil officials. First the *Tome* of 1341 was read, then they turned to examine the anti-Palamite *dossier* which Calecas had presented to Anne and which contained the anti-Palamite interpretation of the events of 1341. Calecas was condemned and the Synodal *Tome* of 1341 solemnly confirmed: those bishops who had not signed the condemnation of Barlaam, had to do so before coming to the meeting of the Council on February 2nd, 1347.

Having been deposed both by the Cantacuzenist Council of Adrianople and by the Synod of Constantinople, Calecas then ceased to be an obstacle to peace between the two opposing factions. On the very evening of February 2nd Cantacuzene made his entry into the

[75] *Marc. gr.* 155, *fol.* 41v, 49v-50.
[76] *P.G.* CLI, 767-70.
[77] Cantacuzene, *Hist.* 98, Bonn, II, 604; Gregoras, *Hist.* XV, 9, Bonn, 781, 783.

capital. But the Empress Anne did not as yet capitulate; she barricaded herself in her palace, and sought reinforcements from outside. Some difficult negotiations, of which we do not know all the side issues, took place between the two parties. Why did Cantacuzene send as ambassador to Anne an obstinate supporter of Calecas, Neophytus, Metropolitan of Philippi, accompanied by the *sakellarias* Cabasilas? Perhaps he imagined that the Patriarch was still all powerful and hoped to establish contact with him. In any case Anne refused to accept his proposals. It was only on the intervention of John V, by then aged 15, that she herself sent an embassy to her adversary, and her ambassador was none other than Gregory Palamas himself, accompanied by Andronicus Asen, the father-in-law of Cantacuzene: both had been let out of prison to go on the embassy. Thus Palamas could again take up the task in which he had failed in 1341; the re-establishment of peace between the two factions who were tearing up what remained of the Empire. This time he succeeded completely. Cantacuzene and John V were recognized as co-Emperors, and in fact things returned to the political regime previous to the autumn of 1341.[78]

The attitude of Byzantine society to the controversy

The turbulent time we have just described shows up a very characteristic side of Palamas's nature; his interest in the affairs of the world. From the beginning he took up a very clear political position and held to it with unswerving loyalty: 'Right to the end,' Cantacuzene wrote, 'in spite of all that he had to suffer in the cause of justice and of truth, he was never guilty of any base action or word.'[79] But he attached no absolute value to this choice, and never forgot the primacy of Christian teaching over every political consideration : as we have seen, he remained loyal to the Empress Anne and the anti-Cantacuzenite government; the inquisitions of his enemies never could prove that he had had secret relations with the rebellion. Moreover Anne's government, while regarding him as a political adversary, was never anti-Palamite in doctrinal matters.

So the Patriarch John Calecas must bear the responsibility for the religious crisis to which the Byzantine Church was subjected during the civil war. Without the Patriarch, Akindynos would have kept silent after his condemnation in 1341. Calecas, who disliked taking any part when purely doctrinal questions were discussed, but who was obliged in 1341 to assert the victory of the Palamites, thought that by disowning his signature he would secure his position in the state. Apart from any

---

[78] These events are described in Cantacuzene, *Hist.* III, 99, Bonn, II, 609–13.
[79] *Hist.* III, 100, Bonn, II, 614.

considerations of morality or theology, that was a political mistake on his part. A great majority of the Byzantines, no matter to what political camp they belonged, approved the Council of 1341 and considered Palamite teaching to conform with Orthodoxy. When writing his *Antirrhetics* in about 1343, Akindynos recognizes that even then, when Calecas was at the height of his power, many anti-Palamites were afraid or ashamed to manifest their views, since they were against the general trend of public opinion.[80] It is also worth noting that Calecas never dared to convene a true Council to condemn Palamas, and the simple decision of the local synod (σύνοδος ἐνδημοῦσα) in November 1344, which excommunicated Gregory and Isidore and could not obtain the Empress's confirmation for several days, was not to be compared to the great Palamite assemblies of 1341, 1347 and 1351, which were sometimes the scene of violent popular demonstrations, as Akindynos and Nicephorus Gregoras complained. During the civil war Akindynos was alone in composing theological treatises against Palamas: it was only in 1347 that he was backed up by the *First Antirrhetics* of Gregoras. On the Palamite side, however, during that same period of time, David Dishypatos, Joseph Calothetos, Isidore of Monembasia, Philotheus, Mark Kurtos and several anonymous writers published refutations of Akindynos. Some high officials, such as Nicholas Matarangos, 'judge general,' who had great moral authority at Byzantium—in 1337 he was the only one of the four 'judges general' of the Empire who was found innocent at the time of a great scandal about corruption—gave his full support to Palamas.[81] During the four years passed in the palace prison, Palamas sought support in the most diverse quarters: worth noting are his repeated contacts with the Genoese of Galata, and with the Grand Master of the Hospitallers at Rhodes to whom he sent his works to explain the doctrine he defended.[82] These contacts considered in conjunction with John Cantacuzene's attempts in 1355 and again in 1367 to explain Palamite theology to Paul, the Legate of Pope Urban V, prove that Palamas and his disciples never had any obdurate aversion to the Latins, and that they did not lack the goodwill to engage in theological dialogue with them.

The undecided
Among the high dignitaries of the Church and Court at Byzantium, many took care not to take open part in the theological controversy, or

---

[80] *Against Palamas*, VII, *Marc. gr.* 223, *fol.* 349v.
[81] Palamas, *Letter to Daniel*, Coisl. 99, *fol.* 99v-100; on Matarangos, see P. Lemerle, *Le Juge général des Grecs et la réforme judiciare d'Andronic III*, in *Mémorial Louis Petit*, Paris, 1948, p. 309.
[82] Akindynos, *Letter to Gregoras*, Marc. gr. 155, *fol.* 79.

changed their opinions so often that one may reasonably assume that they had no profound convictions about the matter. Palamas mentions these 'neutralists' and is indignant against them: Akindynos does the same.[83] A certain number of bishops certainly belonged to this category: thus Joseph of Adrianople, Isaac of Madytos and Paul of Xanthia successively signed the deposition of Isidore in November 1344, and that of Calecas in 1347.[84] James Koukounares himself, who was nominated by Calecas in 1347 to the see of Monembasia to replace Isidore, was among the first to repent before that same Isidore, now Patriarch of Constantinople.[85] The case of Macarius Chrysocephalos of Philadelphia is more complex; in 1342 he was out of Constantinople, probably in his diocese: in November 1344 his signature appears under the condemnation of Isidore, and in April 1345 we find him taking part in Calecas's Synod,[86] with Akindynos writing to congratulate him on his anti-Palamism[87]; but in 1347 he was among the first to sign the deposition of Calecas: finally in 1351 he is numbered among the closest collaborators of the Patriarch Callistos,[88] but he adopts a critical attitude towards the great Palamite Council.[89] The *megas dux* Apocaucos himself was chiefly interested in the political side of the situation, and avoided adopting an anti-Palamite position. Reading the correspondence of Akindynos, we find that a high official, Isaris—probably George Isaris, the *eparch,* who with Nicholas Cabasilas was to participate in a judicial inquiry at Mount Athos in 1350 [90]—suffered in his career for his Palamism and preferred to change his views.[91] Two well-known citizens of Thessalonica, Constantine Harmenopoulos and Thomas Magistros also varied in their attitude. Harmenopoulos, 'universal judge of Thessalonica,' began by proclaiming his anti-Palamism in 1345 and 1346: but he published a work attacking both Palamas and Akindynos with equal violence, accusing them both of polytheism.[92] Thomas Magistros, a well-known scholar and humanist, was also, like

[83] Palamas, *Against Akindynos*, I, 12, *Coisl.* 98, *fol.* 42v; Akindynos, *To Hierotheos, Marc. gr.* 155, *fol.* 83v.
[84] cf. Mercati, *Notizie*, p. 202; *Tome of 1347,* ed. cit., p. 225.
[85] Miklosich, *Acta,* I, 271-2.
[86] ibid., 227-8, 242-3.
[87] *Marc. gr.* 155, *fol.* 65.
[88] Callistos, *Homily, Patm.* 366, *fol.* 418v.
[89] Arsenius, *Appeal to Cantacuzene, Vat. gr.* 1111 *fol.* 237v; Macarius was among the most pre-eminent Byzantine preachers of the century, cf. his life in L. Petit, *Macaire Chrysocéphale,* in *Dict. de théol. cath.,* IX, 2 (1927), col. 1445-9; a list of his homilies in A. Ehrhard, *Ueberlieferung und Bestand . . .* III, pp. 690-5.
[90] Miklosich, *Acta,* I, 298.
[91] Akindynos, *Letter to Isaris, Marc. gr.* 155, *fol.* 75-75v; on Isaris, see R.-S. Loenertz, *Dix-Huit Lettres,* in *Or. Chr. Per.,* XXIII, 1957, pp. 126-7.
[92] Akindynos, *To Hierotheos, Marc. gr.* 155, *fol.* 79v-82.

many humanists, opposed to the theology of the monks. But in 1345 Akindynos wrote to inform him that the new Metropolitan, Hyacinth, was soon to arrive at Thessalonica, and he learnt that he had given up attacking Palamism.[93] Among the most enthusiastic supporters of Cantacuzene one finds both supporters and adversaries of Palamas, but one also finds those who hesitated. Two intimate friends of the Great Domestic, Demetrios Cydones and Nicholas Cabasilas, seem at that time to have fallen into the last category, being united not only by political ties, but also by a common interest in the profane studies which Cantacuzene loved to patronize. Demetrios makes no allusion to the theological controversy in his letters dating from this period; later anti-Palamism increased his sympathy for the Latin West, but in 1346 he wrote a friendly letter to Isidore, his former teacher, and from 1347 to 1349 he was again on close terms with Isidore, then Palamite Patriarch.[94] Whereas Nicholas Cabasilas who, unlike Demetrios, was later to become a convinced Palamite, appears to have hesitated at the time of the civil war; we find both that Akindynos solicited his patronage[95] and that David Dishypatos addressed a long treatise explaining the Palamite thesis to him: the tone of this treatise leads one to suppose that Nicholas did not yet share the monk's point of view.[96]

The anti-Palamites

While many others were undecided and easily changed their convictions with the politico-religious fluctuations of the Byzantine Empire at that time, our sources distinguish several persons who stood firm. From the beginning of his controversy with Palamas, Akindynos found at Constantinople a constant ally in Irene Choumnos, daughter of the learned Nicephorus Choumnos and widow of the despot John Palaeologus, who had become a nun under the name of Eulogia.[97] As a former spiritual daughter of Theoleptus of Philadelphia, and one who, after his death, continued the practice of hesychast spirituality under the direction of another spiritual father, Eulogia should, one would have thought, have joined the Palamite camp. Belonging to one of the richest aristocratic families of Byzantium, she should also have been a Can-

---

[93] Ed. Loenertz, p. 95; Thomas is also presented as Palamite by Philotheus of Selymbria, *Dialogue, Patm. gr.* 366, *fol.* 394.
[94] *Letters* 43 and 86, ed. Loenertz, in *Studi e testi*, 186, Vatican, 1956, pp. 77-8, 118-20.
[95] *Letter* published by I. Ševčenko, *Nicolas Cabasilas' correspondence, Byz. Zeitschr.*, 47, 1954, p. 53, footnote 4.
[96] Text. in *Paris gr.* 1247, *fol.* 1-50.
[97] On Irene, see V. Laurent, *Une princesse byzantine au cloître*, in *Echos d'Orient*, XXIX, 1930, pp. 29-60; *La direction spirituelle à Byzance*, in *Revue des études byz.*, XIV, 1956, pp. 48-86.

tacuzenist, if it was true that the civil war from 1341 to 1347 was only the product of the social struggle between the poor and the aristocracy. We also know that while she presided over a convent of enclosed nuns at Constantinople, Irene-Eulogia had not given up the administration of the immense domain left to her by her father, her husband and her brother, and she had not given up political life; in fact, she continued to have herself called 'Empress' ($\beta\alpha\sigma\iota\lambda\iota\sigma\sigma\alpha$). From 1342 we find her at the centre of the anti-Cantacuzenist clan at the Court, and it was thanks to her protection and that of her family that Akindynos once more gained access to the imperial palace. In her convent she was surrounded by a crowd of relations, importunates and clients, who overwhelmed her with flattery and roused the disquiet of her spiritual director. After he had been condemned in August 1341 Akindynos found himself in that last class, thus escaping pursuit and apparently living in the convent, that of the Christ-Philanthropos, at least until 1344.[98] Akindynos sang her praises, stressing her wealth as much as her intelligence; he compares her both to Croesus and to Semiramis.[99] But for the Palamites, Eulogia is a Jezebel who distributes her money lavishly, and the Akindynists 'Eat at her table' like the false prophets.[100] She is their 'private Empress,' whom Palamas contrasts with Anne, who always appears in his writings, and those of his friends, as Orthodox. Eulogia claims to teach the dogmas of the church, imitating Theodora, who re-establised Orthodoxy after the iconoclast crisis: Palamas grows indignant at this pretension, recalling that she had never been reigning Empress and that after the death of her husband she kept no imperial prerogative.[101]

Another convinced anti-Palamite is fairly well known to us through Akindynos's correspondence. That is the rich Cypriot humanist, George Lapithos, a friend of Irene-Eulogia Choumnos and a correspondent of Nicephorus Gregoras, Hyacinth and Akindynos. The last-named sent him several works of Palamas, accompanied by his own refutations thereof, and Lapithos himself wrote some works against Palamas.

In analysing the works of Gregory Palamas, we come across other examples of anti-Palamites. Akindynos's party was recruited from very diverse spheres, but especially from the humanists. Yet one does not find among them any 'Latinophrone,' open or disguised: quite the con-

[98] cf. Palamas, *Against Akindynos*, VII, 5, *Coisl.* 98, *fol.* 184–184v; *Letter to Arsenius*, *Coisl.* 99, *fol.* 125v.
[99] *Letter to Lapithos*, ed. Th. Uspenskii, *Sinodik*, p. 77; cf. Gregoras, *Hist.* XXIX, 21–4, Bonn, IV, 234–40.
[100] I (III) *Kings*, XVIII, 19; cf. Calothetos, *Vatic. gr.* 704, *fol.* 157v; Anonymous Palamite, *Letter*, *Chalc. Panagh* 157, *fol.* 287v.
[101] *Against Akindynos*, VII, 5, *Coisl.* 98, *fol.* 185.

THE TIME OF CIVIL WAR (1341–1347)

trary, Akindynos, steeped in a formalist and scholastic theology, often parades his anti-Latin feelings [102]; George Lapithos wrote polemical treatises against the Latins [103]; Gregoras nourished no sympathy towards them and accused Palamas of speaking in their favour.[104]

We must also remember that it would be quite incorrect to suppose that the anti-Palamite party was entirely found in the camp of the adversaries of Cantacuzene. The attitude of Demetrios Cydones and Nicholas Cabasilas is interesting in this respect, in that it shows how two men of very similar humanist education and coming from that same aristocratic circle at Thessalonica from which the best friends of Cantacuzene were recruited, could hesitate between 1341 and 1347 to support the renewal of monastic and anti-humanist spirituality, and subsequently adopted opposed doctrinal attitudes. Their case combined with other examples of anti-Palamite Cantacuzenists (Nicephorus Gregoras) and anti-Cantacuzenists who accepted the Palamite theology (Alexis Apocaucos), shows how incorrect it would be to completely identify the religious controversy of that time with the struggle which launched one part of the feudal nobility, grouped around Cantacuzene, against the government of Anne of Savoy. We will again come across this fact in connection with the attitude of Gregory Palamas towards the Zealots of Thessalonica.

---

[102] *Against Palamas*, VI, *Monac. gr.* 223, *fol.* 277v–278, etc.
[103] Akindynos, *Letter to Gregoras*, *Marc. gr.* 155, *fol.* 79.
[104] cf. his letter 156, in Guilland, *Correspondance*, pp. 256–7; cf. Philotheus, *Against Gregoras*, IV, P. 6, CLI, 836D.

CHAPTER V

GREGORY PALAMAS: ARCHBISHOP IN THESSALONICA

The Tome of 1347

The first months after the civil war were still troubled times for the Byzantine Church. On February 8th, 1347, when Cantacuzene entered the imperial palace, the ex-Patriarch John Calecas was still there, shut into his own apartments by the Empress Anne.[1] He refused to recognize his condemnation in his absence. A new Synod was held in the palace, attended by both Anne and Cantacuzene and several senators and monks, but the Patriarch, summoned also, refused to come.[2] A new *Tome* was issued against him which, like that of 1341, included the decisions of two Councils, that of February 2nd presided over by Anne alone, and that of the joint council held by Anne and Cantacuzene.[3] It is expressed as a confirmation of the *Tome* of 1341 (τόμος ἐπικυρῶν ... τὸν πρότερον τόμον) and brings Calecas under the scope of the condemnation which had struck Barlaam. Akindynos was also excommunicated 'although he was already subject to a previous sentence of the Synod.'[4] The *Tome* of February 1347 was originally signed by eleven bishops, those who were at Constantinople at Cantacuzene's arrival. In March he published a decree (πρόσταγμα) confirming the Synod's decision.[5] Some weeks later the bishops who had taken part in the Council of Adrianople arrived; they were headed by Lazarus, Patriarch of Jerusalem; a new Council was held, this time in the precincts of Aghia Sophia, in the presence of Anne, John V Palaeologus and John VI Cantacuzene; twenty bishops signed a confirmation of the two *Tomes* of 1341 and 1347 and this confirmation was annexed to the *Tome* of February. Thus within a few weeks three Synods were held at Constantinople to confirm Palamism.[6]

[1] Gregoras, *Hist.* XV, 9, Bonn, II, 784; Cantacuzene, *Hist.* IV, 3, Bonn, III, 22.
[2] Cantacuzene, ibid., 23; *Proclamation*, P.G. CLI, 772AB; *Tome against Matthew*, ed. Porphyrii Uspenskii, p. 730.
[3] The *Tome* relates the events of February 2nd, but frequently mentions Cantacuzene as Emperor. Ed. Meyendorff, in *Zbornik Radova*, Belgrade, 1963, pp. 209–27; on the text, see also G. T. Dennis, *The Deposition of the Patriarch J. Calecas* in *Jahr. der Österreichischen Byzant. Gesellschaft*, 1960, ix, pp. 51–5.
[4] Ed. cit., p. 222.
[5] *P.G.* CLI, 769–72.
[6] cf. the clear mention of these three consecutive synods in the *Tome against Matthew*, ed. P. Uspenskii, pp. 730–1.

Election of Isidore as Patriarch

Cantacuzene soon had to undertake the hard task of finding a successor to Calecas. Finally Isidore Boukharis, former bishop-elect of Monemvasia, was appointed to the patriarchal see on May 17th, 1347,[7] and consecrated by Athanasius, Archbishop of Cyzicus.[8] The bishops who had opposed this choice vehemently proclaimed that the election had taken place under pressure from the civil power, an allegation naturally denied by official sources. Cantacuzene records that Palamas himself was the most popular candidate because of his virtues, but even more because of his political attitude during the civil war.[9] It is characteristic that the Emperor should specially have stressed such motives; we also know that, before the choice of Isidore, he had long urged Sabbas of Vatopedi to accept the patriarchate: Sabbas apparently was a candidate acceptable both to the opposition and to Cantacuzene.[10] We have seen that this Athonite ascetic, unswervingly faithful to Cantacuzene (that was the essential point for the Emperor), had been, at least for a certain time, rather critical of Palamite theology. It was after Sabbas's refusal that Isidore's name came to the fore, for his ties with some close friends of Cantacuzene, Demetrios Cydones especially, made his candidature acceptable.

Immediately after his election Isidore consecrated thirty-two new bishops,[11] some of whom, after their appointment, signed the *Tome* of February. Gregory Palamas was one of those promoted, being consecrated Archbishop of Thessalonica. It was probably on that occasion that formulas of Palamite theology were added to the confession of faith demanded from bishops at their consecration.[12]

The opposition

Substantial opposition manifested itself against the election of Isidore and the other measures taken by the new government. John Calecas continued not to recognize the sentences against him, and published an *Apology*.[13] For a short time he was exiled to Didymotica and fell ill there. He was brought back to Constantinople where he died on

---

[7] cf. V. Laurent, *La Chronologie des patriarches de Constantinople de la première moitié du XIVs.*, in *Revue des études byzantines*, VII, 2, pp. 154–5.

[8] cf. the *Short Chronicle* publ. by B. Gorianov, in *Vizantiiskii Vremennik*, II, 1949, p. 289.

[9] *Hist.* IV, 3, Bonn, III, 25; Gregoras (*Hist.* XV, 10, Bonn, II, 786), the *Antipalamite Tome of 1937* (*P.G.* CL, 881BC) and the Antiochene *Project of Tome* (fol. 1) confirm the candidacy of Palamas to the patriarchal throne.

[10] Philotheus, *Life of Isidore*, p. 118.

[11] ibid., p. 118.

[12] Isidore, *Last Will*, Miklosich, *Acta*, I, 291; *Tome of 1351*, *P.G.* CLI, 721C–722B.

[13] Cyparissiotes, *Palamiticae transgressiones*, IV, *P.G.* CLII, 708CD.

December 29th, 1347, to the last refusing the political amnesty offered to him by Cantacuzene.[14] Akindynos had fled from the capital. At the beginning of 1348 he addressed a sort of testament to his disciples at Constantinople. It is expressed in moving terms and reflects the drama of this undoubtedly sincere man, fundamentally convinced that he was defending the truth, but unhappily unable to comprehend the problem clearly posed and resolved, though in diametrically opposite ways, by Barlaam and Palamas.[15] He died in exile some weeks later, abandoned by almost all his former friends.[16] Nicephorus Gregoras, who became the intellectual leader of the anti-Palamite party, very seldom refers to him. Those bishops who then put themselves at the head of the opposition, took care to disassociate themselves from Akindynos, as he in 1341 had disassociated himself from Barlaam, while taking up the same arguments against Palamas.[17]

This opposition in 1347 on the part of some bishops seems to have many motives, among which the doctrinal element was not the chief; in their protest they themselves particularly stress the appointment of Isidore as Patriarch.[18] Cantacuzene records that three members of the Synod favoured Calecas, while others pressed political claims of their own to accede to the patriarchate; they had all been just as good supporters of Cantacuzene as Isidore and Palamas had been and, like them, they had suffered for their political convictions.[19] The first three can be identified by the *Tome* decreeing their deposition; they were Neophytus of Philippi, Joseph of Ganos and Metrophanes of Patras.[20] The others were headed by the aged Metropolitan Matthew of Ephesus, who during the civil war had remained in his diocese under Turkish occupation; he had however come into conflict with the Patriarch John Calecas and his Synod.[21] Palamas in 1345 ranks him as one of the wisest of his supporters![22] In September 1346 he signed the appeal to Anne against the Patriarch; but his signature is not found on the *Tome* of February. In May 1347 Matthew belonged to the minority who refused to vote for Isidore, and he carried some other bishops with him, including

---

[14] The date is furnished by a short notice in *Vat. gr.* 778, *fol.* 1 (G. Mercati, *Notizie*, p. 202, n.1); cf. Cantacuzene, *Hist.* IV, 3, 23, Bonn, III, 24-5, 166-8; Gregoras, *Hist.* XV, 10, Bonn, II, 784.
[15] *Marc. gr.* 155, *fol.* 17-34.
[16] On the date of his death (before May 1348), see Philotheus, *Against Gregoras*, VII, *P.G.* CLI, 924C.
[17] This attitude is particularly characteristic of the group which published an *Antipalamite Tome* in 1347 (*P.G.* CL, 878BD).
[18] ibid., 881; cf. Philotheus, *Life of Sabbas*, p. 340.
[19] *Hist.* IV, 3, Bonn, III, 24-5.
[20] *Tome against Matthew*, pp. 730, 735.
[21] Max. Treu, *Matthaios, Metropolit von Ephesos*, S. 2-9.
[22] *Letter to Daniel, Coisl.* 99, *fol.* 99.

Chariton of Apro, who had signed both the appeal to Anne and the deposition of Calecas.

Councils of the anti-Palamites and their condemnation

This heterogeneous opposition included twenty bishops, ten of whom held Councils beginning in May at Constantinople, first in the church of the Holy Apostles, and then at the monastery of St. Stephen Protomartyr.[23] In July 1347 they published a *Tome* of excommunication against Isidore and Palamas. The accusations brought against the hesychast leaders, Palamas especially, recall those formerly brought against Athanasius I, in particular those concerning the 'profanation' of icons and holy objects in the churches.[24] The accession of hesychast monks to positions of authority in the Church, their austerity and their antiformalism aroused the opposition of some bishops. It was among the bishops too that Athanasius had found his bitterest adversaries.

After vain efforts to bring them back to obedience, Isidore and his Synod proceeded in August to depose them in a new Synodal *Tome* countersigned by the Patriarch of Jerusalem.[25] They also took a series of measures concerning the administration of the dioceses which the rebels had been governing. For the time being only a provisional deposition was in question, for it was still hoped to obtain their concurrence.[26]

Palamas and the 'Zealots'

After his election as Metropolitan of Thessalonica, Palamas was prevented from going to his see by the Zealot government which still refused to recognize the accession of John Cantacuzene to the throne: some Thessalonicans were also supporters of Akindynos, though, according to Philotheus, that was only a pretext to mask their political opposition to Cantacuzene.[27]

The revolt of the 'Zealots' had broken out at Thessalonica in the summer of 1342; it was the most spectacular manifestation of the discontent of the poor classes in the Empire in the fourteenth century against the high aristocracy on which Andronicus III and Cantacuzene had relied in their efforts to establish a sufficiently strong central government to face the catastrophic situation confronting the state. The Zealots represented a political force diametrically opposed to centralization, in that they stood out against the 'mighty' who represented the

[23] Gregoras, *Hist.* XV, 10, Bonn, II, 786.
[24] *Antipalamite Tome*, P.G. CL, 884B; cf. 882B.
[25] *Tome against Matthew*, ed. cit.
[26] The actual deposition was postponed until 1351 (*Tome of 1351*, P.G. CLI, 731A).
[27] *Encomion*, 612D–614B.

imperial power, and defended the local interests of the city of Thessalonica, rather than those of the Empire.[28] The government of Alexis Apocaucos in its struggle against Cantacuzene somtimes relied on the support of the middle and poor classes, in particular of the Zealots, though its alliance with the latter was not free from snags; the interests and social doctrine of the Zealots led them to refuse any direct submission to the central government.

As concerned religion, the republic of the Zealots at Thessalonica was not at the beginning unfavourable to Palamism. At the moment when the revolt broke out, the Patriarch appointed to the see of Thessalonica a monk from Athos named Macarius. He had formerly been abbot of Lavra and was a friend of the Hesychasts although opposed to Cantacuzene. It was only at the end of 1345, after a new and violent attack by the Zealots on the nobles, who had tried to open the town gates to Cantacuzene, that Calecas sent the anti-Palamite bishop Hyacinth to Thessalonica with a mission to purify his flock from 'the Palamite disease': that 'disease' must therefore have been particularly prevalent there.[29] No document suggests that the Zealots had ever molested the monks, still less the Hesychasts, who in their own sphere fought against the disastrous spiritual consequences of the substantial enrichment of the great coenobitic monasteries in the thirteenth and fourteenth centuries. Philotheus relates that some Zealots sought the support of their compatriot, Sabbas of Vatopedi who, though he favoured Palamite theology, was one of the spiritual leaders of the monks of Athos; strongly favouring Cantacuzene, Sabbas did not accept this proposal.[30] In the social field, the Hesychasts were conscious of the miserable condition of the poor classes. In an interesting description of the state of the empire in 1347, in which he stresses the general poverty, Philotheus tells how Isidore, now Patriarch, did his best to help the poor and interceded on their behalf with the Emperor[31]; moreover, if one is to trust Isidore's *Will*, he was himself far from being a rich man.[32] One should not therefore say that the Hesychasts always supported the interests of the 'mighty.'

What made the Zealots oppose their new Archbishop was basically his loyalty to Cantacuzene. As we have seen, that loyalty was above all based on the conviction that the new Emperor was the only man

---

[28] On the 'zealots' see P. Charanis, *Internal Strife in Byzantium during the fourteenth century*, in Byzantion 15 (1940–1); G. Ostrogorsky, *Hist.* pp. 459–61; I. Ševčenko, *Nicolaus Cabasilas' 'antizealot' discourse: a reinterpretation*, in *Dumbarton Oaks Papers*, IX, 1957, pp. 80–171.
[29] Akindynos, *Letter to Thomas Magistros*, ed. Loenertz, p. 97.
[30] *Life of Sabbas*, pp. 326–31.
[31] *Life of Isidore*, pp. 124–30.
[32] Miklosich, *Acta*, I, 292–3.

capable of preserving the unity of the Empire threatened by increasingly centrifugal forces. This loyalty, as we shall see, did not at all prevent Palamas in his sermons from violently attacking the social injustices from which Byzantine society suffered. Thus the main point of dispute between the 'political Zealots' and the 'church Zealots' (to use G. Ostrogorsky's expressions) [33] was about the functions and part played by the Emperor of Constantinople. In defending the medieval theocracy in the person of Cantacuzene, Palamas wished simply to preserve a traditional prop of orthodoxy; for him the empire was not an end in itself; we shall moreover see that Palamas was much better prepared than many of his contemporaries to accept the final ruin of the Empire at the hands of the Turks.

Palamas and Stephen Dushan

Since it was impossible to go to his see, Gregory Palamas went to Mount Athos, which he had not seen for eight years. The most important event in the interval had been the establishment of Serb authority there at the end of 1345.[34] When he reached the holy mountain, Palamas met an important pilgrim there, Stephen Dushan, 'Emperor of the Serbs and Greeks,' who was then in process of creating a great Eastern Empire of his own, by uniting both Serbs and Byzantine lands under his authority. To realize his dream more easily, he sought the support of the church and the monasteries. The monks of Athos on whom he showered lands and privileges, had already entered into his political orbit, and the *protos* had been present in 1346 at his coronation at Skoplje. Palamas had several interviews with Dushan who tried to persuade him to follow the example of his brothers at Athos. Perhaps he wished to gain the moral support of Palamas to get possession of Thessalonica. The Archbishop, however, remained unshakeable in his loyalty to the Emperor of Constantinople. If Philotheus is to be believed, he also taught a lesson to the monasteries of Athos which had succumbed to Dushan's generosity: when the Serbian Tsar offered him 'towns, churches and land, and then enumerated the annual revenues and wealth to be added thereto,' the Archbishop answered: 'We have absolutely no need of political power, land, revenues, rents or wealth. . . . We have long since learnt to live on little and to be content with bare necessities . . .' [35] We have in fact there another example of the opposition between the Hesychasts and the coenobitic monasteries concerning monastic property. After this unsuccesful

[33] ibid., p. 460.
[34] See G. Soulis, *Tsar Stephen Dushan and Mount Athos*, in Harvard Slavic Studies, II, 1954, pp. 125–39.
[35] *Encomion*, 615CD.

proposal Dushan sent the Archbishop, whose prestige hindered his authority at Athos, away by entrusting him with a mission to the Emperors of Constantinople. Another source seems to confirm Palamas's opposition to the Serbian Tsar's claims: during his stay on the Holy Mountain, Palamas had undertaken the defence of the *protos* Niphon accused by Serbian monks of Messalianism, but whom his other brothers at Athos, and afterwards the Synod of Constantinople in 1350, found perfectly Orthodox [36]; in fact it would seem that Messalianism was used as a pretext; the real point was that Dushan wanted to install a Serbian *protos* in place of Niphon; by sending Palamas away, the Serbian King was trying to attain his end more easily; in fact we do find the Serbian *protos* Anthony in charge of the Holy Mountain after May 1348.[37]

Entry into Thessalonica

Palamas did not stay long in the capital, and made a second unsuccessful attempt to take possession of his see; the Zealots declared themselves ready to accept him on condition that he made no mention of the Emperor Cantacuzene in the liturgy.[38] Still loyal to his original position, Palamas thought it better to delay his entry into Thessalonica. A decision of the Synod entrusted him with a mission to Lemnos that by his preaching he might soften 'the barbarous manners' of the island's inhabitants.[39] We can assume that the mission was connected with the government's desire to liquidate the last islands of resistance to Cantacuzene.

It was not until the beginning of 1350, when Cantacuzene finally made himself master of Thessalonica, that Palamas took possession of his see. The traditional ceremonial of enthronement included a prayer by the new Bishop at the gates of the city. To this prayer Gregory gave a penitential character: 'We have ceased to know each other: we have gone back to the former state before thou ledst us together to the One God, the one faith, the one baptism and the one communion.' And he prayed God to grant peace and concord to the town.[40] Three days after his entry, which Philotheus describes as a triumph, he preached a sermon on the theme of peace; in it he condemned the excesses of the Zealots which had given to Thessalonica 'the appearance of a town fallen into the hands of enemies': 'who invaded the town?' he demanded, 'who sacked the houses and pillaged what was

[36] Miklosich, *Acta*, I, 297.
[37] *Acts of Zographou*, in *Viz. Vrem.* XIII, 1907, Suppl., p. 90; P. Lemerle, *Actes de Kutlumus*, p. 97; cf. G. Soulis, op. cit., p. 138.
[38] Nilus, *Encomion*, *P.G.* CLI, 672B–673A.
[39] Philotheus, *Encomion*, 161CD; Cantacuzene, *Hist.* IV, 16, Bonn, III, 105.
[40] Ed. S. Oikonomos, p. 309.

found therein? Who was so mad as to drag the owners thereof by the nose, and kill them without pity or human feeling? Was it not the inhabitants of this city?' But at the same time he remained vigilant against any policy of revenge or reaction : 'Think no longer of doing evil, or of returning ill for ill.' [41] Palamas was often in his later preaching to condemn the social injustices which had been the cause of the revolt of the Zealots, and several among them, if we believe Philotheus, became his close friends.[42]

Nicephorus Gregoras

At Constantinople meanwhile some intellectuals continued to attack Palamite theology. The most representative of these was undoubtedly the learned Nicephorus Gregoras, supported by Theodore Dexios, and by the bishops deposed at Ephesus and Ganos, the sole survivors, in about 1351, of those who had protested in 1347. It is true that Matthew of Ephesus, who objected more to the Patriarch personally than to Palamite teaching, became for a while reconciled to the Synod after the death of Isidore; his letter of apology does include an approval of Palamite teaching.[43] Probably he thought that he would thus be better able to influence the election of the next Patriarch. On June 10th however another monk of Athos, Callistos, was elected Patriarch, and Matthew again joined the opposition.

During the civil war, Gregoras, the intellectual head of the opposition, kept out of the theological controversy between Akindynos and Palamas, and it was not until the end of 1346 that at the Empress Anne's request, he began to write, and pronounced against Palamas. It was then that he wrote his *Steliteutic Treatises* or *First Antirrhetics* against Palamas. But he does not seem to have circulated this work very widely. In politics favouring Cantacuzene he was often received at Court, where he strove to exercise some influence to counterbalance that of the Patriarch Isidore, especially with the Empress Irene, wife of Cantacuzene.[44] That was how he came openly to argue with the Patriarch about the liturgical reform which the latter had just introduced, in which a hymn of his own composition in praise of the Trinity was included, a hymn which contained some Palamite expressions. If we are to believe Gregoras, the Emperor had Isidore's hymns burnt, convinced by Gregoras of their heretical character.[45]

[41] *Hom.* 1, *P.G.* CLI, 12D, 16B.
[42] *Encomion*, 618CD.
[43] *P.G.* CLI, 772D–774A.
[44] R. Guilland, *Essai sur Nicéphore Grégoras*, Paris, 1926, pp. 30–3.
[45] Gregoras, *Hist.* XVI, 5, Bonn, II, 827–8; on the rich amount of hymnography attributed to Isidore by Greek and Slavic manuscripts, see Filaret, *Istoricheskii obzor pesnopevtsev grecheskoi Tservki*, Chernigov, 1864, pp. 445–6.

Just then, probably at the beginning of 1348, Gregory Palamas also came back to Constantinople, after his meetings with Dushan at Athos. He had some arguments about theology and canon law with Gregoras in the presence of the Emperor.[46] But it does not seem that the difference between them then was very passionate, for Philotheus, who had been made Metropolitan of Heraclea among those appointed to bishoprics in May 1347 and who remained in the capital for about a year after his nomination, was able, in friendly discussions, to find ground for theological agreement with Gregoras; he thought that only personal reasons kept Nicephorus opposed to Palamas.[47]

Convocation of a new Council

But in 1351 it became clear that a new Council was inevitable. It was convened by the Emperor and the Patriarch Callistos on May 28th, at the palace of Blakhernae, in a room of the *triclinium* built by Alexius Comnenus and decorated with pictures of the Oecumenical Councils.[48] This was a much more numerous and solemn assembly than any of the former Councils of the fourteenth century. John Cantacuzene presided, and with him were his brother-in-law the Sebastocrator Manuel Asen, his wife's cousin Michael Asen, and his other brother-in-law the Panhypersebastos Andronicus Asen[49]; the whole Senate was also there. Twenty-five Metropolitans and seven Bishops took part in the Council, and three absent Metropolitans had sent deputies. All these prelates were beforehand favourable to Gregory Palamas who also was present at the debates. The opposition was represented by two Metropolitans, Matthew of Ephesus and Joseph of Ganos, and by some less eminent personalities, Theodore Dexios, the *hieromonk* Athanasius, the monk Ignatius, and the young humanist Theodore Atouemis. In the course of the debates the anti-Palamites were also supported by Arsenius, Metropolitan of Tyre, the delegate at Constantinople of the Patriarch Ignatius of Antioch, a friend of Calecas.[50] Arsenius has left an account of the debates, and he, like Nicephorus Gregoras, contests their fairness. However, whatever justice there may have been in this criticism, there is no doubt that the anti-Palamites were able, at the Council of Blakhernae, to expound their views at length, and that Cantacuzene

---

[46] Gregoras, *Hist.* XVI, 5, Bonn, II, 829-34.
[47] Philotheus, *Against Gregoras*, VII, *P.G.* CLI, 924C-925C.
[48] Gregoras, *Hist.* XVIII, 6, 8, Bonn, II, 898, 905; *Tome*, *P.G.* CLI, 721A; Philotheus, *Encomion*, 622B.
[49] The text of the *Tome* where these personalities are enumerated is corrupt in all editions, except that of P. Uspenskii, p. 744 and I. Karmiris, *Ta dogmatika, mnemeia*, I, Athens, 1952, p. 313.
[50] Arsenius of Tyre, *Project of Tome, Vat. gr.* 2335, *fol.* 1; cf. Gregoras, *Hist.* XVIII, 5, Bonn, II, 891-4; Mercati, *Notizie*, pp. 210-17.

made a real effort, in the course of the assembly's lengthy debates, to bring those present to agreement before having recourse to the measures of which the minority, once condemned, was generally the victim in like cases.

The Council of 1351 comprised two quite distinct phases; in May and June there were meetings in which both parties were heard, the anti-Palamites, at first *de facto* and later *de jure,* playing the part of accusers, but not succeeding in persuading the assembly to condemn Palamas: in July 'another Synod' assembled without them and pronounced a solemn definition of dogma.

The first meeting

The first meeting took place on May 28th. The anti-Palamites were asked publicly to explain the reasons for their opposition; they put in evidence the addition made to the confession of faith required from bishops before their consecration, and attacked certain expressions of Palamas. The long theological discussion which followed chiefly concerned the acts of the Sixth Oecumenical Council; Palamas claimed that his own theology was only a development (ἀνάπτυξις) of the decisions of that Council about the two 'energies' or wills of Christ.[51] Nicephorus Gregoras answered by accusing him of iconoclasm on account of his doctrine of the 'deified flesh' of Christ; did not that flesh cease to be human, and could it still be represented on icons? To bring that accusation home, Gregoras quoted definite facts; Palamas and his disciples had burnt sacred images [52]; these facts may, as we have already seen, reflect the negative attitude of the most austere hesychasts to the too rich decoration of churches. However, in attacking Palamas, Gregoras and his supporters strongly disavowed both Barlaam and Akindynos. At the end of the day there was a written decision (κεκύρωται ἐγγράφως) that at the next session the anti-Palamites should be heard first, bringing forward their accusations against Palamas; the latter could defend himself later.[53] That was certainly a success for Gregoras who was recognized as the accuser, and describes the first session of the council as a victory.[54]

The subsequent meetings

Two days later, on May 30th, the second meeting proved much less favourable to the anti-Palamites. Gregoras and his supporters attacked

[51] *Tome,* P.G. CLI, 722B.
[52] Gregoras, *Hist.* XVIII, 6; XX, 4, Bonn, II, 898-978.
[53] *Tome,* 722B-723A; cf. Philotheus, *Against Gregoras,* VI, P.G. CLI, 1060C; Arsenius of Tyre, *Project of Tome, Vat. gr.* 2335, *fol.* 2.
[54] *Hist.* XX, 4, Bonn, II, 978.

Palamas on grounds of his terminology; the words 'God' (Θεός) and 'Divinity' (Θεότης), they asserted, should not be applied to the divine *energy,* but only to the essence.[55] Cantacuzene tried unsuccessfully to persuade Gregoras to give way on this point, promising him various favours. Palamas urged, as he had often done in his writings at the time of the civil war and was to do again later, that theological formulas have only a secondary value compared to the truth they express; he recognized that in his polemical writings he might have used a terminology less exact than that in the solemn confession of faith attached to his works; that confession of faith was then read and gained general approbation.[56] However, some of Palamas's adversaries had left the meeting before it was read; that was particularly the case with the Metropolitan of Tyre, who preferred to go away to avoid further complicating his relations with the Church of Constantinople where he was representing the Patriarch of Antioch; the latter had condemned Palamas in 1344.[57]

The third session did not take place till eight days later, on June 8th. The anti-Palamites were asked to present their confession too; they contented themselves with reading the Creed of Nicaea-Constantinople, adding one phrase: 'As to Barlaam and Akindynos our opinion is the same as that of the holy Church of God.' That vague formula was evidently susceptible to various interpretations; Arsenius of Tyre later wrote that by the 'Church of God' he himself meant the Patriarch of Antioch, Ignatius, and that, in his view, the formula condemned Palamas. Discussion continued concerning the Palamite formulas which Gregoras and his supporters had classified in 'chapters.' Each of these chapters was examined separately; the first three at the third session, on June 8th, the fourth at the beginning of the session of June 9th.

This fourth and last session was decisive. The Emperor and the Synod having interrupted accusing speeches of the anti-Palamites, proceeded to have the *Tome* of 1341 read; Palamas also put in evidence writings of his adversaries which manifestly contradicted the text of that *Tome;* that *Tome,* promulgated under Andronicus III, continued to be the basic document about which every one was, in principle, agreed. Extracts from St. Basil, St. John of Damascus, St. Maximus and St. Gregory of Nyssa were also read; when it was proposed to bring in the Acts of the Sixth Oecumenical Council, which were particularly favourable to Palamite theology, his adversaries protested, declaring that only the decision (ὅρος) had authority; then there was read to them

---

[55] Gregoras, *Hist.* XX, 6., Bonn, II, 988-90.
[56] *Tome,* 723C; text of the *Confession* in *P.G.* CLI, 763-8.
[57] Gregoras, *Hist.,* ibid., p. 991; Arsenius in Mercati, *Notizie,* p. 266.

the paragraph of the *Synodicon of Orthodoxy* which anathematizes those who reject the Acts of the Sixth Council, and the reading of the latter continued. These documents having been considered sufficient to prove the heretical character of the accusations against Palamas, Cantacuzene, having addressed a last appeal to his adversaries to recant, ordered the reading of the *Tome* of deposition prepared in 1347 against Matthew of Ephesus and his colleagues, the stipulations of which had not yet been applied. When that had been read, a high ecclesiastical official, Amparis, *chartophylax* of the patriarchate and 'consul of the philosophers,' solemnly asked the Bishops present to express their opinion in turn about the questions in dispute. All confessed both the unity of God and the necessary distinction between the divine essence and *energy*, both being uncreated. The Patriarch Callistos, who was called last, expatiated on this doctrine, again calling on the adversaries to recant and, when they refused, pronouncing the deposition of the Metropolitans of Ephesus and Ganos; their supporters were condemned and excluded from the meeting, with the exception of those who repented.[58]

Protest of Arsenius of Tyre

However no sanction was taken against Arsenius of Tyre who, though he disassociated himself from the Council, apparently adopted a sufficiently prudent attitude to avoid any useless complication. At the end of the meetings he addressed an appeal to the Emperor, John Cantacuzene, against its decisions, basing this both on formalities— unfair distribution of seats at the assembly, unilateral solution of dogmatic questions by the Patriarch of Constantinople alone without the agreement of the other Patriarchs, personal rulings made by Cantacuzene at the Council on the plea that he alone could act as impartial judge between the two parties, and his refusal to read the *Tome* which the Patriarch of Antioch had published against Palamas in 1344—and on theological grounds.[59] The action of Arsenius of Tyre led to complications in the relations between Constantinople and Antioch, and to troubles within the Patriarchate of Antioch itself. It seems that by 1352 Ignatius of Antioch did recognize the *Tome* of 1351; at some date before 1358 he or his successor was already in friendly correspondence with Callistos. But in 1365 the election of the Patriarch Pachomius was contested by some anti-Palamites and, in 1370, Arsenius, elected

---

[58] The debates are described in the texts, quoted above, of Gregoras and Arsenius, and in the *Tome* itself.

[59] Arsenius, *Appeal, Vat gr.* 1111, *pars.* IV, *fol.* 223-321. For the authorship cf. the French edition, p. 409.

Patriarch by an opposition group, drafted an anti-Palamite *Tome*, and was finally deposed.[60]

A second Council

A few days after the fourth session, probably in July, 'another Council' assembled, still in the *triclinium* of Alexius, but without the condemned anti-Palamites, who were mostly in prison or under house arrest. Six questions were examined in turn:

1. Is there in God a distinction between essence and *energy*?
2. If that is the case, is the *energy* created or uncreated?
3. If the *energy* is uncreated, how can one avoid complexity (τὸ σύνθετον) in God?
4. Can one apply the term 'divinity' to the *energy*, while still avoiding ditheism?
5. Is it right and traditional to say that the essence surpasses (ὑπέρκειται) the *energy*?
6. Since participation (μετοχή) in God exists, is that participation a participation in the essence or the *energy*?[61]

The council answered each of these questions in conformity with Palamite theology: there is a distinction between essence and *energy*, and both are uncreated; this distinction does not involve 'complexity' in God, for it is not a question of two essential realities, since both belong to one unique living God; the term 'divinity' was certainly applied to the *energy* by the Fathers who also speak of the essence which 'surpasses' the *energy*: finally, these same Fathers assert very clearly the incommunicability of the divine essence, while they speak of the real and existential revelation of the divine life or *energy*.[62] Then the *Tome* of 1341 was read again and compared with the writings of Akindynos.[63]

Finally, following the same procedure as in June, Amparis, the *chartophylax* and consul of the philosophers, asked each of the members of the Council, lay or cleric, their opinion: the Emperor spoke last—all the members of the assembly standing 'as was the custom'—and drew the conclusions from the debate; the Archbishop of Thessalonica was perfectly Orthodox and his teaching entirely conformed with the tradition of the Fathers.[64]

---

[60] cf. Gregoras, *Hist.* XXVI, 11, Bonn, III, 77, and various documents in Miklosich, *Acta*, I, 380, 407–9, 412–13, 463–5; cf. Mercati, *Notizie*, pp. 214–18.
[61] *Tome*, 732AB.
[62] *Tome*, 732C–754B.
[63] *Tome*, 754C–756B.
[64] *Tome*, 756D–757B.

The voice of Athonite monasticism was also to have been heard, its representatives having been invited to the Council, but 'the difficulty of the times' (war between Genoa and Venice, and fresh conflict between Cantacuzene and John V) prevented them coming; two *hieromonks* only conveyed the adhesion of the Athonites to the decisions of the Council, and presented, as expressing the opinion of the whole Holy Mountain, the treatises written by Philotheus and sent to Constantinople in 1346.[65] Besides this, a sort of theological commission met several times in St. Sophia to examine the chapters extracted from Palamas's works and considered heretical by his adversaries; there again Palamas was declared innocent of all blame.[66]

The Synodal Tome of 1351

The Synodal *Tome* incorporating all these decisions, which was apparently written by Philotheus, Metropolitan of Heraclea, decreed excommunication against all those who did not accept Palamism as conforming with Orthodoxy. Prepared in July, the *Tome* was not signed until August; on the 15th of that month, the day of the Assumption, between 7 and 8 in the morning, after matins, the Emperor John Cantacuzene entered the sanctuary of Aghia Sophia and solemnly handed the Synodal *Tome,* signed by himself, to the Patriarch Callistos, after that he went back to his place and listened to a reading of the document by the *protecdicos* George Galesiotes, by a certain 'Maximus the wise,' and finally by Philotheus, Metropolitan of Heraclea, who, when he had finished the reading, commented on the decisions of the Council in a short homily.[67]

The young Emperor John V Palaeologus, who was not in Constantinople at the time of these ceremonies, signed the *Tome* later, probably in February or March 1352.[68] According to Nicephorus Gregoras, after 1355 the young Emperor declared that he had signed the *Tome* under constraint by Cantacuzene.[69] But Palamas vehemently denies that assertion of Gregoras, and recalls John V's personal sentiments which were always favourable to Palamite theology, and which he particularly expressed at the time of the civil war.[70] Palamas is right in so far as John V never publicly opposed Palamite doctrine which was accepted as Orthodox by the immense majority of clergy and people; but he probably would gladly have avoided associating himself

---

[65] *Tome,* 757CD; the treatises are unedited (cf. French edition, p. 414).
[66] *Tome,* 759–60.
[67] Philotheus, *Against Gregoras,* I, *P.G.* CLI, 781BC; Cantacuzene, *Hist.* IV, 23, Bonn, III, 170.
[68] R.-J. Loenertz, *Wann unterschrieb Johannes V. Palaiologos den Tomos von 1351?,* in *Byz. Zeitschrift,* 47 (1954), p. 116.
[69] *Hist.* XXX, Bonn, III, 268–9.
[70] *Against Gregoras,* I, *Coisl.* 100, *fol.* 233–233v.

with something for which Cantacuzene was mainly responsible. In fact, the Synodal *Tome* of 1351 was not only an ecclesiastical decision, but also a state document rebounding to the glory of the Emperor John Cantacuzene.

A third imperial signature will finally figure on the document, that of Matthew Cantacuzene; this addition, dating from February 1354, was made at the time of the solemn coronation of the son of John Cantacuzene by the Patriarch Philotheus.[71]

The episcopal signatures vary greatly in number on different manuscripts. There are various reasons for these differences. As Philotheus indicates, the text of the *Tome* was very widely circulated and frequently copied. Moreover new Metropolitans signed the *Tome* when they came to Constantinople to be consecrated, or did so in their dioceses. Other prelates, who had been present at the deliberations, were away on the day of solemn signature in August. Relying on what appears to be the most ancient list of episcopal signatures, twenty-two Metropolitans signed in August; later copies carry some forty episcopal signatures to which are added those of the ecclesiastical officials of the Great Church. In 1358 Palamas writes that it had already been signed by 'more than fifty bishops.' [72]

The Synod of 1351 was the most solemn act by which the Orthodox Church confirmed the doctrine of Gregory Palamas. It was not, properly speaking, an Oecumenical Council, but a Synod of the episcopate of the patriarchate of Constantinople; but its decisions were accepted, in the course of the fourteenth century, by the whole of the Eastern Church. Thus in 1360 a Council of the Bulgarian Church assembled at Trnovo urged on by St. Theodosius, a disciple of Gregory of Sinai, confirmed the condemnation of Barlaam and Akindynos.[73]

The opponents

But there was opposition, notably on the part of Theognostos, Metropolitan of Russia. He was a Greek from Constantinople, and a friend of Nicephorus Gregoras.[74] But Theognostos died on March 11th, 1353, and was replaced by Alexis, a Russian. The latter was consecrated at Constantinople in 1354 by the Patriarch Philotheus, and must surely have subscribed to the synodal decisions. The results of the appeal

---

[71] P. Lemerle, *Le Tomos du concile de 1351 et l'horismos de Matthieu Cantacuzène*, in *Revue des études byzantines*, VIII, 1950, pp. 55–64.

[72] *Against Gregoras*, I, Coisl. 100, fol. 233v.

[73] P. Syrku, *K istorii ispravleniia knig v Bolgarii*, St. Petersburg, 1898, pp. 268–70.

[74] Gregoras, *Hist.* XXVI, 47–8, Bonn, III, 113–15; cf. E. Golubinskii, *Istoriia Russkoi Tserkvi*, II, 1, Moscow, 1900, p. 170.

of Arsenius of Tyre were more durable; at least up to 1370 a group of clerics in the patriarchate of Antioch opposed the rest of the Byzantine Church. The island of Cyprus, then under Lusignan rule, long provided a refuge for numerous anti-Palamites. Cantacuzene, after his abdication, wrote to a Cypriot bishop pointing out the Orthodox character of Palamism and refuting the arguments of the Akindynists.[75] It was through these anti-Palamite refugees in Cyprus (among whom was John Cyparissiotes. who in the end was converted to the Roman Church and became a Thomist theologian), and through Byzantine humanists, such as Demetrios Cydones, who were culturally and politically attracted to the West, that Latin theologians learnt the little they knew about Palamism.

The last official act by which the Orthodox Church gave Palamas's doctrine a formal approval was its insertion in the *Synodikon of Orthodoxy*. The anathemas against the anti-Palamites which are still found to-day in the liturgical *Triodion*, were first pronounced on the first Sunday in Lent 1352; they are six in number, and were followed by six proclamations of 'eternal memory' for those who had struggled for Orthodoxy against the Barlaamites: among the heroes of the faith first place was given to Andronicus III. Thus the Council of 1341 remained the witness *par excellence* to the Palamite triumph, and all that happened afterwards in the troubled time that followed, was only taken as confirming a Council held by an Emperor whose legitimacy was unquestionable. Andronicus therefore is the only sovereign glorified in the 'Palamite' part of the *Synodikon*.

Except for his personal enemies, Cantacuzene does not seem to have treated his adversaries with excessive severity. The condemned bishops ended their lives in the capital; Joseph of Ganos in his own house, Neophytus of Philippi at the monastery of St. Basil in which John Calecas also had been imprisoned, Macarius of Serres in a monastery dedicated to the Virgin, and Matthew of Ephesus must have been set at liberty.[76] Apart from a few people grouped round Nicephorus Gregoras, no one any longer opposed Palamism in the Church of Byzantium.

---

[75] J. Darrouzes, *Lettre inédite de Jean Cantacuzène relative à la controverse palamite*, in *Revue des études byz.*, XVII, 1959, pp. 7–27.
[76] Joseph Calothetos in *Angel, gr.* 66, *fol.* 199v.

CHAPTER VI

THE LAST YEARS

THE fresh triumph gained at Constantinople in 1351 did not bring Palamas's tribulations to an end. Having braved a great storm on his journey from the capital to Thessalonica, he again found himself refused entry into his episcopal see. John V Palaeologus, who was living there under the protection of the Sabastocrator Andronicus Asen, his wife's grandfather and the father-in-law of Cantacuzene, profited by his protector's absence to try and get free from the supervision under which he had lived. To that end he negotiated with the Serbian King, Stephen Dushan. The arrival of the Archbishop, whose loyalty to the Emperor of Constantinople was well known, was not particularly convenient for this project. As in 1347 Palamas had to go to Athos and wait three months there, until the Empress Anne, coming from Constantinople, momentarily, dissuaded her son from following the rebellious path.[1]

Gregory Palamas as pastor
Re-established in his see in the autumn of 1361 Gregory devoted himself to preaching and to the administration of his diocese. The austere monk and indefatigable polemicist proved also a zealous pastor; taking an interest in the spiritual and material needs of his church, he tried to re-establish peace and justice after the troubled years of the civil war and Zealots' revolt. The situation was, in truth, far from brilliant. The Archbishop, who in 1347 had condemned the excesses of the Zealots, now turned against the rich who had come out victorious in the civil war: 'We are known for nothing,' he exclaimed, 'except the wrongs we do each other and our insults to the poor. . . . And even if for a moment we put on an appearance of making peace between us, we, the powerful, still further increase our oppression of the poor, imposing heavier taxes on the work of their hands. What soldier is content with his pay? What magistrate does not plunder? . . . That is why the poor cry out against you all, all you in high places, you who hem them in, and you army officers and those who serve you! They cannot bear the pitiless and inhuman spirit of the tax gatherers, and the constant violence and injustice with which you afflict them, because you are more powerful than those who cultivate the land; already the torrent of injustice has reached the monasteries themselves.'[2]

[1] Philotheus, *Encomion*, 623–4; cf. Cantacuzene, *Hist.* IV, 27, Bonn, 208–9.
[2] *Hom.* 63, ed. Oikonomos, pp. 287–8.

Fresh political difficulties

In the autumn of 1352 [3] Palamas suffered the first serious attack of the illness which was to carry him off seven years later. On rising from his sick bed he was entrusted with a new political mission. The Emperor John V resided at Thessalonica, and since 1351 his mother Anne lived with him there too. So Palamas was in daily contact with the Court which had held him prisoner for four years at Constantinople. John had restarted the civil war against Cantacuzene; in the spring of 1353 he suffered a series of setbacks which resulted in the coronation of Matthew Cantacuzene at Constantinople, and he was obliged to take refuge in Tenedos; there he was soon joined by the Patriarch Callistos, who had been deposed, and replaced by Philotheus, because he refused to crown Matthew. John V's conduct towards Palamas had been correct, and the Archbishop does not seem to have intervened, on his own initiative, in the ups and downs of the renewed struggle between Palaeologi and Cantacuzenes. At the beginning of 1354 the young Emperor, perhaps on the advice of his mother who remained at Thessalonica, approached Palamas asking him to effect a reconciliation with his enemy.[4] Palamas was well suited for such a task; he was an old supporter of Cantacuzene, but he backed the claims of the poor classes who pleaded for the return of John V, and he was also the undisputed spiritual master of the two Patriarchs, Callistos and Philotheus, who both claimed the throne of Constantinople. Moreover all his earlier political activity and the favourite theme of his sermons were all devoted to the re-establishment of peace in the Empire.

Prisoner of the Turks

An imperial warship was put at Palamas's disposal to take him to Tenedos, where he received Palaeologus's instructions, and waited till the earthquake of March 2nd was over. Continuing his journey to the capital, he was forced by the wind to land near Gallipoli where, to his surprise, he found the Turks who had taken advantage of the earthquake to occupy the town.[5] So to his troubled career was added a long sojourn in Asia Minor under Moslem occupation. The Turks took prisoner the Archbishop and all his suite, including a *chartophylax*, probably the one attached to the Metropolitan see of Thessalonica, two hieromonks, Joseph and Gerasimos, and a certain Constas (Constant) Calamares.

[3] Philotheus, *Encomion*, 625D.
[4] ibid., 626A.
[5] cf. P. Charanis, *On the date of the occupation of Gallipoli by the Turks*, in *Byzantinolavica*, 16, 1955, pp. 113–17.

Palamas has himself described his sojourn with the Turks[6]; we have both two letters which he wrote in captivity, and the detailed account of a theological argument in which he had to take part. These are documents of great historical interest.

The most immediately striking feature thereof is the comparatively favourable picture he gives of the life of the Christians under the Turkish yoke, and the positive attitude he adopts towards the Turks themselves. This attitude is in contrast to that of many of his contemporaries; Matthew of Ephesus, in his prayer at his enthronement, merely bewailed the 'barbarian' occupation, and longed for the return of the Empire of the Romans.[7] And Nicephorus Gregoras, describing Palamas's captivity, manifestly exaggerates the insults to which he was subjected, and interprets them as divine punishment for his support of the pro-Turkish policy of Cantacuzene.[8] Palamas too considered the occupying forces as 'the most barbarous of the Barbarians,' but he regarded his captivity as providential in giving him a chance to reveal the Gospel to them. Philotheus's two accounts of his captivity also record his missionary preoccupations. Palamas nowhere refers to the possibility of a Byzantine reconquest of Asia Minor; quite the contrary, he considers the victory of Islam as something normal: 'This impious people boasts of its victory over the Romans, attributing it to their love of God. For they do not know that this world below dwells in sin, and that evil men possess the greater part of it ... that is why, down to the time of Constantine ... the idolaters have almost always held power over the world.' In contrast to the humanists who were often ready to sacrifice everything, even the Orthodox Faith, for the salvation of the Empire, the Archbishop of Thessalonica, though he obviously did not desire the victory of the barbarians, did not in the least consider that it put a final end to the history of Christianity. He describes the life of the Christians under the Turkish yoke, and reveals their new responsibilities, favoured by the great tolerance of the occupying power. Such an attitude was not peculiar to Palamas, but seems to have been very widespread among fourteenth century hesychasts and among the poor classes in general.[9] Philotheus records that St. Sabbas of Vatopedi, when he journeyed in Syria and Palestine, enjoyed the respect of the Moslems

[6] For the story of Palamas's captivity, based on his own letters, cf. G. Georgiades Arnakis, *Gregory Palamas among the Turks and documents of his captivity as historical sources*, in Speculum, XXVI, 1951, pp. 104-8; J. Meyendorff, *Grecs, Turcs et Juifs en Asie Mineure*, in the Acts of the Congress of Byzantine studies, Ohrid, 1961.
[7] Max. Treu, *Matthaios*, pp. 51-2.
[8] *Hist.* XXIX, Bonn, III, 227-9.
[9] cf. for example, I. Ševčenko, *Alexios Makrembolites and his 'Dialogue between the Rich and the Poor,'* in Srpska Akademija Nauka, Vizant. Institut, Zbornik Radova, 6, 1960, p. 196.

and had friendly interviews with their leaders. The tolerance of Islam towards the Orthodox Christians was, in Philotheus's eyes, in sharp contrast to the persecutions to which they were subjected by the Latins in Cyprus.[10] This attitude towards Islam of one part at least of the Byzantine monks, aroused the indignation of their adversaries. 'You summon the invasion of the Ismaelites,' wrote Akindynos, 'and you throw all your zeal into glorifying the manners of the Persians (the usual Byzantine term to designate the Turks), provided no one contradicts you, and fights to defend piety.'[11] One can see the incalculable influence of these ideas, which acquired increasing influence in Byzantine society.

The grandson of Orkhan

Palamas and his companions travelled from town to town under the light control of guards who freely allowed them to dwell with their compatriots in the towns through which they passed. Only during the journeys did they suffer privations. In this way they visited Lampsacus, Pegae, Brussa and Nicaea. Everywhere the Christians joyfully welcomed them. Their first theological discussions with the Moslems took place at Lampsacus; at Pegae, where they stayed three months, they were the guests of a *heteriarch* named Maurozumes, and took part in the relatively flourishing local church life. After a short stay at Brussa, they were taken in June 1354 to the summer residence of the Emir Orkhan, not far from the town; there they met the grandson of Orkhan, called Ismael, a young man of whom Palamas gives a very sympathetic description. They took a meal with him and had a long theological conversation in which he showed the tolerant spirit of a Turkish prince. The prisoners also had the chance to visit the Imperial Ambassadors who transmitted money to them. Taronites, a Greek doctor from Nicaea who had been summoned to Brussa to treat Orkhan's liver, intervened in their favour and arranged for them to be transferred to Nicaea. Before leaving the Emir's Court, Palamas had a long discussion, at which Taronites was present, with people whom he calls 'Chiones' (Χίονες).

The 'Chiones'

A detailed account of this discussion, written by the doctor, has survived,[12] and is interesting for many reasons. The discussion took place at the suggestion of the Emir, who had been impressed by the theological arguments put to his grandson by Palamas, and wanted to confront him with worthy antagonists. When they arrived, the Chiones tried to

---

[10] *Life of Sabbas, ed. cit.*, pp. 220–43, 264, 285–6.
[11] *Against Palamas*, VII, *Monac. gr.* 223. *fol.* 357v.
[12] Taronites, *Dialogue*, ed. A. I. Sakkelion, in *Soter*, XV, 1892, pp. 240–6.

persuade Taronites, Palamas and the Emir to save them from the necessity of arguing with the Archbishop; they did not succeed in this, but were allowed to hold the conversation without the presence of the Emir, who appointed deputies to preside over the meeting in his place.

The first thing one would like to know is who the Chiones were. Recent suggestions have been, first, that they were a fraternity of sailors (*Al Akhiyan*) which may have included some religious activity or, alternatively, that they were doctors of the Moslem faith (*akhond* or *khoja*). But Taronites's account shows that these somewhat far-fetched hypotheses are not correct. Here is the first address of the Chiones to Palamas, as it is reported by the doctor: 'We have heard the ten words which Moses brought down (from the mountain) engraved on stone, and we have learnt that the Turks hold firmly by them; therefore we have given up our former opinions, have gone to them, and have become Turks also.' Therefore the Chiones were not Turks by birth: they gave up their former faith, and found in the Mosaic law a means of assimilating themselves to the conquerors. Palamas's answer is also clear: 'These people, from what I have heard about them and from what they have said here, are clearly Hebrews and not Turks; but I have nothing to say to the Hebrews.' But the Chiones are not Jews by birth, for they 'gave up their former faith' to adopt the law of Moses. On the other hand, the term 'chiones' appears, in a slightly different form, in a patriarchal act dating from twenty years before the captivity of Palamas: a 'Chionios' (Χιόνιος) and 'his brothers' were brought to trial at Thessalonica for denying the true faith and embracing Judaism.[13] There is therefore no doubt that their conversion had been from Christianity, and that is how Philotheus speaks of them: 'Palamas had an argument with the Chiones, traitors to Christianity.'[14] That is what explains their repugnance to having a discussion with Palamas in the presence of the Emir; they could more easily explain their case in a 'family' reunion! Their attitude, and their presence at Brussa, is certainly due to the particular favours which the Jews enjoyed at the capital of the Osmanli Emirs; they there had a quarter to themselves, round the great synagogue called *Etz-Hayyim*. The Jews, in the fourteenth century, generally accepted the Ottoman conquest gladly. And, while many Christians frankly embraced Islam, some may have been tempted to adopt Judaism, which gave them the social privileges

[13] Miklosich, *Acta*, I, 174; the document has been studied by B. Melioransky, *K istorii protivotserkvnykh dvizhenii v Makedonii v XIV-m veke*, in "Ερανος, *Sbornik statei v chest' Th. Th. Sokolova*, St. Petersburg, 1895, pp. 62–72.

[14] Philotheus, *Encomion* (passages omitted in the printed text), Coisl. 98, *fol.* 264v, 267.

extended to the Jews, and allowed *rapprochement* with the Turks ('we have become Turks,' as they said to Palamas), without giving up the Scripture equally venerated by the Christians. This is a unique case, in many ways interesting for the history of the relations between Islam, Christianity and the Jews under the Ottoman Empire.

Taronites records a conversation between Palamas, the Turks and the Chiones. The Archbishop tried to address the Moslems directly, over the heads of the renegades, but they intervened, and the conversation veered between Moslem dogmas and the relation between the old and the new law. Finally the Archbishop succeeded in convincing the Moslems that the Jewish interpretation of the Law of Moses is not the true one, and that the Old Testament leads on to the realities of the New. The Turks complimented him and left the meeting. This success of Palamas aroused the anger of the Chiones, who could no longer use Judaism as a link with Islam, and one of them actually struck the Archbishop; the Turks intervened to protect him, and led the offender before the Emir. The main point of the *Dialogue* therefore is to show the inconsistency of the position the Chiones claimed to occupy between Christianity and Islam.

At Nicaea

Moved to Nicaea, Palamas lived in the monastery of St. Hyacinth. While walking in the streets of the town, he chanced on a Moslem burial, whose ceremonies he described; he also records a friendly conversation with the Mullah (ὁ τασιμάνης) in the presence of a crowd of curious Moslems and Christians; to all these the prisoner Archbishop preached the truths of the Christian Faith, and his own letter to his church concluded thus: 'One of them said, the time will come when we shall understand one another; and I am glad, and pray that that time may come soon.' So the Archbishop of Thessalonica saw the conversion of Islam to Christianity as a possible consequence of the Turkish conquest.

Return to Constantinople

These events all date from the first months of Palamas's captivity. His sojourn at Nicaea dates, according to his *Letter to his Church,* from July 1354 and no later episode is mentioned. So the letter must have been written at that time. But the Archbishop stayed in Asia Minor till the spring of 1355. According to Philotheus, events during that time at Constantinople delayed the sending of the ransom demanded for him by the Turks: in November 1354 John V succeeded in entering the capital. Cantacuzene was obliged to abdicate, and became a monk under the name of Joasaph. Philotheus too had to surrender the patriarchate to which Callistos returned. The young Emperor was in no particular hurry to bring back Palamas who had always supported Cantacuzene. According to Philotheus it was the Serbs who sent the necessary money.[15] According to Gregoras [16] it was Cantacuzene who, although dethroned, sent to his son-in-law Orkhan the ransom for Palamas in order to give him a better chance of defending his theology, the new political situation being more favourable to the anti-Palamites.

Nicephorus Gregoras, condemned in 1351, did now again have access to the Court, and John V allowed him to propagate his theology. According to Gregoras, in intimate conversation John V was unfavourable to Palamas; only the instability of his political position did not allow him to speak up. The Patriarch Callistos who had presided at the Council of 1351, the bishops generally and the great majority of public opinion was Palamite. In 1355 the Emperor could not formally oppose the doctrine confirmed by the Council of 1351. Palamas describes how, after his return from captivity, he celebrated the liturgy with the Patriarch in Haghia Sophia in the presence of John V and recalls that the latter could not but remain loyal to the pro-Palamite decisions of his father, Andronicus III, his mother, the Empress Anne, and 'if you like,' Palamas adds, with a trace of irony, 'of his father-in-law,' Cantacuzene.[17] What is certain, however, is that John V, whose dogmatic convictions were in general not very stable, had since his accession to power initiated *pourparlers* with a view to religious union with the West, and he therefore wanted to avoid the Byzantine Church giving an appearance of division in face of the Latins. This policy had the full support of Cantacuzene who continued to play an important role at Constantinople. The former Emperor also received Gregoras.[18] So there was not, under John V, any spectacular reversal of religious policy.

Public discussion with Gregoras

A Legate of Pope Innocent VI, Paul of Smyrna, had just arrived at Byzantium.[19] He was ill disposed towards Palamas. Perhaps his information came from Barlaam himself. An effort was therefore made to give him more complete information; John V arranged a meeting between him and Palamas, and asked him to be present at a discussion between the latter and Nicephorus Gregoras. This discussion took place in the

[15] *Encomion*, 627B.
[16] *Hist.* XXIX, 42, Bonn, III, 252.
[17] *Against Gregoras*, I, *Coisl.* 100, *fol.* 235v; cf. Philotheus, *Against Gregoras*, XII, *P.G.* CLI, 113B.
[18] Gregoras, *Hist.* XXXII, 4, Bonn, III, 377.
[19] On Paul and his relations with the Byzantine, see O. Halecki, *Un empereur de Byzance à Rome*, Warsaw, 1930, pp. 30–7; J. Meyendorff, *Projets de Concile oecuménique en 1367*, in *Dumbarton Oaks Papers*, XIV, 1960, pp. 169–77.

THE LAST YEARS

evening, in the Imperial Palace, in the presence of John V, his wife Helen, who was Cantacuzene's daughter and very favourable to Palamas, and some lay officials. We have two accounts thereof, one by Nicephorus Gregoras,[20] and the other by the *Protostrator* George Phacrases,[21] an imperial official who had been present. The two accounts are very different; Gregoras, incapable of objectivity where his own role in the theological controversies of his time was concerned, pleads his own case and himself admits that he has not recorded all Palamas's speeches, as they were not worth mentioning. His account is very long, and Palamas fairly remarked that if Gregoras had really delivered every speech he pretended to have made, the discussion would have lasted not one evening, but several consecutive nights and days.[22] Phacrases's account, which constitutes more or less the official record of the conference written by a high official, is certainly more impartial. It has been copied in many manuscripts. But probably, to maintain the dignity of the debate, Phacrases allowed some omissions; for instance, he says nothing about a rather unfortunate philological digression of the Archbishop of Thessalonica, which Gregoras records sarcastically.[23] The discussion did not add much that was new to the theological debate; the two adversaries resorted to the battle of Patristic texts usual in the circumstances. Though professing a formal conservatism and unswerving loyalty to the letter of scripture, Gregoras defended his view which applied to God, in an absolute manner, the philosophical conception of simple essence. The Emperor John V remained silent throughout the debate; according to Phacrases, he announced at the beginning that the assembly had no decision to take, for that had already been taken by the Church, but that he personally wished to learn about the problem, not having been present at the Council of 1351. This passage of Phacrases so contradicts what Gregoras records of the attitude of John V that one is tempted to see it as a sort of official dementi of the *History* of Nicephorus: the latter states that the Emperor declared that he had signed the *Synodal Tome* under constraint, and expressed his desire to review the question. Against this assertion of Gregoras, Palamas and Philotheus quote concrete examples of John V's loyalty to the decisions of 1351.[24] The Emperor certainly did not want to make new difficulties for himself in Byzantium. His object was to make a favourable impression on the

---

[20] *Hist.* XXX and XXXI.
[21] cf. M. Candal, *Fuentas palamiticas: dialogo de Jorge Facrasi sobre el contradictorio de Palamas con Niceforo Gregoras*, in *Or Chr. Per.*, XVI, 3-4, 1950, pp. 328-56.
[22] *Against Gregoras*, I, *Coisl.* 100, *fol.* 233.
[23] *Hist.* XXX, 81, Bonn, III, 324.
[24] Palamas, *Against Gregoras*, I, *Coisl.* 100, *fol.* 235-235v; Philotheus, *Against Gregoras*, XII, *P.G.* CLI, 1130B.

Papal Legate. The discussion at the Palace was certainly not enough to attain that end. The legate, Paul of Smyrna, appointed Archbishop of Thebes and then Titular Patriarch of Constantinople, remained down to 1369 at the centre of the *pourparlers* for union. At first these *pourparlers* envisaged the assembly of a veritable oecumenical council at Constantinople, but they ended in the personal conversion of John V to the Latin Church. Cantacuzene, who took part in these *pourparlers*, again tried to explain to Paul that Palamism was in no sense a new doctrine, formulated in opposition to the West, but was an appropriate expression of the tradition of the Fathers of the Church. If one trusts a letter written by Paul to Pope Urban V, he was not at all convinced by Cantacuzene, but we must note that at the Council of Florence, which was the distant result of the *pourparlers* of the second half of the fourteenth century, Palamism, which was always treated by the Greeks as the official doctrine of the Church, was not considered as a point of separation between the two Churches.

At Thessalonica

In the summer of 1355, Palamas returned to Thessalonica bearing letters from John V testifying to his perfect loyalty to the new political and ecclesiastical regime established in Constantinople. He began again to preach and, according to Philotheus, performed several miraculous healings. He often visited the monasteries of the town, and took part in many services and traditional processions of the Byzantine liturgy. He preached on all these occasions, and the collection of his homilies covers practically the whole of the liturgical year.

But Gregoras's activity in Constantinople continued to disturb him. Friends sent him certain passages of the *Second Antirrhetics* of the philosopher; from these he learnt that Gregoras denied the correctness of a quotation of St. Basil as it was given in the *Synodal Tome* of 1351. The anti-Palamites wished to prove that the grace of deification was created and put forward Patristic quotations in which God was called *hypostates* (ὑποστάτης) of that grace; against that assertion, the *Tome* quotes the *Against Eunomius* of St. Basil of Caesarea in which the Greek verb ὑφίστημι is applied to the Generation of the Son, and therefore does not necessarily mean 'to create'; 'He who engendered drops of dew (Job 38 : 28) did he not establish (ὑπεστήσατο) in the same way both the drops and the son?'[25] Gregoras asserted that the authentic text of St. Basil did not have the word ὑπεστήσατο but ἐτεκνώσατο ('had engendered').[26] Palamas then collected manuscripts of St. Basil's works,

[25] P.G. XXIX, 624A; cf. *Tome of 1351*, P.G. CLI, 744B.
[26] *Laur. Plut.* LVI, 4, *fol.* 129.

especially the oldest ones, to be found at Thessalonica, and had it established first, by a learned commission, and then by the Logothetes τοῦ γενικοῦ that both readings were found in the manuscripts and that anyhow the two expressions meant the same.[27] The question seems to have disturbed other men besides Palamas then, for the deposed Patriarch Philotheus also refutes Gregoras's interpretation in a treatise of like date, addressed to the Great Domestic Palaeologus.[28]

When Gregoras's own writings reached Thessalonica, Palamas wrote two treatises refuting his account of the dialogue of 1355. For some reason unknown to us he published these under the pseudonym of Constantius, *hagiorite hieromonk*. Then in 1358 the deposed Patriarch Philotheus asked him to refute the *Antirrhetics* of Gregoras about the light on Mount Tabor; the Archbishop's two last treatises deal with that matter.

His last days

In 1358 Gregory Palamas had another attack of the internal disease from which he had been suffering for some years. However he continued to conduct the services and to preach. As his illness grew worse, his sermons concentrated on the theme of death. On August 1st he spoke of the origin of human illness—the Devil and the sin which he brought among men—and the suffering caused thereby. Clearly he was thinking of himself when he spoke of the month of August whose heat he found hard to bear.[29] In passing he attacked the magicians and charlatan healers who kill the soul without healing the body. The next Sunday he could no longer get up, and delivered his sermon from his sick bed.[30] Contemplating his own approaching death, he spoke, after commenting on the Gospel for the day, of the true danger which lay in wait for Christians, which is not the death of the body, but the eternal loss of body and soul.

His canonization

He died on November 14th, 1359, the day after the feast of St. John Chrysostom, aged 63 years, and having been a bishop for twelve years and a half.[31] His body was buried in his cathedral, Haghia Sophia at Thessalonica, and, according to Philotheus, many miracles were per-

---

[27] *Letter on St. Basil*, Coisl. 100, *fol.* 287v–288.
[28] *P.G.* CLI, 1139–43.
[29] *Hom.* 31, *P.G.* CLI, 397D.
[30] Philotheus, *Encomion*, 635AB, referring to *Hom.* 32.
[31] ibid., 635BD; cf. K. I. Dyovouniotes, Τὸ ἔτος τοῦ θανάτου Γρηγορίου τοῦ Παλαμᾶ, in Ἐπιστημονικὴ Ἐπετηρὶς τῆς θεολογικῆς σχολῆς, I, 1924, p. 74.

formed at his intercession immediately after his death.[32] An inquisition was ordered by the Patriarch Callistos in 1363, who then addressed himself to the suffragan bishops of the metropolitan see of Thessalonica, which shows that no successor was immediately appointed. The bishops, at a meeting over which the Empress Anne of Savoy, who still lived at Thessalonica, presided, proceeded to hear witnesses and wrote an official document which they sent to Constantinople. Using this document, Philotheus, who again succeeded Callistos in 1363, himself wrote the *Encomium* of Gregory and also a liturgical service in his honour, and presided at a ceremony at the monastery of the Incomprehensible (τοῦ 'Ακαταλήπτου) where Palamas had been imprisoned by Calecas in the autumn of 1342. Elsewhere too the cult of Palamas commenced; at Lavra on Mount Athos in spite of protests from Prochoros Cydones, and at Kastoria where a church had already been dedicated to him in 1368. So local and popular veneration, as was almost always the case in Byzantium, preceded his official canonization. That then took the form of a Decree of the Synod authorizing the inclusion of the Saint in the calendar of the 'Great Church' (Haghia Sophia at Constantinople), whose example was followed by the other churches. This decision was taken by the Patriarch and Synod in 1368. A quite special place was chosen for St. Gregory's commemoration in the liturgical year, the Second Sunday in Lent. A sort of continuation of the Feast of Orthodoxy was thus established. Liturgical hymns composed by Philotheus were integrated into the service for the day, while the *canon* for the Feast was composed by a certain George.[33] The *Synodicon of Orthodoxy* was also enlarged by a proclamation of eternal memory to 'Gregory, the Most Holy Metropolitan of Thessalonica.'

The troubled life of this great Byzantine theologian passed in one of the periods most critical for the Eastern Christianity; torn by intestinal conflicts, forced to defend its land foot by foot against the invaders from the east, tempted by a Western alliance and by union with Rome, the Byzantine Empire was on the eve of its final ruin. None of the events of this period can be explained simply, so diverse were the religious, political and social motives inextricably intertwined. That certainly applies to Palamas's activity. But careful examination of the different attitudes he adopted, clearly brings out the essential motive which constantly guided him, and which always took precedence over the other elements of the situations with which he tried to deal. That motive was loyalty to dogmatic Orthodoxy as he understood it. That

---

[32] Besides Philotheus's *Encomion,* the *Tome of the Council of 1368 (P.G.* CLI, 711–12) gives some information about the death and canonization of Palamas.

[33] Karabinov, *Postnaia Triod,* St. Petersburg, 1910, p. 200.

loyalty led him to engage in the controversy with Barlaam and to pursue the struggle against Akindynos, and it was that loyalty which enabled him to adopt a comparatively conciliatory attitude towards the Turkish conquerors, in so far as they allowed religious liberty to the Christians. Though psychologically prepared to face the ruin of the Byzantine state, he was far from adopting a purely fatalistic attitude thereto: as long as that State existed, it was to be supported, and its traditional unity and Orthodoxy safeguarded. To Gregory, Cantacuzene seemed the man for this policy of continuity, and his enemies did not strike him just as being defenders of the poor classes oppressed by the high nobility, but rather seemed to him to be rash politicians preferring the local interests of their town or their profession to the common weal of the Empire. Such was the case with the Zealots of Thessalonica. The wealth and lands promised to the Archbishop of Thessalonica by the rich Serb Emperor Stephen Dushan were not an argument that could make Palamas deviate from his loyalty to Byzantium as the sole legitimate heir of the Christian Empire.

Although he took a decided part in political affairs, Gregory continued to distinguish between the relative and the absolute. Openly favouring Cantacuzene, he remained loyal to Anne of Savoy and the government actually holding power at Constantinople; he by no means scorned the support of Alexis Apocaucos, and only repulsed the offers of the Patriarch because the latter had betrayed Orthodoxy. When the Zealots' revolt had been crushed, he was not afraid publicly to castigate the rich and the officials of the State who, having helped the victory of Cantacuzene, forgot the bitter lesson of the revolt, and persisted in those social injustices which had provoked it.

Thus the impartial history of this stormy period makes the moral character of Palamas stand out in an altogether exceptional light. None of his adversaries ever attacked him on moral grounds. It was only his written works and the theological teaching which he had elaborated, which were attacked by the Byzantine humanists, some of whom had adopted the Latin Faith and so helped to represent the Palamites as the fiercest adversaries of religious union with Rome.

Admitting that the theology of Palamas in no way favoured dogmatic compromises, and for that reason was opposed to the method too often employed in the negotiations for union, after the manifest checks to these attempts, we should to-day consider whether the Western Church was not wrong in avoiding a true dialogue with the best that Byzantine spirituality and theology had produced.

PART TWO

THE THOUGHT OF PALAMAS

THE thought of the greatest Greek theologian of the Middle Ages was never presented as a system. It was expressed in a series of polemic writings answering the needs of the moment. Hence there would be a risk of misrepresenting Palamas's thought, and certainly a risk of diminishing its relevance, if an 'Introduction' to his work did not follow the logical order of events which led him to elaborate his views. His mind had a strong dogmatic turn, enabling him to interpret the spiritual tradition of Byzantine monasticism in terms of doctrinal concepts, but yet he never attempted to shape his thoughts to the norms of any philosophy. To some this seems a weakness, but it was of the essence of his peculiar strength, which led to his canonization by the Byzantine Church, and to his being called a teacher of Orthodoxy.

Therefore in tracing the main outlines of his thought, we will follow the logical order in which Palamas himself became conscious of the doctrine he was teaching. It will become clear that the different aspects of this doctrine are linked by an essential unity which is not the product of intellectual speculation, but which springs from the inner necessity of life in the Church as Palamas understood it.

CHAPTER I

OPPOSITION TO PROFANE HELLENISM: MAN DEPRIVED OF GRACE

A discussion on the knowledge of God

It was opposition to profane philosophy which led Palamas to write his first theological treatises. In Barlaam of Calabria's thought he found a form of humanism which was trying to introduce new criteria into the domain of theology, with the special object of facilitating *pourparlers* for Union.[1] This humanism was not opposed to tradition as such, and it was very far from proclaiming the complete freedom of the human mind. At Byzantium, as in the West, the phenomenon conventionally designated as the 'Renaissance' was exceedingly complex. Barlaam and his like professed to reverence 'authorities,' but among those authorities they counted Aristotle and Plato. Moreover, in the field of natural philosophy, the authority of the Ancients was regarded as exclusive, as that of Scripture and the Fathers was in the field of theology. In common with his Western contemporary, William of Ockham, Barlaam was sceptical about the power of the human intellect by itself to know God, but such nominalism led to an even greater exaltation of the authority of Scripture and the Fathers, as sources of an *ex machina* incomprehensible revelation.[1a] Revealed writings, in his view, could not have been intended to stimulate thought, for thought could not derive the smallest corollary from a unique Revelation. So the proper field for the development of the human mind must be elsewhere than in the field of theology, and his own particular interests inclined him to study the profane sciences. Thus, while he accepted in their own spheres the authority of Scripture and of the philosophers, he had a different attitude towards them. Scripture for him was a source of quotations and references, and not a means of living communion with the spirit of God. But the philosophers stimulated the real activity of his intellect, and provided the permanent criteria of his thought. So an abyss, which the humanists made no claim to cross, yawned between intellectual activity and the religious life, between philosophy and theology.

When Barlaam had the chance to air his views about the Union of

[1] On Barlaam's thought see my article *'Un mauvais théologien de l'unité: Barlaam le Calabrais,'* in *L'Eglise et les Eglises*, II, Chevetogne, 1955, pp. 47–64.
[1a] My *tentative* interpretation of Barlaam's thinking was sharply challenged by J. S. Romanides in the *Greek Orthodox Theological Review*, VI, 2, 1961. According to Fr. Romanides, Barlaam is to be placed in the line of classical Western Augustinism. If sufficient evidence was to be found for that interpretation in Barlaam's mostly unpublished writings, the controversy would be reduced to a simple episode in the debate between East and West.

the Churches, he decided to apply his philosophy to that question. When he considered the Latin propositions about the procession of the Holy Spirit, he easily demonstrated that the premises and conclusions of the syllogisms in which this was expressed did not conform to the conditions of an 'apodictic syllogism' as defined by Aristotle; the Deity in fact surpassed every syllogism and all human logic. Therefore the Latin arguments had only a 'dialectic' value. It went without saying that the Greek arguments were convincing only in that same sense.

Palamas at first had difficulty in refuting this reasoning which shocked his religious experience. He too had been formed in his youth in the school of Aristotle, and he did not want to admit that there was any opposition between Aristotelian method and theology. He sought therefore to prove that demonstration can be well applied to divine realities: 'We have learnt from the Fathers how to reason ($\sigma\upsilon\lambda\lambda o\gamma i\zeta\varepsilon\sigma\theta\alpha\iota$) about such matters in a practical way, and no one should blame the Latins for that (as Barlaam does). But I confidently assert that they do not reason in an apodictic manner . . . for they do not use the truths of the faith as principles and axioms . . . nor in a dialectic manner, for they construct their syllogisms starting from premises which are foreign to us . . .'[2] Hence it is possible to judge theological arguments from the point of view of simple formal logic, and it is from that simple point of view that the Latin arguments are seen to be erroneous. 'Nobody,' Gregory continues, 'has ever expressed, or sought, or thought what God is, but it is possible to seek and demonstrate that God exists, that he is a Unique Being and not a unique thing, that he has not surpassed the Trinity, and many other things . . .'[3] He seeks to show that all true theological reasoning is necessarily apodictic, for it is founded on sure premises, and therefore cannot simply be considered as 'dialectic,' as Barlaam would have it.

But Gregory was not slow to see that his attempts to use Barlaam's methods and terminology in order to refute him, could lead to nothing. Barlaam found it easy to answer that, on the basis of Aristotelian logic only, no 'theological' premise could be considered sure, for it could not be perceived by the senses; for Barlaam, like Ockham, considered that 'only knowledge provided by the senses is sure when existing things are in question.'[4] The difference between the two disputants concerns the theory of knowledge: can God be directly perceived by man? Is there any sure and immediate knowledge, apart from that provided by the senses?

[2] *First Letter to Akindynos*, 8, ed. Meyendorff, in *Theologia*, XXVII, 1955, p. 83.
[3] ibid., p. 84.
[4] E. Gilson, *La philosophie au Moyen Age*, Paris, 1952, p. 641.

When he had fully appreciated exactly where Barlaam contested his view, Palamas began to develop his conception of the knowledge of God, on which he had only touched in his *First Letter to Akindynos*, and in which he contrasts the two states of man, the natural and fallen state and the state of union with grace.

As Augustine had done in his writings against Pelagius, Palamas insists on the basic incapacity of man to reach God by his own efforts: in this respect Palamas is one of the most 'Augustinian' writers of the Christian East. Moreover he had at his disposal all the 'apophatic' terminology of the Fathers to express the inaccessibility of God, due to the two obstacles rising between man and God, that is to say the created state, and sin. We shall see later that, in Palamas's view, man, even when he breaks through these two obstacles, remains entirely dependent on divine grace for his knowledge of God. We must now examine in turn Palamas's conception of man as a creature, and as a fallen creature.

Knowledge through creatures

As a creature man holds a pre-eminent position in the world; he is the goal of the whole creation,[5] 'the conclusion of the universe' (συνδρομὴ τοῦ παντός) 'the recapitulation (ἀνακεφαλαίωσις) of the creatures of God'; 'that was why,' Palamas wrote, 'he was brought into existence last of all, as we end a treatise with an epilogue; for we can say that the universe which we see is, as it were, a writing of the hypostatic Word.'[6] In developing, in his sermons especially, this very Patristic idea, in which the Biblical conception of man as 'king of creation' is combined with the Platonic and Stoic conception of the microcosm, Gregory stresses the purely preparatory character of this original kingship; it was but the firstfruits whose fulfilment depended on obedience to the divine command: 'If he had obeyed this command he could have enjoyed a still more perfect union with God.'[7] The world which served as Adam's dwelling place had not been created just to serve him, but to lead him to knowledge of the Creator; the first man had before him a mirror (κάτοπτρον) in which to see supernatural realities, and in his heart he possessed a *natural law* (ἔμφυτον νόμον) and conscience (συνείδησιν) which allowed him to distinguish the good.[8] In Paradise therefore already man at the time of his creation possessed an external and an internal way of access to God.

[5] *Hom.* 51, ed. Oikonomos, p. 109; *Hom.* 3, P.G. CLI, 33B; *Hom.* 6, ibid., 81A.
[6] *Hom.* 53, ed. Oikonomos, p. 172; cf. *Hom.* 26, col. 332CD.
[7] *Hom.* 57, ed. Oikonomos, p. 213.
[8] *Hom.* 3, col. 36B.

The conception of the world as the mirror of God was clearly taken by Palamas from the Greek Fathers, and it is founded on the doctrine of divine *logoi* present in the creation, which all the Fathers, after St. Justin, had adopted, and which goes back to the Stoics. Palamas speaks of them too, but he insists that, for Christians, these *logoi* are the *energies* of a unique God, and have no separate existence.[9] Therefore it is to him that a true understanding of beings leads, and in that lies their principal justification. Palamas, though the general line of the argument in which he was involved did not lead him to elaborate his ideas about natural knowledge of God, had a positive attitude about the matter. 'Knowledge of creatures,' he wrote, 'brought mankind back to knowledge of God before the Law and the Prophets; to-day also,' he continues, alluding to the progress of Islamic monotheism, 'it is thus bringing men back; and almost the whole of the inhabited world, all those parts which do not obey the mandates of the Gospels, now possess, by that means alone, a God who is none other than the Creator of this universe.'[10] Even when he is bent on diminishing the importance of this analogical and indirect knowledge of God, he specifically admits that, by paying attention to the *logoi* of beings, one comes to realize 'the power, wisdom and providence of God.'[11] 'Are knowledge and profane science evil things? Never,' he answers, 'our Father, our Master and our Creator has given them to us,'[12] but 'I say that among the gifts of God some are natural; they are given to all without discrimination, before the Law, under the Law, and after the Law; others are supernatural, spiritual, and in a special sense mysterious; I consider the latter superior to the former, just as those who have been found worthy to receive the wisdom of the Spirit are superior to the whole tribe of Greeks.'[13] This distinction between 'natural' and 'supernatural' keeps recurring when Palamas is dealing with profane wisdom. 'As in lawful marriage,' he writes, 'the pleasure of procreation cannot strictly be called a divine gift of God, for it is carnal and a gift of nature, not of grace, even though nature was created by God, even so knowledge derived from profane education, though it be well used, is yet a gift of nature and not of grace, God giving it to all without exception by means of nature, and it is something that can be developed by practice. This last point, the fact that no one attains it without effort and practice, is clear proof that it is a natural, and not a spiritual, gift.'[14] Natural

[9] *Tr.* III, 2, 24, 26–7.
[10] *Tr.* II, 3, 44.
[11] *Tr.* II, 3, 15–16, 69–70; *Against Akindynos*, III, 18, *Coisl.* 98, *fol.* 89v; IV, 18, *fol.* 110v–111.
[12] *To John and Theodore*, ed. Oikonomos, p. 306.
[13] *Tr.* II, 1, 24; II, 3, 71.   [14] *Tr.* I, 1, 22.

faculties are thus contrasted with the completely gratuitous quality of grace.

Knowledge of God 'through the creatures' is incomplete and limited: 'there is,' writes Palamas, 'a knowledge *about* God and his doctrines. ... The use and activity of the natural powers of the soul and of the body do shape the rational image of man, but that is not the same as the perfect beauty of the noble state which comes from above; that is by no means the supernatural union with the more than resplendent light, which is the sole source of sure theology.'[15] Natural philosophy is not the same as *union* with God; it mostly proceeds by the method of exclusion, defining *what is not God,* and does sometimes see the beauty of the First Cause, but it does not put us face to face therewith. That is not its proper aim: 'The aim of profane philosophy, by which means we examine the laws of nature and of movement, analogies, and the configurations and quantities of the indivisibly divisible parts of matter, is the study of the truth which lies in existing things; when this study consciously goes beyond the truth which is within its scope, it is perfidious and deceives its hearers; if it does this unintentionally, it is a stranger to philosophy and void of understanding.'[16] Palamas therefore leaves the way perfectly free for autonomous philosophic and scientific research, on condition that the limits of such research are recognized, and that no one claims that its conclusions are absolute. 'To know God, and to know man himself and the dignity belonging to him ... that is knowledge superior to physiology, astronomy and all philosophy linked with such sciences; moreover it is incomparably more profitable to our understanding if we recognize its weakness and try to cure that, rather than to know and study the greatness of the stars ...'[17]

Image and likeness

However, as we have seen, besides natural external knowledge, man in Paradise also possessed an inner 'natural law' leading him to God. The Creator had given him his own image, and so, within himself, he found another mirror reflecting God, giving a more exact reflection than that which he could discover by contemplating the external world. Palamas considered this image of God in man as an existential and dynamic reality; nowhere in his works is teaching about this image elaborated by itself, without relation to the divine grace which in Paradise gave it its full force or, as we shall see later, without reference to the sin which obscured it, and to Christ who again established its former state.

[15] ibid., 3, 15.
[16] *Against Akindynos*, VI, 1, Coisl. 98, fol. 149v.
[17] *Cap. phys.* 29, P.G. CL, 1140C.

'God created Adam,' writes Palamas, 'in his own image and likeness
... and introduced no evil disposition into him; rather, with the soul
that he breathed into him, he also gave him the divine grace of the
Spirit to preserve him in his first state and confer on him the (divine)
likeness.'[18] By thus taking up again the Patristic conception according
to which 'nature' does not possess an autonomous existence, but *supposes* grace and communion with God, in order to fulfil its own true
destiny, Palamas affirms that the likeness too is an effect of grace while
presupposing the collaboration (συνεργία) of man : hence man *needs
God* to attain the likeness, but God can only give what man accepts ...

At the beginning of his theological activity, in his *First Letter to
Akindynos,* Gregory is already speaking 'of the (divine) goodness by
which (the creatures) receive the being and inherent grace (χάρις
ἐγγεγενημένη) by which each creature shares in the well-being suited to
it'[19]; in this context 'well-being' is a term of St. Maximus to designate
the supernatural state,[20] as Palamas himself says later when he speaks,
in the same passage of the *Letter,* of the grace which 'comes afterwards'
(ἐπιγεγενημένη), the grace by which what had been fallen is restored
to well-being. It was therefore a particular grace which allowed Adam
to share, partially and by anticipation, in the divine life, and this privilege was not inherent in his created state, as such. 'In the beginning man
was not only a creature of God, but also his son in the Spirit; this
grace was given to him at the same time as his soul by the life-giving
breath; it was in the nature of an earnest; if he had observed the
covenant of which this was the earnest, he could thereby have enjoyed
a still more perfect union with God, and have become coeternal with
God, clothed in immortality.'[21] Elsewhere Palamas says that divine grace
'by many benefits completed the insufficiency of our own nature.'[22]
Essentially, therefore, nature *supposes* grace, and grace means participation in divine life. But the sin committed by man separated him from
this grace, and left man alone with all the insufficiencies of his created
nature.

Original sin

Besides the necessary limitations of every creature, original sin was the
basic obstacle between man and God.

'We hold within ourselves,' Palamas wrote, 'the images of the *logoi*
which reside within the creative Intelligence.' These images are that

[18] *Hom.* 54, ed. Oikonomos, p. 185.
[19] 5, ed. Meyendorff, p. 80.
[20] *Cap.* IV, 54, *P.G.* XC, 1329A; V, 13, 1353B, etc.
[21] *Hom.* 57, ed. Oikonomos, P. 213.
[22] *Hom.* 36, col. 452A.

inner mirror by which we are able to understand God through his creatures. 'But why,' he asks, 'have these images from the beginning proved ineffective? Is it not because of sin, and also because of ignorance and scorn of divine commandments? Why do we need teaching to see these images, although they are inscribed within us? Is it not because the passionate part of the soul, roused to commit evil, has corrupted them? Is it not because it has overthrown the power of sight of the soul, and driven it away from its primal beauty?'[23] Instead of joy in the presence of God, man preferred a selfish joy of which he himself was the object[24]; he broke the fast ordained by God to preserve his immortality,[25] and thenceforth a veil had fallen over his soul (2 Cor. 3: 13–16) and obscured the divine reflection.[26]

By disobeying the divine command, Adam, though he preserved the divine image, was deprived of resemblance to God.[27] We have seen that in Palamas's scheme this resemblance—a dynamic conception—was the effect of peculiar divine grace, or, more precisely, represented a participation by man in the divine life. That was what man lost by his own fault, and the immediate consequence thereof was death, for 'God alone possesses immortality' (1 Tim. 6: 16).

To understand Palamas's thought about sin and death, it is necessary correctly to analyse his use of the word 'nature' ($\varphi\acute{\upsilon}\sigma\iota\varsigma$). For him 'nature' is not a static conception, but must always be considered in one or other of its existential states. Its state before the Fall implied life in God, for which it had been made, although that life was not its own, but that of God; this was essentially the 'natural' state of nature; after the Fall, deprived of that life, it was left to rely on its own powers alone, a condition basically contrary to its destiny, and involving death. Which of these two states was the 'natural state' of man? One can immediately see where these views, basically formulated already by Maximus the Confessor, differ from the views on 'grace' and 'nature' developed in the West after St. Augustine.

Sin and death

On the one hand Palamas asserts that the human soul possesses life both by essence ($\kappa\alpha\tau'o\dot{\upsilon}\sigma\acute{\iota}\alpha\nu$) and through *energy* ($\kappa\alpha\tau'\dot{\epsilon}\nu\acute{\epsilon}\rho\gamma\epsilon\iota\alpha\nu$), for it does not only live itself, but communicates life to the body; that is its essential difference from the animal soul which possesses life only through

---

[23] *Tr.* I, 1, 3.
[24] *Tr.* I, 3, 32.
[25] *Hom.* 6, col. 81C.
[26] *Tr.* I, 3, 47.
[27] *Cap. phys.* 39, col. 1148B.

energy, as a function of the body which it makes alive, and which it does not survive.[28] On the other hand he asserts equally explicitly that the soul 'dies' as a result of sin, stressing the paradox of the 'natural' immortality of the soul, and its actual death. 'The soul which, separated from its spiritual Spouse ... gives itself to pleasures and lives in delights, is dead, though it yet remains alive (ζῶσα τέθνηκε), for in essence it is immortal.'[29] This conception of the death of the soul frequently appears in Gregory's works as the central theme of his doctrine concerning man and of his spirituality; it is by no means a figure of speech, but rather a real death the true significance of which is the separation from God caused by sin: 'After the transgression of our ancestors in Paradise ... sin came into life, we ourselves are dead and, before the death of the body, we suffer the death of the soul, that is to say the separation of the soul from God.'[30] 'When the soul leaves the body, and is separated from it, the body dies; in the same way, when God leaves the soul and is separated from it, the soul dies, although, in another sense, it remains immortal'[31]; that is 'the eternal death of the immortal soul' (θάνατος αἰώνιος τῆς ἀθανάτου ψυχῆς)[32]; as we shall see, only baptism can deliver us from that death. For those who are not baptized, their souls remain dead.[33] This death of the soul, though it is not immediately followed by bodily death, renders the latter inevitable with all the ills that that entails. On the day of sin the soul of Adam 'was put to death ... for it separated itself from God; but in a bodily sense it remained alive for nine hundred and thirty years (cf. Gen. 5: 3-4), but the death which the soul had suffered through transgression, not only made the soul unprofitable and man accursed, but also subjected his body to many sufferings and evils, and made it corruptible.'[34]

This death of the soul, which is balanced by the 'resurrection of the soul' through baptism, was the ontological catastrophe which struck Adam after the Fall. Was his 'immortality' nevertheless preserved, as Palamas affirms? Yes, but it was a state worse than death. Adam and Eve 'hid themselves from shame, naked and bereft of the glory to which even immortal spirits owe their life, and without which the life of spirits is far worse than many deaths.'[35] In that Palamas is com-

[28] ibid., 30-2, col. 1140D-1141A.
[29] ibid., 45, col. 1153A; cf. *Hom.* 31, col. 389D (cf. 1 Tim. 5: 6).
[30] *Hom.* 11, col. 125A; cf. *Cap. phys.* 36, col. 1148B; 51, col. 1157CD; cf. *Hom.* 13, col. 157C; *Hom.* 16, col. 208A; *Hom.* 32, col. 409CD.
[31] *Hom.* 16, col. 196A; *To Xene*, col. 1048C.
[32] *Hom.* 34, col. 424D; *To Xene*, col. 1048A.
[33] *On participation to God*, Coisl. 99, fol. 23.
[34] *To Xene*, col. 1048C; cf. 1049AD.
[35] *Cap. phys.* 48, col. 1156C.

pletely faithful to the Biblical conception of death, which is nothing but a semi-existence in a dim place, or Hades,[36] from which God alone can deliver it. God alone possesses immortality, and it was by sharing in the divine life that man, in Paradise, was immortal.

Palamas often stresses the fact that God's design had destined man for such immortality. The fires of Hell were destined for Satan, not for man, and it was by their free choice that men must dwell there with the devils.[37] 'Not only did God not create death,' he writes, 'but he forbade it to be... In his wisdom and goodness he found a means of forbidding death to man, and at the same time preserving his free will'; he left man free choice between life and death.[38] According to Palamas, man's freedom is at the very heart of his being; it is that which essentially distinguishes a 'rational' being from the animals. 'Is there a great difference between us and mice?' Palamas asks. 'Is not this body of ours made of the same substances? Is not our food the same? However we surpass ourselves by the rational quality of our soul.' But 'for what use would we have for this rational character,' he continues, 'if it did not include the power to choose, and free decision? And how could one be free and possess power of choice, if one was unable, on one's own account, to choose evil?' [39]

It was therefore in full freedom that Adam and Eve chose the way which separated them from God, and at the same time deprived them of life. The sentence which condemned them and made them vassals of the Devil was no arbitrary act, but the just and necessary consequence of their own choice.[40] Nevertheless God in his compassion still tried to preserve their freedom for them; with that object he delayed their bodily death, so that they might have time freely to choose the way of life through penitence,[41] and thus to prepare for the coming of Christ.

How death was passed on

Having thus asserted that the first sin was Adam's personal responsibility, Palamas plainly asked the question how it came to be transferred.[42] Why should the *descendants* of the first man suffer the con-

[36] cf. *Hom.* 16, col. 196A.
[37] *Hom.* 4, col. 60C.
[38] *Hom.* 31, col. 388D; cf. *Hom.* 29, col. 369C.
[39] *Hom.* 41, col. 517AC.
[40] *Hom.* 16, col. 198C; *Hom.* 25, col. 324B.
[41] *Hom.* 22, col. 289AB; *Hom.* 31, col. 389A, 392A; *Hom.* 39, col. 492C.
[42] For an interpretation by the Greek Fathers of the crucial Pauline passage on original sin (Rom. 5: 12) see S. Lyonnet, *Le sens de ἐφ' ᾧ en Rom. V, 12 et l'exegèse des Pères grecs*, in *Biblica* 35 (1955), pp. 436-56; J. Romanides, *Original sin according to St. Paul*, in *St. Vladimir's Seminary Quarterly*, Vol. IV, Nos. 1-2, 1955-1956, pp. 5-28.

sequences of a sin they did not commit? He answered that question in accordance with the almost universal view of the Greek Fathers, which held that Adam's misdeed was not a collective sin of the human race, but was like some corruption of human nature. Men's personal responsibility does not come into the picture, except in so far as they *imitate* Adam; their only congenital *inheritance* from him is the corruption (φθορά) and death which, in turn, lead them to sin; men are thus involved in a sort of vicious circle of death and sin. Hence Palamas in one of his sermons refers to '*our* original disobedience to God,' and '*our* ancestral sin in Paradise,'[43] but when he comes to put the question of our real responsibility for sin more precisely, it is to our personal sins, even more grave than that of Adam, to which he attributes it: 'There are many who accuse Adam of obeying an evil counsellor, scorning the commandment, and by that scorn transmitting death to us. But it is not so serious to wish to taste a deadly plant before you have tried it as to want to eat it all knowing by experience that it is deadly! The man who knowingly takes poison is more to blame.... Thus every one of us deserves, more than Adam, to be blamed and condemned...'[44] So what we have received from Adam is *death,* not guilt; that Gregory affirms in strong terms very near to those of Cyril of Alexandria: Adam, 'having voluntarily given himself up, was conquered and rendered useless; being the root of our race, he produced us who are mortal branches....'[45] It is basically by heredity that the corruption has been transmitted to the whole human race.[46] According to Palamas, it was to deliver us from hereditary mortality that the Son of God was made flesh, and not because of the sin of Adam; where a Westerner would have said *felix Adae culpa* (fortunate sin of Adam), Gregory proclaimed *felix mors* (fortunate death). 'If there was no death,' these are his actual words, 'and if, before dying, our race coming from immortal stock had not become mortal, we should not have been enriched with the firstfruits of immortality, we should not have been summoned to heaven, and our nature would not have been enthroned above all Principalities and Powers (Eph. 1 : 20–1).'[47] Natural human generation could only produce corruption,[48] for man 'no longer lived according to God, that is to say he no longer possessed the resemblance to God, and could not engender beings similar to God, but similar to

---

[43] *Hom.* 31, col. 388C.
[44] *Cap. phys.* 55, col. 1160D–1161A.
[45] *Hom.* 52, ed. Oikonomos, p. 121.
[46] *Hom.* 5, col. 64B.
[47] *Cap. phys.* 54, col. 1160D.
[48] *Hom.* 16, col. 192C.

himself, ageing and subject to corruption.'[49] 'Even if, thanks to God, marriage is irreproachable, nature always carries the marks of condemnation.'[50] Christ is 'the only man who was not conceived in iniquity, nor born in sin (cf. Psalm 51 : 5)'[51]; 'If he had been born of a sperm, he could not have been a new man, and could not have received within himself the fullness of the Divinity without alloy, because he would have been struck from the old stamp and would have been heir to the Fall.'[52] He alone could inaugurate a new race of humanity, into which man enters by the new birth of baptism.

Did the Philosophers know God?

This Patristic system of thought did not, one can see, agree with the convictions of Barlaam of Calabria. Palamas's reaction was lively when he read in one of the 'Italian's' writings that 'knowledge of beings, that is to say philosophy, is the best thing we possess,'[53] and 'those whose hearts are pure can see God, either by analogy, or as Cause, or by negation, *but not otherwise;* the man who knows the most, or the most important parts of the world, and especially the man who knows best what he does know, wins the best vision of God. . . . For if *God makes himself known only through his creatures,* one cannot know God through something unknown to one, but only through something one knows; hence the more, and the more wonderful, things one knows, and the better one knows them, the more does one surpass other men in knowledge of God. . . .'[54] For Barlaam it was clear that 'theological wisdom and the philosophy of the profane sciences had the same end,'[55] and he declared that what he lauded was 'wisdom in itself (τὴν αὐτοσοφίαν), the idea of true knowledge, which is one.'[56] Consequently, if there is direct revelation of God, it is not restricted to the Apostles and the Fathers of the Church, and the philosophers of antiquity were no strangers to it. 'When I find those,' he writes, 'who consider that methods of demonstration and analysis, and methods of definition and distinction, and also all science of division and transition, appertain to the *logoi* present in the soul, and when they declare that material and physical things are ruled by the principle proper to them, whereas in the things which surpass us, so they affirm, it is they who receive a vision from on high and are illuminated by an intelligible light enabling them

[49] *Hom.* 54, ed. Oikonomos, p. 186.
[50] *Hom.* 43, ed. Oikonomos, p. 22.
[51] *Hom.* 16, col. 192C.
[52] *Hom.* 58, ed. Oikonomos, p. 230.
[53] Quoted in *Tr.* II, 3, 73.
[54] Quoted in *Tr.* II, 3, 64.
[55] Quoted in *Tr.* II, 1, 5.
[56] Quoted in *Tr.* II, 1, 21.

to unite themselves with divine things which possess, better than by demonstration, the contemplations of transcendental things . . . when I hear them (the profane philosophers) say such things, I cannot conceive that God has not illuminated them in a certain manner, and feel that they must surpass the multitude of mankind.'[57]

Simple confrontation of these quotations from Barlaam with Gregory Palamas's thought, shows up the point of disagreement between them. For Barlaam the way to God is essentially natural *gnosis,* whose limited scope he admits, but which is perfectly autonomous with regard to the conception of sin and—even when it takes on a visionary aspect borrowed from the Neo-Platonists—is foreign to any idea of a specifically Christian supernatural life. For Barlaam the philosophers of antiquity provided the essential criteria for all thought and for all mysticism, without the coming of grace through Jesus Christ substantially modifying the relations between God and man.

Throughout his works Palamas keeps returning to violent criticism of the Greek philosophers in whom he found the origin of the errors of his successive adversaries, Barlaam, Akindynos and Nicephorus Gregoras.

Knowledge and salvation

As we have seen, Palamas admits the genuine character of natural knowledge; but the difference between it and revealed wisdom is that, by itself, it cannot procure salvation. To Barlaam's assertions about a 'single knowledge,' common to Christians and Hellenes, and seeking the same end, Palamas answers by stressing the reality of two forms of knowledge having distinct ends and based, as we shall see in the next chapter, on two different organs of perception. 'It is perhaps not totally false to say that profane philosophy by itself introduces us to a knowledge of beings. . . . But that is not the knowledge of beings and the wisdom which God has directly granted to the Prophets and the Apostles.'[58] Moreover, and most importantly, 'that which is true in external wisdom is not necessary, and does not lead to salvation'[59]; one could know nothing of the sciences and nonetheless attain eternal life.[60] In a passage of the *Second Triad* Palamas summarizes his thought in the following way: 'In the field of knowledge and doctrine, saving perfection lies in accord of thought with the Prophets, the Apostles and all the Fathers through whom the Holy Spirit has certainly spoken

---

[57] Barlaam, *First Letter to Palamas,* ed. G. Schirò, in *Barlaam epistole,* p. 262.
[58] *Tr.* II, 1, 7; cf. also 8–9 and *Tr.* I, 1, 10, 17.
[59] *Tr.* I, 1, 5.
[60] *Tr.* I, 1, 18, quoting Basil, *In Ps.* XIV, *P.G.* XXIX, 256C.

of God and of his creatures. Whereas those things which the Spirit has omitted and which have been discovered by others, are useless to the salvation of the soul, even if they are true: for the teaching of the Spirit does not leave out what is needful. That is why we cast no blame on those who disagree about things which the Spirit disregards, and why we do not say that those who have wider knowledge in this field have attained blessedness.' [61]

Wisdom turned mad

In dealing with this problem Palamas is not considering profane science in general, but a definite system of thought, that of the Greek philosophers, to which Barlaam refers, and which, for him, represents a supreme authority; 'What we are now saying,' he writes in careful qualification, 'is not said about philosophy in general, but about the philosophy of those people.' [62] St. Paul proclaims that the wisdom of the Greek philosophers 'has been turned to folly' (Rom. 1: 21). 'The wisdom to which this misfortune has not occurred,' Palamas comments, 'has therefore not been turned to folly. How could this not be so, since it has succeeded in attaining the end naturally proper to it, and since it has turned towards God, the Cause of nature? Such is the wisdom of the pious and venerable men among us, the wisdom which has truly the courage to reject evil, to choose what is profitable, to draw men to the Church of God, and harmoniously to conform with the wisdom of the Spirit. For my part, I believe that it holds the truth.' [63] As for Hellenic wisdom, it is not in its aspect as natural wisdom that it has been 'turned to folly,' but 'in so far as it does not come from God.' 'The intelligence which discovered it, as intelligence, came from God, but the wisdom itself, in so far as it has strayed from its proper end which is knowledge of God, should not be considered as wisdom.' [64] 'If it had seen and announced the wisdom of God through his creatures, if it had revealed what had been hidden, if it had been an organ of truth making ignorance vanish, if by participation it had been what the Object of its message is as Cause, how could it have been turned to folly by him who gave this wisdom to creation?' [65] The Law of Moses was imperfect; it too was given to a 'natural' and fallen humanity; but yet when Christ had appeared, he said that Moses was as worthy of trust as himself (John 5: 45), whereas he 'turned to folly' the wisdom of the

---

[61] *Tr.* II, *1*, 42; cf. also 44.
[62] *Tr.* I, *1*, 16; cf. also 17.
[63] *Tr.* II, *1*, 23.
[64] *Tr.* I, *1*, 12; cf. also 18.
[65] ibid., 13.

Greeks! [66] 'We are all filled with praise and wonder,' Palamas concludes,'when we contemplate that great work of God, I mean the whole visible creation; the sages of the Hellenes also praised and wondered at it, when they examined it; we do so to the glory of the Creator, but they against his glory.' [67]

The errors of Greek philosophers are numerous, and Palamas often enumerates them in his works. 'Enveloped in that wisdom full of stupidity and folly,' he cries, '. . . they calumniated both God and nature; to nature they gave the sovereignty, and they deprived God of that sovereignty . . . ; they gave credit to the view that the divine name belonged to demons, and they were so far from finding knowledge of beings—the object of their desires and zeal—that they asserted that inanimate beings had a soul, and shared in a soul superior to our own, and that irrational beings had reason, as they were able to receive a human soul . . . they classed among things coeternal with God, uncreated and without beginning, not only matter and what they called the soul of the whole world . . . but our souls too.' [68] All the arguments which Palamas employs to demonstrate the errors of the Hellenes, are far from being equally powerful; for instance, he cites the elements of Old Testament cosmology and Biblical miracles to prove the impossibility of admitting the absolute value of Aristotle's cosmological laws. However such doubtful arguments were not, for him, the essential point. We have seen that he specifically allowed the freedom of scientific research in the physical field, and we may note that he reproaches the philosophers for not succeeding in agreeing about the laws of creation, which is a classical Patristic argument to prove the relativity of non-Christian philosophic doctrines.

He is as violently opposed to Plato and the Neo-Platonists, as to Aristotle.

Plato

The idealism of Plato is in fact incompatible with the Christian conception of a living God, absolutely free in his creative activity : 'These models and exercises which,' Palamas writes, 'existed in the thought (of God) before the actions, and which are no strangers to passion, are they better suited to men who are building a house and fear some check due to lack of circumspection, or to a God whose thought is already action? And since his thought is already action, would he have

[66] ibid.
[67] *Hom.* 34, col. 424AB; cf. *Tr.* I, *1*, 18.
[68] *Tr.* I, *1*, 18; the doctrines referred to here are the Platonic idea of the world's soul and metempsychosis.

need for other plans and other models? Would he not then have ideas of ideas, and so *ad infinitum?*' [69] And Palamas recalls immediately Plato's theological conceptions, notably those in the *Timaeus,* where certain cosmic forces are deified, and where a whole hierarchy of 'demons' rules the life of the universe. These conceptions are enough to render Platonism unacceptable to Christians, who cannot admit any intermediate substance between the Creator and the creatures, nor any mediating *hypostasis;* we shall see later, in his teaching about *'energies,'* that Palamas stressed this point to demonstrate the 'existential' character of divine operations which are neither essences, nor *hypostases.*

Nor did Neo-Platonic contemplation find favour in Palamas's eyes; 'Their visions,' he proclaimed, 'drive truly divine things away. . . . The intelligible light which shone in their eyes, does not draw them to the realm of light, but condemns them to eternal shadows. . . . There is therein a bait and terrible snare, invented by the Prince of Darkness, and devised with such minute care, lest it should be noticed, so that it might deceive even those who have only heard talk of it.' 'The Devil has plunged the contemplatives into the greatest possible error, and he has led on their disciples, who considered them enlightened men, into his twisted nets, and he hastens, by the intermediary of their writings, to act on those who shall come afterwards . . . leading the crowd astray by the beauty of their language.' [70] In common with the Christians of the first centuries, Palamas considered Pagan divinities (δαίμονες) as having really existed, but as angels of Satan. It is thus that he accounts for the 'demon' which accompanied Socrates, for the 'dragon' which, according to Porphyry, appeared on the day of Plotinus's death, and the oracle of Apollo received by Amelios about the arrival of Plotinus 'at the assembly of demons.' [71] He has no difficulty in finding in Plato, Homer and Hesiod other references to demons, which are, for him, so many proofs of the Satanic inspiration of their works. This attitude of Palamas towards the philosophers of antiquity, an attitude shared by many of his contemporaries, especially in the monastic world, shows how far the Byzantines could preserve the spirit of the Patristic literature of the first centuries; it is clear that Gregory's long tirades against the demonic character of classical literature, echo, sometimes word for word, Christian polemical writings against Porphyry or Julian the Apostate—especially those of St. Gregory of Nazianzus— which date from an age when Paganism represented a real danger to

---

[69] *First letter to Barlaam,* ed. Papamikhail, p. 471.
[70] ibid., pp. 464–5.
[71] *First letter to Barlaam,* pp. 469–70; *Tr.* I, *1,* 15.

the Church. The echoes of the struggle between the Eastern Christians and the representatives of Pagan Neo-Platonism—a struggle which lasted right through the fourth and fifth centuries—thus go on reverberating down to the end of the Byzantine Middle Ages.

Aristotle

In general Palamas's attitude towards Aristotle was more moderate than his treatment of the Platonists. Aristotle's *Logic* and *Physics,* as taught in schools and universities, were the essential basis of all 'profane' education at Byzantium. They formed part of the 'general education' (ἐγκύκλιος παιδεία), a programme in which Palamas himself had excelled in his youth and which, normally, excluded Platonic metaphysics. Nevertheless Palamas does not use velvet gloves with Aristotle, especially when Barlaam gives his principles of logic absolute value. His first correspondence with Akindynos and Barlaam is almost entirely devoted to an impassioned demonstration that Aristotle's logic cannot, by itself, define divine transcendence. This logic is not absolute even for knowledge of beings, for being based in origin on experience, it remains the fruit of the human mind which actually cannot have experience of all the facts which serve as its premises: 'How can you, man, seek for the antecedent element for the demonstration?' he asks. 'Is it in time? Then you will never attain any demonstration either in the sky ... or on the earth or in the sea ... or in the air among the phenomena thereof, or in the ether among the meteors; for common notions, axioms and definitions, premisses, demonstrations and reasonings, distinctions and all analyses come after them; in fact they depend on the intelligence of him who was last created (man).' [72] If it is impossible, by following Aristotle, to construct an apodictic argument about the phenomena of the created world, it is even more futile to seek there for a theological demonstration, and finally to find, as Barlaam did, a proof that God is not demonstrable, for God is not alone in escaping the experience of the senses, as many created beings also escape therefrom. It is not to any formal criterion, defined by Aristotle, that one owes the knowledge that God is unknowable, but through a religious experience, which may in part be due to a true understanding of beings, but which equally constitutes a revelation of the living God. That is why this 'what-surpasses-the-demonstration-of-Aristotle is pointless.' [73]

Serpents subjected to dissection

However opposed Palamas might be to classical philosophy, he could

---

[72] *First letter to Akindynos,* 10, ed. Meyendorff, p. 86; cf. *Second letter to Barlaam, Coisl.* 100, *fol.* 101v–102.
[73] Title of the *Second letter to Barlaam.*

not completely overlook the fact that the Fathers of the Church to some extent made use of philosophers to express the true faith. Were not these philosophers also the essential source used by Christians to attain a certain 'natural' knowledge of beings, a knowledge which could lead according to St. Paul (Rom. 1 : 19–20) to a certain perception of the Divinity? Palamas did not refuse to answer these questions, either by himself giving in his *Physical Chapters* an account of the cosmos and of man largely derived from the then accepted classical notions, or by supplying a simile, which seemed suitable to him, of the method to follow in using the writings of the Greek philosophers. He likens them to poisonous snakes from whom doctors succeed in deriving useful drugs: 'the flesh of snakes,' he writes, 'is useful to us if we kill them, and dissect them, and if we make preparations from them, and use them with discernment as a remedy against their own bites.' [74] The sense of this original simile is that one can have recourse to the philosophy of the Greeks on condition that one knows how to use it, and possesses enough of the discernment which comes from the Spirit and which belongs to the life in Christ. 'The sciences are a gift of God,' his adversaries said to him. 'But how,' Palamas answered, 'does that justify those who make a bad use of them, both employing them wrongly and, in the end, thanks to the sciences, turning the Gospel of Christ into something imperfect? For one cannot justify debauch and intemperance on the ground that God, who in the beginning created the body and breathed the soul into it, gave it the power of procreation and of nourishing itself. This is what my words try to prevent; the evil and perverted use, and the exaggerated veneration of which the sciences are the object.' [75]

The case of the Pseudo-Dionysius

Still Barlaam had one objection in reserve which was of a nature to rouse echoes in a Byzantine audience very loyal to the letter of Patristic tradition; 'If you want to know,' he writes to Palamas, 'whether the Greeks have understood that the superessential and anonymous Good transcends intelligence, science and all other achievement, read the works of the Pythagorians, Pantenetos, Brotinos, Philolaos, Charmidas and Philoxenos, which are devoted to that subject; there you will find the same expressions as the great Dionysius employs in his *Mystical Theology*. . . . And Plato has also well understood divine transcendence'; there follow quotations from the *Parmenides* and from the *Republic* which are to be found again, almost word for word, in the

[74] *Tr.* I, 1, 11; cf. also 20–1, and *Second letter to Barlaam, Coisl.* 100, *fol.* 98.
[75] *Tr.* II, 1, 27.

works of the Pseudo-Dionysius.[76] Was the undoubted link existing between the pagan authors and the man whom every one then considered to have been the disciple of St. Paul, compatible with the demoniacal character attributed by Palamas to the writings of the philosophers? The case of the Pseudo-Dionysius and, to a lesser extent, that of all the Fathers who found inspiration in Neo-Platonism, is thus found at the back of the whole controversy between Barlaam and Palamas, who both, while constantly referring to the 'Great Dionysius,' interpreted him each in his own fashion. For Barlaam it was Dionysius, more than any of the other Fathers, who knew how to use Neo-Platonism, and who, by his apophatic theology, had established the solid basis of a nominalist philosophy; did not God infinitely surpass all the names that could be applied to him? On the other hand Palamas relied on the passages where the Areopagite speaks of union with God—passages which Barlaam deprived of their realist sense—to find therein the principles of mystical knowledge; in fact, he was thus forced to introduce a Christocentric corrective into Dionysius. We shall have occasion several times to return to this aspect of Palamas's thought, for it throws light on his capacity for integrating in a balanced theology elements which before his time had made Eastern Christian thinkers stumble.[77] Palamas, after St. Maximus the Confessor, thus took another step forward in giving a completely Christian meaning to the Corpus Areopagiticum, by freeing it from some ambiguous concepts, which had become all the more dangerous in the fourteenth century as they furnished arguments favouring the nominalism of the humanists.

Palamas's attitude to classical philosophy in general, and especially his correspondence on this subject with Barlaam, prove how far from correct it is to regard him as heir to the Neo-Platonists in Christian thought. Though he continued to use the terminology of Plotinus, borrowed from St. Gregory of Nyssa or from Dionysius, he never had recourse directly to the authority of the ancients, and he definitely wished to turn his contemporaries away from them. His thought, taken as a whole, certainly marked a step forward in the progressive liberation of Eastern Christian theology from Platonic Hellenism, and his final victory in 1351 amounted, for Byzantine culture, to a refusal of the new humanist civilization which the West was in process of adopting.

---

[76] *Second letter to Palamas*, ed. Schirò, pp. 298–9.
[77] cf. our brief *Notes sur l'influence dionysienne en Orient*, in *Studia patristica*, Vol. II (*Texte und Untersuchungen*, 64), Berlin, 1957, pp. 547–52.

CHAPTER II

THEOLOGICAL INTEGRATION OF HESYCHASM: THE LIFE IN CHRIST

THE argument about the spiritual life of Byzantine monks and their methods of prayer only emerged as the second stage in the quarrel between Barlaam and Palamas. It is important to see clearly the connection between the two aspects of the controversy, which, in the beginning, were distinct. As a sceptic philosopher Barlaam was concerned with those who, in opposition to him, claimed the supreme reality of a mystical knowledge of God, and his examination of the matter logically led him to deny the spirituality of the monks. Palamas, as a result of the Christological argument which he had used against Barlaam concerning profane philosophy, had come to realize the abyss which separated them on the most essential points of Christian doctrine. For it was the Christian faith itself, and not just one form of spirituality, which he felt himself to be defending in his *Triads in Defence of the Hesychasts*.

We cannot here undertake to give an historical account of 'hesychasm,' nor even to analyse the voluminous literature devoted to that subject in the last decades. We shall limit ourselves to pointing out certain features which seem essential to the understanding of Palamas's works, giving references to the most important authorities.

Hesychasm before the fourteenth century

The term 'hesychast' (ἡσυχαστής, ἡσυχάζων) was for long only used in the West in connection with the disputes of the fourteenth century, and so came to designate the uneducated Byzantine monk who practised a strange and suspect method of prayer, which Barlaam ridiculed as 'omphalopsychos.' Actually the word *hesychia* (ἡσυχία) had entered into the vocabulary of Christian mysticism from the fourth century, and had become a technical term to designate the state of inner rest and silence which victory over the passions gained for a monk and so allowed him to proceed to contemplation. St. Gregory of Nyssa applied it to Moses, whom he described as the model of all Christian mystics. 'Moses,' he writes, 'went into forty years' exile from the society of man and, living alone with himself, applied his vision, not allowing himself to be disturbed and in tranquillity (δι' ἡσυχίας), to the contemplation of invisible things.'[1] The hermits who chose that way of life, in preference to the liturgical and ascetic discipline of the great monastic communities, were called 'hesychasts,' and it was especially in that *milieu* that there developed the spirituality of 'mental prayer' of which Evagrius Ponticus was the first great teacher.[2]

Evagrius

Understanding of the part played by Evagrius in the history of Eastern Christian spirituality has certainly greatly helped our knowledge of this spirituality, especially showing us the link with Origen. It was the great Cappadocians who popularized the 'theology' of the Alexandrian master by giving it the Orthodox form approved by the Councils. It was Gregory of Nyssa who persuaded future generations to adopt the essential principles of Origen's mysticism. But it was Evagrius who taught the monks of the Egyptian desert a way to pray and unite themselves with God in conformity with Origen's conception of the relations between God and man.[3]

This 'discovery' of Evagrius as the common father of Eastern Christian mystics poses a problem of very great historical and dogmatic importance. Was not this Pontic deacon a heretic condemned together with Origen, by the fifth Oecumenical Council for his Platonic spirituality? But whereas the Origenian doctrines—and we do not always know how far they all go back to Origen—had been, at least in part, corrected by the Cappadocians or by St. Maximus, the teaching of Evagrius had penetrated clandestinely, in its original form, and with the borrowed name of St. Nilus, into the most venerable Patristic tradition! It is true that the works of Evagrius, which we find quoted in almost all the Greek spiritual writers down to and including Palamas, do not substantially include the Origenian errors condemned under Justinian. But it is nonetheless true that the purely intellectual mysticism of Evagrius, as we find it for instance in his *De Oratione*, faithfully reflect Neo-Platonic spirituality with hardly any corrective; scattered references to the Word and the Trinity certainly reveal a Christian author, but it is enough to say that in this little work there is *no* reference to the Incarnation as such, nor any to the Church or the

---

[1] *In Psalm. P.G.* XLIV, 456C.
[2] cf. I. Hausherr, *L'hésychasme, Etude de spiritualité*, in *Or. Chr. Per.*, XXII, 1956, pp. 5–40, 247–85.
[3] cf. M. Viller, *Aux sources de la spiritualité de s. Maxime*, in *Revue d'ascétique et de mystique*, XI, 1930, pp. 156–84, 239–68, 331–6; I. Hausherr, *Les grands courants de spiritualité orientale*, in *Or. Chr. Per.*, I, 1935, pp. 114–38.

sacraments, and that prayer is essentially conceived as an immaterial contact of the intelligence with God, as a 'preface to immaterial knowledge,' to prove that the Incarnation *could not* have any place in a philosophy of existence and a spirituality on such lines. So one may well ask how we are to understand the historical phenomenon of Evagrius's influence, for it was through him, as I. Hausherr has written, 'that the grand conceptions of Origen and Gregory of Nyssa descended from their inaccessible heights, and came within the reach of men of ordinary understanding. Nilus by lending his name, Maximus by giving the guarantee of his Orthodoxy, and the Sinaites by continuing to aspire to the delights of contemplation, simply succeeded in preserving the teaching of the philosopher monk of Scete down to the day when Gregory of Sinai was to revive the flame in Byzantine monasteries, and cause that explosion of mysticism which we call "hesychasm" . . .' [4]

Actually, though throughout the history of Eastern spirituality the *terminology* of Evagrius is almost continuously in use, it is far from being the case that Evagrius's ideas, in particular his spiritualistic teaching about the nature of man, had an equally permanent effect. In the minds of writers nearer to the Bible and to the main tradition of the Church, spiritual notions derived from Evagrius or from Origen were manifestly subjected to a Christological corrective; that has been pointed out especially in the case of *The Life of St. Anthony* by Athanasius,[5] and, above all, in the ascetic and spiritual works of Maximus the Confessor.[6] But, along with this progressive self-defence of the Fathers against Platonic spirituality, we must also take into account the existence, at the very start of Christian hesychasm, of another Master who represented a tendency diametrically opposed to Evagrius: the unknown author of the *Corpus Macarianum*.

We cannot here solve, or even fully discuss, the problem of the Pseudo-Macarius. For the last thirty years or so several writers have accepted the view of Dom Villecourt, which makes the author belong to the sect of Messalians and even tries to identify him with one of their leaders, a certain Symeon of Mesopotamia.[7] But that remains rather questionable; W. Jaeger, following J. Stiglmayr, has argued brilliantly

---

[4] *Le Traité de l'oraison d'Evagre le Pontique*, in *Revue d'ascétique et de mystique*, XV, 1934, pp. 34–93, 113–70.
[5] M. Marx, *Incessant prayer in the Vita Antonii*, in *Studia Anselmiana*, 38, Rome, 1956, pp. 134–5.
[6] I. H. Dalmais, *Le doctrine ascétique des Maxime le Confesseur d'après le Liber Asceticus*, in *Irénikon*, XXVI, 1953, pp. 17–39.
[7] L. Villecourt, *La date et l'origine des Homélies spirituelles attribuées a Macaire*, in *Comptes-rendus des séances de l'Académie des inscriptions et belles lettres*, 1920, pp. 29–53; M. Dörries, *Die Ueberlieferung des messalianischen Makarius-schriften*, in *Texte u Unters.*, 4 Reihe, 10. Bd., I. Heft, Leipzig, 1941.

on the other side, proving an undoubted link between the writings of the Pseudo-Macarius and the mystical works of St. Gregory of Nyssa.[8] In the present state of our historical and textual knowledge, it remains probably impossible to give a final solution to this problem. The main Messalian texts are lost and the textual tradition of Macarius is far from being cleared. Whatever was the original connection between them, the Macarian *Corpus,* with its insistence on the role of baptism and the sacraments of the Church, cannot be considered as consistently Messalian, unless one applies to it confessional or personal criteria of what Christian spirituality should be. Macarius has been accused of a tendency either to admit the coexistence in the soul of the demons and of grace, and perhaps to distinguish too clearly the signs of that grace, thereby coming close to *Pelagianism.*[9] These elements existed in the Messalian doctrine. In the first case, however, it is not at all clear whether Macarius meant to say anything more than St. Paul ('For I delight in the law of God after the inward man. But I see another law in my members warring against the law in my mind, and bringing me into captivity to the law of sin, which is in my members,' Rom. 7 : 22–3) explaining this accepted text of Christian spirituality in the terms generally used by the common monastic tradition, but *which also have been used by Messalians* in a heretical dualistic sense. As for the reproach of semi-Pelagianism, that might be directed against the whole of Eastern mysticism, especially, and with greater reason, against St. Gregory of Nyssa and his school.[10]

Two doctrines concerning man

If we turn from this interesting dispute whose conclusion cannot yet be seen, but which does touch on a central point in the relations between Eastern and Western Christians, and pay attention to the *influence* of the writings of the 'great Macarius' on the spiritual literature of the East, we easily see that, for readers from the fifth to the fourteenth centuries, these writings opposed a *Biblical terminology and a Biblical doctrine concerning man*—with perhaps some Stoic connections—*to a Platonic terminology and Evagrius's spiritualizing doctrine of man.* These two doctrines concerning man are latent in the history of hesychasm, and writers can be roughly classified as disciples of Evagrius or of Macarius, provided, of course, that that classification is not applied too strictly and, especially, too much stress is not put on the terminology

[8] *Two rediscovered works of ancient christian literature: Gregory of Nyssa and Macarius,* Leiden, 1954.
[9] For the latter point, see I. Hausherr, *L'erreur fondamentale et la logique du messalianisme,* in *Or. Chr. Per.,* I, 1935, pp. 328–60.
[10] cf. W. Jaeger, op. cit., pp. 89–92.

which tends to get the two schools confused even where they most preserve their peculiar characteristics.[11] Thus the word 'heart' used in the Bible to mean the centre of all man's psycho-physiological life, in Origen and Gregory of Nyssa becomes practically a synonym for the mind (νοῦς) or for the Platonic soul (ψυχή), whereas Macarius and his school want to give the word its full Biblical meaning, while still taking into account Evagrius's terminology widely adopted in monastic circles, localizing the mind (νοῦς) in the heart, which, terminologically, allows them to reconcile the two vocabularies. Actually it is a question not of words only but of *two doctrines concerning man*—that of Plato and that of the Bible—between which it was necessary to choose, if one was to construct the foundations of a coherent spiritual life. Is man only an intelligence imprisoned in matter and longing to be free, or is he a psycho-physiological whole to whom God brought salvation by his Incarnation? Does grace only touch the mind (νοῦς), purified not only of all 'passion' but also of all material attachment, or does the whole man, by virtue of the baptismal water into which he is plunged, receive the first fruits of bodily resurrection? It is clear that Evagrius's mysticism chose the first alternative, and exactly that was the reason for which it was condemned. Since, nonetheless, the writings of Evagrius had clandestinely penetrated into the Christian tradition, there was need for the Orthodox corrective supplied by the Fathers. Thus whatever the Platonic character of his system and of his terminology, such a man as St. Maximus could write: 'Man remains wholly man in soul and body, and by grace becomes wholly God in soul and body.'[12] That was a dogmatic necessity imposed on Maximus not by his education in philosophy, but because he was in touch with the Scriptures and because of his religious experience. In the same way the 'pure prayer' of Evagrius, a sort of *gnosis* foreign to the piety of which Christ is the centre, was progressively transformed into the 'prayer of Jesus,' in which all spiritual progress was linked, not to knowledge of an impersonal Divinity, but to living communion with the Saviour.[13]

Barlaam's published writings clearly show that he shared the essential principles of the Platonic doctrine of man, and expressed them directly without modifications. But Palamas's quotations from Barlaam's treatise

---

[11] On this see P. Minin, *Glavnyia napravleniia drevne-tserkovnoi mistiki*, in *Bogoslovskii Vestnik*, 1911, December, pp. 823–38; 1913, May, pp. 151–72; 1914, June, pp. 304–26; I. V. Popov, *Ideia obozheniia v drenei vostochnoi tserkvi*, in *Voprosy filosofii i psikhologii*, 97 (1909), pp. 165–213; A. Guillaumont, *Le coeur chez les spirituels grecs*, in the article *Cor et cordis affectus* of the *Diction. de Spiritualité*, col. 2281–8.
[12] *Ambigua*, P.G. XCI, 1088C.
[13] cf. L. Gardet, *Un problème de mystique comparée*, in *Revue thomiste*, 1953, I, pp. 197–200.

devoted to 'pure prayer,' and Barlaam's own constant references to the Platonizing Fathers, especially Dionysius, show that Barlaam was fairly well acquainted with the hesychast tradition and with the mysticism of the Fathers in general. He had read the classics of 'pure prayer' and founded his opposition to the fourteenth century hesychasts on formulas derived from Evagrius. For instance we find him quoting the passages closest to Evagrius from St. Maximus in order to contrast them with the spirituality of the monks of Athos: 'The supreme state of prayer is when the mind passes out of the flesh and the world and remains entirely untouched in prayer by matter and forms.'[14] Basing himself on such venerable authorities, Barlaam recommended 'causing the complete death of the passionate part of the soul' and 'of all activity common to soul and body,' for such activity attaches the soul to the body and fills it with darkness'; it 'blinds the divine eye.'[15] So Barlaam did not reject *the whole* of the hesychast tradition, but only that part which contradicted his Platonic and dualistic conception of man, according to which he considered the spiritual life as a disincarnation and an intellectual contemplation.

Christian Yoga?

That was the adversary against whom Palamas had to defend his hesychast brothers, and this defence was all the more difficult because the dominant trend in hesychasm, and the trend to which he himself adhered, had substantially adopted the psycho-physical *method* of prayer, which reflected the 'Macarian' tendency in Eastern monasticism in its most extreme form, and might sometimes have led to abuses. We have no certain evidence of the existence before the twelfth century of an elaborated form of this method of linking the 'prayer of Jesus' with breathing, fixing the eyes on one point in the body, and 'making the spirit thus descend into the heart'[16]; any connection between it and Hindu *yoga*, which some people have tried to establish, could only have been indirect and fairly remote. But it does seem extremely probable, if not certain, that there was some Islamic influence; the parallels between the Moslem *dhikr* and the method of Nicephorus

---

[14] *De caritate*, II, 61, *P.G.* XL, 1004C; transl. by P. Sherwood in *Ancient Christian Writers*, 21, 1955, p. 165; cf. Palamas, *Tr.* II, 2, 17.
[15] Quoted in Palamas, *Tr.* II, 2, 4, 12, 23.
[16] For the thirteenth and fourteenth centuries the essential texts on this method are those of Nicephorus the Hesychast (*P.G.* CXLVII, 945–66) of the Pseudo-Symeon (ed. I. Hausherr, in *Or. Chr. Per.* IX, 2, 1927) and of St. Gregory of Sinai (*P.G.* CL, 1313–36). They are found in an English translation from the Russian (thus to be used with caution) in E. Kadloubovsky and G. E. H. Palmer, *Writings from the Philocalia on prayer of the heart*, London, n.d., pp. 22–37, 152–61, 74–6.

the Hesychast are too striking, and personal contacts—journeys of monks to Palestine and Egypt, and the Moslem occupation of Asia Minor—were too frequent for it to have been possible for such similar religious phenomena to have existed at the same time without mutual influence. But there is a distinction between the two practices; both *yoga* and *dhikr* are physical *techniques,* which by themselves and immediately produce the desired effect, whereas the hesychast method is never more than a means to gain the attention and silence of the spirit, and the practice of the virtues and fasting are specific conditions for it [17]; it is the combination of these factors, of which breathing is by no means the most important, which make man receptive of grace.

Nevertheless Barlaam's attacks put the hesychasts out of countenance. The little works of Nicephorus and the Pseudo-Symeon certainly gave them a practical receipt, but contained no doctrinal argument with which to answer Barlaam. Palamas provided such a doctrine and a strict hierarchy of values. He did so by integrating the spiritualist vocabulary derived from Evagrius, and the more recent psycho-physical methods of prayer, with a harmonious conception of life in Jesus Christ. In this way he continued the work of the Fathers who, without avoiding those elements whose non-Christian origin could not be in doubt, adapted them—as reflections of natural mysticism—to the unique reality of the Christian mystery. It goes without saying that this adaptation inwardly modified the meaning of the terms employed, and put them in harmony with the Biblical teaching on man.

During the long years which he spent on Mount Athos, Palamas absorbed the whole of monastic hesychast spirituality. As we have already pointed out, if circumstances had not forced him into doctrinal polemics, he would nonetheless have left behind fairly important spiritual works, but with no original feature. The spirituality, centred on the prayer of Jesus, which he taught to his disciples, is very closely in the tradition of Diadochus of Photice, St. John of the Ladder and Theoleptus of Philadelphia, with an even more marked dependence on Macarius. It is important to notice that none of these works of Palamas contain any reference to the breathing method; he only talked about it in order to defend it against Barlaam. It is therefore rash to say, as has sometimes been done, that the silence of some great spiritual writers of the age—Theoleptus and Nicholas Cabasilas—on this subject indicates hostility thereto on their part. Palamas was not hostile, but he found it unnecessary to mention a secondary and very localized aspect of the hesychasm of his time.

[17] cf. L. Gardet, op. cit., p. 678.

THEOLOGICAL INTEGRATION OF HESYCHASM

Purification and continuous prayer
To attain contemplation, man must first pass through the negative stage of intellectual purification. Dealing with this common theme of mystical literature, Palamas uses the language of Evagrius which had become classical. 'Illumination,' he writes, 'appears to the pure intelligence to the extent that it is liberated from all concepts and becomes formless.' [18] 'All vision having a form to the intelligence, that is to say to act on the passionate part which is the imagination . . . comes from a ruse of the enemy.' [19] The saints have been able to attain true vision through 'purity of heart,' that is to say by freeing themselves from the passions.[20] A glance at passages from the *Discourse to Xene* about the 'blessed affliction' are enough to show how close Palamas was to the ascetic tradition of John of the Ladder.[21]

The positive element in his spirituality, acquisition of grace and of life in Jesus Christ, is based on the uninterrupted 'monological prayer' (προσευχὴ μονολόγιστος ἀδιάλειπτος). This prayer is a 'memory of God' (μνήμη τοῦ θεοῦ),[22] and is not simply, as Barlaam said, a passive state, but a conscious activity of the human being; when the Apostle recommended us 'to pray continually' (1 Thess. 5 : 17), it was to a continuous activity that he called us, and to a supplication addressed to God : 'We supplicate with this continual supplication,' Palamas writes, 'not to convince God, for he acts always spontaneously, nor to draw him to us, for he is everywhere, but to lift ourselves up towards him.' [23] Elsewhere Gregory recalls that continuous prayer is also a *thanksgiving* [24]; hence in both cases it is above all a communion with a personal God. Palamas's view of prayer as conscious and active shows how far hesychast spirituality was from adopting any mechanization of prayer. The words contained in this 'monological prayer' were generally the following : 'Lord Jesus Christ, Son of God, have mercy on me' [25] : about that form of prayer Barlaam complained that it contained no confession of the Divinity of Christ. But Palamas also recognized that more simple and ancient use of the 'Lord have mercy' (Κύριε ἐλέησον),[26] and he considered that the Publican's prayer (Luke

[18] *Dialogue*, Coisl. 99, fol. 40v.
[19] *Letter to Athanasius*, Coisl. 99, fol. 6; *Against Akindynos*, VI, 12, Coisl. 98, fol. 163-4v.
[20] *To Xene*, 1064D, 1085A, etc.; *Chapters on Prayer*, 1117C, 1120C-1121A; *Theophanes*, 956BC.
[21] Col. 1076-7; cf. *Tr.* II, 2, 15.
[22] *Chapters on prayer*, 1120C; *Hom.* 2, col. 28A, etc.; *Letter to Athanasius*, Coisl. 98, fol. 7v.
[23] *Tr.* II, 1, 30.
[24] *Hom.* 2, col. 21C.
[25] *Tome of 1341*, P.G. CLI, 689A.
[26] *Chapters. Vatic. Reg. Svec.*, 43, fol. 169. (These *Chapters* may however belong to Symeon the New Theologian, according to information given to us by Abp. Basil Kzivocheine.)

141

18 : 13) was also a form of 'monological supplication.'[27] All this was in fact nothing but traditional in Eastern Christian spirituality.

Prayer and anthropology

However the true significance of Palamas's teaching about prayer comes out when he starts polemics against the platonizing spirituality of Barlaam. He forcefully opposes a monist conception of man to the Platonic view making 'intellectual prayer' a disincarnation of the soul. 'Beware of thyself,' writes Palamas with reference to Deuteronomy 15 : 9, 'that is to say to the whole of thyself, not to one part of thyself, neglecting all the rest.'[28]

Father Kiprian Kern has devoted a whole chapter of his book on *St. Gregory Palamas's anthropology* to Gregory's teaching about the superiority of man compared to the angels: in his view this superiority is based on the bodily existence of the human being, which enables him to exercise dominion over the universe.[29] This particular, but very characteristic, aspect of Palamas's thought is, as we shall show here, an integral part of his Soteriology and his Christology. As a result of sin, fallen man has both lost his supra-angelic state, for he is no longer king of the universe and lets himself be dominated by cosmic forces, and lost his inner equilibrium, for his spirit is subject to the laws of the flesh and even his soul, destined for immortality, has become mortal. It was to re-establish the kingship of man, and to give back his lost equilibrium, that the Word was incarnate, 'to make him share the divine immortality . . . to honour the flesh, even this mortal flesh, so that the proud spirits should not consider themselves, and should not be considered, worthy of greater honours than man, so that they should not deify themselves on account of *their incorporality and their apparent immortality.*'[30]

Barlaam, in his treatise against the hesychasts, wrote: 'The fact of loving activities common to the passionate part of the soul and to the body, attaches the soul to the body and fills it with darkness.' Palamas refused to accept that point of view. In creating man, a rational animal, God gave his soul a particular quality which distinguishes it from the Angels—*the power to make the body alive*: 'The soul has by nature such a link of love with its body that it never wants to leave it, and would never leave it unless forced to do so by some great illness, or by some wound coming from outside.'[31] There is therefore no question

---
[27] *Hom.* 2, col. 28A.
[28] *Tr.* I, 2, 9.
[29] *Antropologiia S. Grigoriia Palamy*, Paris, 1950, pp. 353–85.
[30] *Hom.* 16, col. 204A.
[31] *Cap. phys.* 38, col. 1148A.

of Gregory considering the body as an evil thing or as 'a prison of the soul': 'Apart from sin,' he proclaims, 'nothing is wrong in itself in the present life, not even death, but (everything) can lead to evil.'[32] Only the Messalian heretics say that the body is evil in itself.[33]

The body takes part in prayer . . .

So it is above all against a dualistic conception of man that Palamas raises his voice. 'What pain or joy or movement of the body is there, which is not shared by soul and body? . . . There are blessed passions, activities common to soul and body, which do not attach the spirit to the flesh, but which draw up the flesh to a dignity near to that of the spirit, and make it to turn towards the height. . . . In the same way as the Divinity of the Word Incarnate is common to soul and body . . . so, in spiritual men, is the grace of the Spirit transmitted to the body by the soul as intermediary, and this gives it to experience of divine things, and allows it to feel the same passion as the soul . . . Then the body is not driven any more by bodily and material passions . . . but turns on itself, rejects all relation with evil things, and itself inspires its own sanctification and an inalienable deification . . .'[34] As a 'common activity of soul and body' particularly 'agreeable to God,' Palamas cites the 'blessed affliction' and the tears of repentance which Eastern mystics, especially Isaac of Nineveh and John of the Ladder, had regarded as a true spiritual baptism.[35] If Barlaam was right, 'there would be no need to fast, watch, kneel, fall on the ground or, still less, hold oneself erect; the man who applies himself to intellectual prayer would need do none of those things. For all that forces the sense of touch into activity, provoking pain, and introduces, as Barlaam would say, tumult into the soul in prayer.'[36] Now the Fathers in the tradition of Macarius speak of physical pain as conducive to prayer, and mention the altogether bodily joy which results therefrom.[37] Palamas has a very lively sense of the contradiction between the Gospel and Platonic spirituality; for him the body is not the seat of evil in man. 'This body united to us has been joined to us by God as our collaborator, or rather put under our dominion; we must therefore suppress it, if it revolts, and accept it, if it behaves as it should.'[38] In many places Palamas speaks of 'scorn of bodily things' using the Platonic language usual with the

---

[32] *Hom.* 16, col. 213C.
[33] *Tr.* I, 2, 1.
[34] *Tr.* II, 2, 12.
[35] ibid., 17–18.
[36] ibid., 4.
[37] ibid., 6–7, 10.
[38] ibid., 5.

Fathers, but he qualifies it thus: 'I call a bodily thing that which comes into our thoughts from the pleasures of the body, and is drawn to them, finding them agreeable, and pulling our thoughts down. But that which, coming from a soul full of spiritual joy, takes place in the body, is a spiritual reality, though it acts on the body. Spiritual joy, coming from the spirit into the body, is in no way corrupted by communion with the body, but transforms that body, and makes it spiritual, because it rejects the evil appetites of the flesh, and no longer drags the soul down, but rises with it, so that the whole man becomes spirit ($\pi\nu\epsilon\tilde{\upsilon}\mu\alpha$), according to what is written: He that is born of the spirit, is spirit (John 3 : 6–8).'[39] There is no great merit in purifying the mind alone: 'What is that that is purified,' Palamas asks, 'by this longing for God? The mind alone? No. According to the Fathers no great effort is needed to purify the mind, and yet, by nature, it easily relapses from purity; that is why it can be purified without divine longing . . . and such a purification is better suited to beginners. True divine longing purifies all the faculties and powers of the soul and of the body, and by an enduring purification of the mind makes man receptive of deifying grace.'[40] So it is the *whole man* who loves God and receives him in himself.

. . . and supernatural life

How can one follow the Gospel path to holiness without bodily activity in accord with the life of the spirit? Is not love of one's neighbour, of which St. Paul gives such a living and intensely active example, necessary to union with God?[41] 'It is not the soul alone which receives the pledge of blessings to come,' Palamas declares, 'for the body, which to this end also follows the Gospel path, receives it too.'[42] Gregory constantly quotes from St. Paul, and refers to his example. In terms of Barlaam's dualistic mysticism, what meaning could be given to such a text as Rom. 12 : 1 : 'I beseech you therefore, brethren, by the mercies of God, that ye present your bodies a living sacrifice, holy, acceptable unto God'? 'We must then,' Palamas comments, 'offer to God the passionate part of the soul, living and active, that it may be a living sacrifice. . . How can our living body be offered . . .? (It is offered) when the look in our eyes is gentle . . . when our ears are attentive to the divine teachings, not hearing them only, but, as David says, 'remembering the commandments of God to accomplish them' (Psalm 103 : 18) . . . when our tongue, our hands and our feet are at the

[39] ibid., 9.
[40] *Tr.* III, 3, 12.
[41] ibid., 21.
[42] *Tr.* I, 3, 33; cf. *To Xene*, 1081D.

service of the divine will.'[43] Palamas easily finds quotations from the New Testament to prove that the Apostles, while calling us to 'perpetual prayer,' did not practise a passive mysticism, and that the Spirit manifested itself through the body, for the 'body also shares in the sanctification, having acquired inactivity of evil.'[44] It is therefore evil, especially the evil use of the senses, which one should combat, not abandoning the body and the senses themselves.[45]

Hence Palamas is as far as possible from any sort of 'quietism,' and his spirituality has nothing in common with a Hindu or Neo-Platonic flight from matter. On the contrary, he has a Biblical sense rather rare in the Middle Ages. Our few quotations show his great spiritual debt to the Pseudo-Macarius.

The true meaning of the psycho-physical method

One can see that, in the context of such teaching about man, the psychophysical method of prayer could more easily find a place than in Barlaam's philosophy. Before looking at the passages in which Palamas justifies the principle of that method, we must point out his refutations of Barlaam's interpretation. Palamas above all denies the view that the method was a *mechanical way* of obtaining grace. Barlaam spoke of 'intelligible entries and exits happening at the same time as the breath,' and other strange phenomena closely linked with the physical practices of prayer; he accused the hesychasts of wanting to produce a spiritual result by forcing the inhalation of breath.[46] According to Palamas, these are calumnies; the method of prayer is essentially a practical way for beginners to avoid distraction and the wanderings of the mind. 'It is not out of place,' he writes, 'to teach, especially with beginners, people to look at themselves, and by means of breathing to send the mind back inside themselves. No man of sense would forbid anybody to use certain procedures in order to collect his mind within himself, when it is not yet contemplating himself. People who undertake this struggle continually find their mind flying off as soon as it has been collected; continual too is the need to bring it back to themselves; in their inexperience they do not realize that nothing in the world is so difficult to contemplate, or so mobile, as the mind. That is why some have recommended control of inhalation and exhalation and holding the breath a little, so as to hold the mind too . . . '[47] Palamas very often stresses the educational and instrumental character of the

[43] *Tr.* II, 2, 20.
[44] ibid., 13-14; cf. *Hom.* 12, col. 153C; *Life of Peter*, 1012D-1013A.
[45] *Tr.* II, 2, 5, 9.
[46] *Letter to Ignatius*, ed. Schirò, p. 323; *Tr.* II, 2, 25.
[47] *Tr.* I, 2, 7.

method,[48] which, for him, is allied to all other corporal ascetic practices: 'Any one who considers as abominable the beginning of prayer ... that prayer accompanied by tears and repentance which comes from grief truly felt in fasting and vigilance, and the care with which novices are taught to lift up their divided minds, in uniform and harmonious prayer, the man who scorns all that, should be consistent enough also to scorn the end pursued in prayer ...'[49] There is no question here of an easy and mechanical way of rising to a vision of God, but of an ascetic exercise based on the need for the monk to 'assemble' his mind by attention ($προσοχή$), and to come back into himself: St. John of the Ladder was already speaking of 'circumscribing the sea of the mind within oneself'[50] and, differing from Evagrius for whom this return into oneself was a purely intellectual act, he defined the hesychast as 'he who tries to circumscribe the incorporeal in his body.'[51]

Justified criticisms

While defending the psycho-physical method, Palamas freely admitted that care was needed in practice: Barlaam 'used the pretext of some human weaknesses.'[52] Palamas also specifically admitted that the little work of Nicephorus the Hesychast, which had been the main object of attack, was not above criticism: 'Nicephorus,' he wrote, 'composed a simple book without research; Barlaam has been able to find holds against him in it.'[53] Moreover he seems to recognize that some of Nicephorus's expressions may have been ambiguous, as Barlaam had been able to find 'apparent grounds' for condemning him.[54] The context suggests that these ambiguities of Nicephorus concerned his doctrine of man, especially the respective roles of the mind ($νοῦς$) and the heart; Barlaam quoted Gregory of Nyssa to prove that 'the intellectual essence, that is to say God, unites itself to the fine and illuminated part of the sensuous nature,'[55] whereas Palamas, defending Nicephorus, relies on the Pseudo-Macarius, and especially this famous passage in his *Spiritual Homilies*: 'The heart directs the whole organism, and when grace receives the heart as its share, it rules over all the thoughts, and all the members; for the intelligence and all the thoughts of the soul reside there.'[56]

[48] *Second letter to Barlaam, Coisl.* 100, *fol.* 100v; *Tr.* I, 2, 8; II, 2, 2, 25; II, 3, 14.
[49] *Tr.* II, 2, 15.
[50] *Ladder,* 28, *P.G.* LXXXVIII, 1132C.
[51] ibid., 27, col. 1097B (quoted in *Tr.* I, 2, 6).
[52] *Tr.* I, 3, 49.
[53] *Tr.* II, 2, 3.
[54] ibid., 26.
[55] *De opif. hominis,* 8, *P.G.* XLIV, 145C; cf. *Tr.* II, 2, 27.
[56] *Hom.* XV, 20, *P.G.* XXXIV, 589B; often quoted by Palamas (*Tr.* I, 2, 3; *Tr.* II, 2, 27, etc.).

The role of the heart

In this way Nicephorus the Hesychast's method of prayer brings to the fore the contrast, of which we have already spoken, between an 'intellectual mysticism' based on a Neo-Platonist dualistic doctrine of man, and the 'mysticism of the heart,' which is more Biblical and, sometimes, Stoic. We have said already that Palamas and the fourteenth century hesychasts plainly belonged to the latter tendency. Most of them thought the heart was the centre of all spiritual and bodily life; they did not in the least think of this as a metaphorical expression for the emotional centre of man, but rather as a Biblical term broadly adopted by Macarius to mean the prime organ of life. Certainly also for many mystics, as for Jewish writers, it fitted in with a physiological conception of the heart as centre. In that conception, 'the heart is the master part; it holds the leadership of the body, and it was in it that the Creator put the innate source of warmth; linked with the lungs, the source of coolness, it played a part in breathing, and in the emission of speech.' [57] It is therefore to the heart that the intelligence must 'descend' to refind its 'stability,' and thus re-establish the inner harmony destroyed by sin. In this psycho-physiological process, breathing and the position of the body had a large part to play, as had also psychological dispositions and ascetic exercises. It is clear that the little works on prayer dating from the thirteenth century, such as those of Nicephorus and the Pseudo-Symeon, assumed a psycho-physical system of that sort.

But, Palamas knowing the Fathers well, could not be quite ignorant of the tradition of purely 'intellectual' prayer. He was also too much of a Byzantine to allow himself to make a formal choice between the two doctrines of man, for that would have involved more or less veiled criticism of authorities such as 'St. Nilus' (the pseudonym of Evagrius) and even Gregory of Nyssa. But inside himself his choice was already made. Hence he sought to give a Biblical and 'Monist' interpretation to the dualist and Neo-Platonic quotations of Barlaam from the Fathers, and thus to re-establish the *consensus Patrum;* at the same time, with a critical sense rare in his age, he stood clear of any dogmatism in the field of pure physiology. Here we will give just one example of this method used several times by Palamas.

'The Great Macarius,' Gregory writes, 'was instructed by the action of grace, and he teaches that the mind and all thoughts of the soul are in the heart as an organ; the Bishop of Nyssa, for his part, says that the mind, in so far as it is incorporeal, is not within the body.'[58]

[57] A. Guillaumont, *Le Coeur*, pp. 77–8; cf. also A. Bloom, *Contemplation et ascèse*, in *Etudes carmélitaines*, 28 (1949), pp. 49–67.
[58] *De opif. hominis*, 12, col. 156.

We draw a single conclusion from these two apparently contradictory statements, and show that they are not really opposed; we say: even if, following Gregory of Nyssa, the mind is not within the body, since it is incorporeal, it is yet inside . . . because it is attached to it, and because, in inexpressible fashion, it makes use of the heart as the prime organ of the flesh, according to the Great Macarius. . . . In the same way, those who assert that the Divinity is in no place, as it is incorporeal, do not contradict those who say that the Word of God came in time within the pure virginal womb, for it was there that, in inexpressible fashion, it was united with our nature. . . .'[59]

This reference to the Incarnation allows Gregory, more or less artificially, to reconcile the contraries. However it may be that the method he uses is not so artificial as it seems: did such Fathers as Gregory of Nyssa and Maximus share, otherwise than verbally, the spiritualizing doctrine of the Neo-Platonists, and would they not have agreed with Palamas's exegesis of their thought? Palamas himself, in his sermons, when he did not have the precise aim of giving a theological foundation to hesychast spirituality and refuting the nominalist spirituality of Barlaam, used traditional spiritual clichés about the necessity of giving up love of the body, and loving the soul alone. In his *Chapters on Prayer* he uses language just like that of Evagrius. Plainly he was not going back on his ideas about the role of the body in spiritual life, but solely intended to re-establish the *equilibrium* in the composite human being broken by sin, by restoring the spirit to its primacy over the body.

There are no dogmas in physiology

While maintaining the general Biblical conception of the ontological unity of man's composition, Palamas had no desire to dogmatize about any physiological system, and so left full freedom to scientific research. Revelation was only concerned with eternal verities necessary to salvation, and not with physiology. 'If we ask how the mind is attached to the body,' Palamas writes, 'where is the seat of imagination and opinion, where is memory fixed, what part of the body is most vulnerable and so to say directs the others, what is the origin of the blood, whether all the humours are quite pure and without admixture, and which organs serve as receptacles for each of them, in all such matters each man may speak his opinion . . . it is the same . . . with all questions of this sort about which the Spirit has given us no plain Revelation; for the Spirit only teaches us to know the Truth which penetrates everything. Therefore, even if you find that on such a point we contradict

[59] *Tr.* II, 2, 29; cf. *Hagioretic Tome*, 1232AB; *Tr.* III, 3, 4.

the holy and wise Gregory of Nyssa, you should not attack us for that.'[60]

Mystical doctrine of the Incarnation

But the essential point in Palamas's thought about hesychasm is not this ontological unity of spirit and body in the natural man. It is on the Incarnation that his main argument depends. One finds an interesting and original example of this in his *Treatise on the Entry of the Virgin into the Temple,* which is a sort of spiritual biography of the Virgin Mary, written by Gregory in his youth. Whereas the Fathers in the line of development from Origen chose Moses to illustrate the stages of spiritual ascent, Palamas turns to Mary when treating a similar subject, and he brings the contemplative life to a climax not with a simple vision of the Divine, but with the corporal and intimate contact of the Incarnation. According to Palamas, in the temple the Virgin practised 'holy hesychia' (ἱερὰν ἡσυχίαν); 'she fixed her spirit to turning in on itself, and attention and holy uninterrupted prayer.' This conscious use of the hesychast vocabulary to describe the life of the Virgin in the temple, clearly shows that Palamas meant to cite her as an example, but it also makes plain his desire to see the practice of hesychasm as a *means,* and not as the very end of mystical life; for the Virgin Mary, the result of that 'uninterrupted prayer' was the discovery that 'nothing could stop the common rush of men to destruction and the unchecked flight of our race to Hades' : it was then that she glimpsed the mystery of the divine Maternity of which she was to be the vehicle : 'She opens the way to the greatest and most perfect things; she discovers, realizes and transmits to future generations a practice higher than contemplation, and a contemplation as different from that which had been spoken of before, as reality is from imagination.'[61] This superiority of the *Christian fact* over all psychological aspiration or mysticism outside the grace of the Incarnation, is certainly the essential idea underlying all Palamas's theology. More than the teachers of spirituality before him, he felt the reality of the *radical change* which took place in the relations between God and man as a consequence of the Incarnation; in this way he gave an objective foundation to Christian mysticism, independent of all psychology, and even more independent of all spiritual 'technique.' It is Christ, and more precisely his Body conceived in the Virgin's womb, which is our unique contact with God; it is he, the Mediator of sanctifying and deifying grace, and his presence is objectively real in the Church. Palamas integrates

[60] *Tr.* II, 2, 30.
[61] *Hom.* 63, ed. Oikonomos, pp. 168–9, 170, 176.

monastic spirituality with the *story of Salvation,* and thus frees it from the last vestiges of Platonic idealism. In undertaking the defence of the corporal method of prayer, he in fact defends the teaching of Paul about the human body as a member of Christ.

The aim of the Incarnation

In speaking of the Virgin birth of Christ, he chiefly has in mind the manifestation of transfigured flesh. 'If Christ had been born by natural procreation, he could not have been the initiator and giver of new life, destined never to vanish: made in the old mould, he could not have received within himself the fullness of the Divinity and *made the flesh an inexhaustible source of sanctification.*'[62] There is a sacramental link between our body and the transfigured flesh of Christ: 'Christ has become our brother, having shared flesh and blood like ours, and so having become like us. . . . As does a husband his wife, so has he drawn us to him . . . by sharing in his blood, having become one flesh with us.'[63]

Christian meaning of 'return into oneself'

By this Christocentric and sacramental mysticism, Palamas gives a new and strictly Christian meaning to the theme of return into oneself.[64] In returning into himself, a man who is not in real sacramental unity with Christ, can only contemplate a humanity fallen and subject to error. Palamas well knew that the Ancients also recommended return into oneself, in order to rejoin the divine and incorporeal spark which, in their view, could bring them back into an intelligible world. 'But,' wrote Palamas, 'if you look at the end envisaged by them as the object of this precept, you find an abyss of impiety; they teach metempsychosis; one cannot know oneself, they thought, and be faithful to that precept, without knowing the body to which one was formerly attached, the place one lived in, what one did there and what one knew. . . . That is where they lead you with their "know thyself".'[65]

Christ within us

Plainly that is not the goal for Christians; what they seek is the Kingdom of God, which *really is there,* and is manifest in the soul as well as in the body. Recalling the passage in St. John of the Ladder,

---

[62] *Hom.* 16, col. 193B; cf. 217A; *Hom.* 21, col. 276D.
[63] *Hom.* 56, ed. Oikonomos, p. 207.
[64] cf. our article, *'Le thème du retour en soi dans la doctrine palamite du XIV-e siècle,'* in the *Revue de l'histoire des religions,* CXLV, No. 2, 1954, pp. 188–206.
[65] *Tr.* I, *1,* 10.

in which he recommends the hesychast to 'circumscribe the incorporeal in the body,' Palamas comments: 'If the hesychast does not circumscribe it within the body, how could he allow entry within himself to him who put on the body ... and who penetrates all organized matter?'[66] Palamas's thought is equally plainly expressed in another passage of the *Triads*: 'Since the Son of God, in his incomparable love for men, did not only unite his divine Hypostasis with our nature, by clothing himself in a living body and a soul gifted with intelligence ... but also united himself ... with the human hypostases themselves, in mingling himself with each of the faithful by communion with his Holy Body, and since he becomes one single body with us ($\sigma\nu\sigma\sigma\omega\mu\sigma\varsigma$ $\dot{\eta}\mu\tilde{\iota}\nu$ $\gamma\acute{\iota}\nu\epsilon\tau\alpha\iota$)[67] and makes us a temple of the undivided Divinity, for in the very body of Christ dwelleth the fullness of the Godhead bodily (Col. 2: 9), how should he not illuminate those who commune worthily with the divine ray of his Body which is within us, lightening their souls, as he illuminated the very bodies of the disciples on Mount Tabor? For, on the day of the Transfiguration, that Body, source of the light of grace, was not yet united with our bodies; it illuminated from outside ($\xi\xi\omega\theta\epsilon\nu$) those who worthily approached it, and sent the illumination into the soul by the intermediary of the physical eyes; but now, since it is mingled with us ($\dot{\alpha}\nu\alpha\kappa\rho\alpha\theta\grave{\epsilon}\nu$ $\dot{\eta}\mu\tilde{\iota}\nu$) and exists in us it illuminates the soul from within ($\ddot{\epsilon}\nu\delta o\theta\epsilon\nu$).'[68]

This passage of Pauline inspiration shows why Palamas felt that defence of the hesychasts was defence of the Gospel itself: it was the actual presence of Christ in the sacramental life of the Church which was put in question by Barlaamite nominalism. The light on Tabor is brought in only as an illustration, but he often returns to it, for it was as light that the mystical tradition derived from Origen and Gregory of Nyssa described the divine presence and sanctifying grace; the Apostles, on Tabor, saw 'the very grace of the Spirit which later came to dwell among them ...'[69]

Therefore the life of Christ in us is, according to Palamas, the foundation of hesychast spirituality. The contrast between knowledge coming from the outside ($\xi\xi\omega\theta\epsilon\nu$)—a human and purely symbolic knowledge—and 'intellectual' knowledge coming from within ($\xi\nu\delta o\theta\epsilon\nu$) is found already in the Pseudo-Dionysius: 'It is not from without ($\xi\xi\omega\theta\epsilon\nu$) that God moves them towards the divine, but in intelligible fashion, by

---

[66] *Tr.* I, 2, 4, 6.
[67] The word $\sigma\nu\sigma\sigma\omega\mu\sigma\varsigma$ is from Eph. 3: 6; it is used by Gregory of Nyssa (*In Cantic.* 15, ed. Jaeger, p. 461), and often by Palamas, especially in a Eucharistic context (*Hom.* 56, ed. Oikonomos, pp. 202–3).
[68] *Tr.* I, 3, 38.
[69] *Tr.* III, 3, 9.

illuminating them from within (ἔνδοθεν) with the most divine will by means of a pure and immaterial light.'[70] Clearly Palamas knew this passage and was inspired by it, but he understands Dionysius in a Christological sense, and frees it from his intellectualism; for him 'within' (ἔνδοθεν) does not designate the purely intellectual reality of man—his *nous* (νοῦς)—but refers to the whole composite human being. It is *within our body,* grafted on to the body of Christ by baptism and the Eucharist, that the divine light shines.

The grace of baptism
The inner regeneration of man through baptism is also identified with what he calls 'the resurrection of the soul' of which we have already spoken. The soul, in this case also considered as the vital principle of the composite human being, has been finally liberated from the Devil by Christ. It only remains for man to free himself from the consequences of his past mortality: 'Although the Lord,' he says, 'has caused us to be reborn by Divine baptism and, on the day of redemption seals us with the seal of the grace of the Holy Spirit, he allows us still to possess a mortal and passionate body; although he has chased away the master of evil from the treasures of our soul, he does allow him *to attack it from without,* so that man renewed by the new covenant, that is to say the gospel of Christ . . . should learn to drive back the attacks of the enemy, and so prepare himself to receive immortality.'[71] Hence the whole of the Christian spiritual fight is directed *outwards,* for it is from thence that danger may still come.[72] So we see that the notion of 'the inner man' so common in the spirituality derived from Evagrius, is interpreted by Palamas in a sacramental context and in this way all spiritual individualism is excluded. The fight against the 'distractions of the mind,' 'sensations' and 'external images' is not for him a mystique of disincarnation, but a means to keep safe the earnest given to the Christian at his baptism: 'Those who have become new beings in the bath of regeneration, and who have preserved themselves from the ancient shame by new life and conduct, or have been purified by repentance . . . see from within their own renewing.'[73] The 'inner' character of redemptive grace opposing the 'external' attacks of the Devil shows once again how far Palamite thought is from Messalianism: moreover, Palamas himself several times condemns the Messalian doctrine about the consubstantiality (συνουσίωσις) of the Devil with the soul.[74]

[70] *Hier. eccl.* I, 4, P.G. III, 376B; cf. R. Roques, *L'univers dionysien,* p. 160.
[71] *Hom.* 16, col. 213B.
[72] *Hom.* 23, col. 304C.
[73] *Against Akindynos,* V, 23, Coisl. 98, *fol.* 139v–140.
[74] *Tr.* I, 3, 2; II, 3, 13.

The morning star

There is another particularly clear passage to which Palamas attached so much importance that he reproduced it word for word at least three times, while his biographer, Philotheus, includes it in his *Encomion* of Palamas: 'When the day breaks, and the morning star rises in our hearts, as the Chief of the Apostles has said (2 Peter 1 : 19), when, according to the word of the Prophet, the true man goes forth to his true work (Psalm 104 : 23) and with this light guiding him, he rises or is transported up to the eternal mountain tops; he begins, oh miracle, to see supracosmic realities, *without separating himself and without being separated from the matter* which has been with him from the beginning. . . . For he does not rise with the imaginary wings of his reason . . . but really, through the inexpressible power of the Spirit . . . becoming really on earth an Angel of God, and by himself drawing to God *all created things.*' The context of what Palamas writes afterwards—particularly the quotation from Chapter LXXIX of Diadochus —clearly shows that the illumination in question comes from baptism.[75]

What the hesychast seeks in 'leading back his spirit into his heart' is that 'star of the morning' which the coming of Christ has caused to rise; such are 'the laws of the Spirit' which, using Macarius's expression, grace has 'carved' there.[76] He then discovers the true human destiny which consists in reigning over the whole creation while leading it to God. He finds his 'true work,' that with which the Creator had entrusted to him in Paradise. In this way a Palamite hesychast broke free from a passive conception of contemplation which reduced the value of man's personal activity to nothing. Contrariwise, as we shall see again later, for Palamas 'works' constituted an absolutely necessary condition for the reception of supernatural grace. 'As the rising of the visible sun,' he writes, 'tells men the time for bodily work, so the sun of Justice which has appeared to us in the flesh tells us that the time following its appearance is all entirely destined to a spiritual work.'[77] However Palamas is far from any Pelagian or Messalian substitution of human 'merit' for the effects of divine grace; that he explicitly states in arguing against a conception of Barlaam's of Platonic origin, according to which the luminous vision accessible 'within the self' was only a vision of the 'essence of the (human) mind.' 'In seeing itself,' Palamas writes, 'the mind sees something else than itself : it does not only contemplate something different, not simply its own image, but the refulgence of

[75] *Discourse to John and Theodore*, ed. Oikonomos, p. 299; *To Xene*, 1080D–1081C; *Against Akindynos*, VII, 11, *Coisl.* 98, *fol.* 190v–191; Philotheus, *Encomion*, 577AB.
[76] *Hom.* XV, 20, *P.G.* XXXIV, 589B; *cf. Tr.* I, 2, 3; I, 3, 41.
[77] *Hom.* 42, ed. Oikonomos, p. 2; *Hom.* 47, ibid., pp. 63, 67.

the grace of God mirrored in its own image; this refulgence strengthens the mind's power to surpass itself, and accomplishes that union with the Best which passes beyond understanding.' So it is not human effort— still less any psycho-physical technique!—which reveals God to us: 'We see in ourselves the glory of God, when it pleases God to lead us to the spiritual mysteries.' [78]

Let us try to recapitulate Palamas's thought about hesychasm. We have seen that with him various tendencies and various terminologies of the hesychast tradition became integrated in a Christocentric doctrine of man. As with Evagrius, the mind is the part of the composite human being which has the faculty 'to surpass itself' and to attain grace; true prayer must be a 'mental prayer' (νοερὰ προσευχή), because the mind (νοῦς) is the very basis of the person, the very self of the man: 'The prayer of the perfect is *par excellence* an intellectual activity; their mind is not turned towards the body, nor towards anything that concerns the body; it does not act through the senses, nor through imagination linked to the senses; it does not dive with its reason and with its faculty of contemplation into the study of beings; but remains constant in prayer alone.' [79] It is the mind too which is the image of God in man, and that which 'knows God.' [80] Nevertheless, *in so far as man cannot save himself on his own, the mind needs grace and can find it nowhere but in the Body of Christ united to our bodies by Baptism and the Eucharist*. Therefore, to exercise its proper activity, intellectual prayer, it must 'descend into the heart,' for it is there that the 'Spirit of the Living God' has written his message (2 Cor. 3: 3). For all that, the mind does not become 'corporal,' nor 'turned towards the body'; it remains immaterial and turned towards God, and accomplishes afresh the function assigned to it by God, namely to lead the whole human organism, body and soul, towards its Creator. Sin and death have broken the harmony of the human person, provoking the revolt of the body against the spirit, and so robbing it of life; that is what Palamas calls, as we have seen, the death of the soul, considering the soul to be the basis and the vital unity of the human being.

The resurrection of the soul

To establish the lost balance man needs the 'resurrection of the soul': that is granted in baptism. 'The resurrection of the body,' Palamas writes 'is now above all contemplated by faith . . . whereas that of the soul . . . begins with divine baptism.' [81] In this way the 'little resurrection

[78] *Tr.* II, 3, 11, 17.
[79] *Tr.* II, 2, 15.
[80] *Hom.* 26, col. 333A.
[81] *Hom.* 16, col. 217A; cf. *Hom.* 54, ed. Oikonomos, pp. 186–7.

of the soul' ($\mu\iota\kappa\rho\grave{\alpha}$ $\tau\tilde{\eta}\varsigma$ $\psi\nu\chi\tilde{\eta}\varsigma$ $\dot{\alpha}\nu\acute{\alpha}\sigma\tau\alpha\sigma\iota\varsigma$), a concept which Evagrius [82] understood in a purely spiritual sense and which, taken by itself, constituted for a Platonizing trend of thought an acceptable variation on the Christian doctrine about the resurrection, was thus given an objective and sacramental interpretation by Palamas : the 'resurrection of the soul' was no more than an anticipation of the bodily and general resurrection on the Last Day. It was an earnest of the new life, brought by Christ, and already active in the heart of man. It is to this earnest that the intelligence should cling, finding it in the heart, and by this means sharing, in the intellectual and incorporeal fashion proper to it, in the complete activity of man turned towards his God.

This total activity in which man participates through his soul and through his body, is *the faith* : 'I hold,' Palamas writes, 'that our holy faith is . . . a vision of our heart which passes beyond all sensation and all understanding, for it transcends all the intellectual faculties of our soul. Faith is a firm assurance of the things for which we hope . . . (Heb. 11 : 1), an intellection of the heart.' [83]

Christian materialism

In this way Palamas combines integration of the terminology of Evagrius, theological assimilation of the mysticism of St. Symeon the New Theologian, and a justification of thirteenth century methods of prayer. In his Christocentrism, his Eucharistic spirituality and his theology concerning the light, Palamas certainly owes much to that great mystic of the eleventh century, to whom however he scarcely ever refers. Nevertheless, these elements in the personal and prophetic mysticism of Symeon find expression in his writings with a theological strictness that they did not have in that author himself. Whereas Symeon reveals experiences he lived through, Palamas speaks as a theologian responsible for accuracy of expression and conscious that he is defending dogmatic orthodoxy. The same concern for theology and spiritual balance leads him to provide a sound interpretation for the psycho-physical method of prayer, without regard to the perhaps non-Christian origins of that method. After Palamas, such misunderstandings as provoked Barlaam would no longer be possible.

The arguments which Palamas elaborated to defend his brothers, the monks, against the attacks of an opportunist philosopher, nevertheless have a value going far beyond their immediate objective. He was really attacking a dualistic doctrine of man which would effectively have removed from the domain of grace a great part of human existence,

---

[82] *Cent.* V, 22, Bousset, *Evagrius Studien*, p. 306.
[83] *Tr.* II, 3, 40.

transforming Christianity into a religion of disincarnation. Barlaam's error in this respect was all the more dangerous because he might have found credence far beyond the nominalist and definitely Platonizing circles of Byzantium. Through Origen and Evagrius a Platonic terminology had invaded Christian literature, and the Biblical correctives applied by the Fathers had not always been enough to limit its effects on spirituality, theology and practice. Palamas's thought was undoubtedly one further step forward in an anti-Platonic reaction, based on a Biblical doctrine of man, that is to say, founded on the essential unity in man of spirit and matter. We thus find here the elements of *Christian materialism* which, instead of wishing to suppress matter which has revolted against the spirit through the effect of sin, gives it the place the Creator assigned to it, and discovers the way which Christ opened for it by transfiguring it and by deifying it in his own body.

These few preliminary conclusions will be confirmed when we come to examine more closely Gregory's Christology and his doctrine of deification.

CHAPTER III

CHRIST AND DEIFIED HUMANITY: REDEMPTION, DEIFICATION AND ECCLESIOLOGY

Spirituality and history

When criticizing profane philosophers and expressing his conception of hesychast mysticism, Palamas, as we have seen, is constantly referring to the new relations established by Christ between God and men by his incarnation, death and resurrection. The essential in these new relations was that man was allowed to have a life in common with God, to unite himself with him, and to 'deify' himself. Palamas's adversaries were prepared to admit the doctrine of *theosis* elaborated by the Greek Fathers, but only as a static notion, an eternal ideal to which men of all times had aspired without ever perfectly attaining it. That was not at all the conception of the monks of Athos. For them deification was an objective reality, become attainable in *history* and in the *person* of Jesus Christ.

Barlaam, in defending his nominalist positions, denied the possibility here below of attaining a supernatural knowledge of God, as distinct from analogical knowledge 'starting from the creatures.' If no such knowledge truly existed, Palamas answered, Christianity would have brought nothing fundamentally new to man. 'To know the actor by analogy from his actions,' Palamas writes, 'and to realize the transcendence of the [divine] Wisdom through the harmony of the world, may be the achievement of the wise ones of this world, as the holy Gregory of Nyssa says.'[1] But the Christian has a much more perfect knowledge: 'We have all known the Son through the voice of the Father who announced this doctrine from on high (cf. Matt. 3 : 16-17), and the Holy Spirit, the inexpressible light itself, has assuredly shown that here is the Well-beloved of the Father; the Son himself has manifested the name of his Father, and has promised, returning to heaven, to send us the Holy Spirit to dwell with us for ever (John 16 : 7): and the Holy Spirit has descended, remained with us and declared and taught us the whole truth (John 16 : 8).'[2]

This insistence on the *historical* character of Revelation is combined

---
[1] *De beat. hom.* VI, P.G. XLIV, 1269B.
[2] *Tr.* II, 3, 67.

in Palamas with an acute sense of the supernatural, opposed to Barlaam's Neo-Platonic conception which would make deification only a 'state of intellectual and rational nature which has existed since the first creation of the world, and comes to fulfilment in the most developed rational beings.' [3] He who says that, Palamas answers, 'plainly contradicts the very Gospel of Christ. If deification only perfects the rational nature, without lifting those who have the sight of God above that level, if it is only a state of the rational nature, since it cannot be set in motion except by a natural power, then the deified Saints do not transcend that nature, they are not born of God (John 1 : 13), they are not of the Spirit because they are born of the Spirit (John 3 : 6), and Christ, by coming into the world, has not given the power to become children of God to those who believe in his name (John 1 : 12.)' [4]

Before studying Palamas's thought about deification more closely, we should briefly analyse his conception of the work of Christ, which in his view was at the centre of human history. His *Homily 16* [5] is devoted to this subject, and is in fact a theological treatise on Redemption.

The Redemption

The Son of God made man 'was born of a woman to put on the nature which he had created and which had been corrupted by the counsel of the Evil One; he was born of a woman who was a virgin to create a new man.' Thus of his free will he made himself like unto us, in our weakness and our mortality, but he brought in himself the germ of a new life : 'Having become son of man and having assumed mortality ($θνητότητος$ $μεταλαβών$) he transformed men into sons of God, having made them share the divine immortality' ($κοινωνοὺς$ $ποιήσας$ $τῆς$ $θείας$ $ἀθανασίας$). Thus the whole work of redemption is conceived in terms of death-life, corruption-immortality. We have seen above that the transmission of Adam's sin was essentially understood by Palamas as a hereditary corruption entailing *at the same time* mortality of the flesh and sinfulness; the voluntary death and resurrection of Christ delivered man from this vicious circle of death and sin. 'By a single death, that of his own flesh, and by a single resurrection, that of that same flesh, he has healed us from a double death and delivered us from a double captivity, that of our soul and that of our body'; 'by his bodily death he has struck down the one who, in death, reigned over soul and

---
[3] Barlaam, *Against the Messalians*, quoted in *Tr.* III, 1, 25.
[4] *Tr.* III, 1, 30.
[5] *P.G.* CLI, 189–220.

body.' 'For us he suffered a death which he did not deserve . . . to ransom us from slavery to the Devil, and to death, death of the soul and death of the body. . . .'

The death of Christ was above all necessary to break the corrupted heredity of 'the old man'; it was a sacrifice of purification, in the Biblical sense of that term. 'A sacrifice was necessary,' wrote Palamas, 'to reconcile us with the heavenly Father and to sanctify us, we who had been soiled by contact with the Evil One. . . . And we need not only a resurrection of the soul, but also the resurrection of the flesh.' The loyally Patristic line of the soteriology of Gregory uses throughout expressions derived from St. Paul and from the Byzantine liturgy, especially the Sunday liturgy. For him, Redemption is not a 'satisfaction' granted to divine justice, but a reconciliation of human nature, fallen and mortal, with a living God. By accepting that his own Son, in the flesh of the old Adam, dies on the cross, and by communicating his own life to man in Jesus, God re-established his own legitimate power and suppressed the deadly usurpation of the Devil; the Trinity again became accessible to man in immediate, direct and intimate fashion. Palamas uses phrases about this subject which clearly show his existential approach to the Christian mystery: 'If the Word of God had not been incarnate, the Father would not have in plain fact manifested himself as Father, nor the Son in plain fact as Son, nor the Holy Spirit as proceeding also from the Father; then God would not have revealed himself in his essential and hypostatic existence, but only as an *energy* contemplated in creatures, as used to be said by the wise ones of old who had become man, and is said now by the partisans of Barlaam and Akindynos.' The doctrine of deification is for Palamas a direct consequence of the historical work of Christ; without him, divine life would have remained inaccessible to man.

The sacraments

Just as sin and death were transmitted from Adam by natural generation, so life has been given to us by the new birth through baptism and the Eucharist which incorporates us with Christ. Thus the salvation brought by Christ touches us all personally. 'He grants a perfect redemption,' Palamas writes, 'not only to the nature which he assumed from us in an unbreakable union, but to *each* of those who believe in him. . . . To that end he instituted holy baptism, defined the laws leading to salvation, preached repentance to all, and communicated his own body and his own blood. It is not nature only, but the hypostasis of each believer that receives baptism, lives according to the divine commandments, aad shares the deifying bread and the chalice.' [6] The

---

[6] *Hom.* 5, col. 64D.

regeneration of human nature accomplished by Christ once for all, is realized in each of us, taken individually, in the sacraments. Baptism and the Eucharist have for Palamas an incomparably greater importance than all the other Christian mysteries, for it is in them that the whole divine economy is manifested. At that time Byzantine theologians did not know the system of the 'seven sacraments' which is in danger of presenting the mystery of Christian initiation as 'one of the means' of salvation, and not the means *par excellence*. Speaking of baptism and the Eucharist, Palamas asserts: 'From these two acts depends our entire salvation, for in them is recapitulated the whole of the divine-human economy.' [7]

Baptism is one of the commonest themes in Palamas's sermons, as it is in his theological and spiritual writings. The sheer number of his references to Christian initiation shows the importance he attached to it; for him neither Christian experience nor spirituality could exist outside the sacramental grace which, in the Church, communicated the divine life to the faithful. It was 'to make a new being of us, and to renew us by baptism,' that Christ was incarnate [8]; 'he has broken on the cross the record of our sins (Col. 2: 14), and he has rendered innocent those who by baptism are buried with him (Rom. 6: 4; Col. 2: 12).' [9] Baptism, by delivering us from the original corruption, is a 'resurrection of our soul,' and to us 'communicates strength to conform to the body of the glory of Christ' (Phil. 3: 21).[10] The triple immersion is a symbol of the three days' sojourn of the soul of Christ in Hades that it might go out thence, and rise again in the body.[11] At baptism we receive a disposition to do good,[12] and we conclude a pact with God, but it depends on us to give real value to this grace.[13] 'If a man called obeys the call, and accepts baptism to be called a Christian, but does not behave in a way worthy of the name he bears, and does not in fact accomplish the promises given at his baptism, he is called, but he is not chosen.' [14] Then the promises are of no avail to him, but rather condemn him.[15] By baptism all Christians are holy—'If the vessel consecrated to God is holy,' Palamas says, 'how much more is the man holy who is joined to him by the bath of regeneration' [16]—and they are

[7] *Hom.* 62, ed. Oikonomos, p. 250.
[8] *Hom.* 56, ed. Oikonomos, p. 186; cf. *Hom.* 3, col. 36D; *Hom.* 16, col. 200D. 213B; *Hom.* 29, col. 368C.
[9] *Hom.* 16, col. 216B.
[10] ibid., col. 217AD.
[11] *Hom.* 62, ed. Oikonomos, p. 250.
[12] *Hom.* 29, col. 368D.
[13] *Hom.* 30, col. 385A.
[14] *Hom.* 41, col. 516B; cf. *Hom.* 60, ed. Oikonomos, p. 245.
[15] *Hom.* 60, ed. Oikonomos, p. 246.
[16] *Hom.* 54, ed. Oikonomos, p. 189.

sons of God,[17] but they are still required to prove by their works that they have received this gift; 'Renewal and new creation of the characteristics of the soul are accomplished by grace in the bath of regeneration; they grow and reach perfection through just actions in accord with faith.' [18]

Baptism and deification

We have seen above that Palamas justified the mysticism of the prayer of Jesus and the bodily method of prayer by a sacramental theology. The basis of his doctrine of deification is also found in his theology of the sacraments and in his ecclesiology. Nothing is further from Palamas's thought than to connect deification with man's own merits, and to consider it merely as an 'exploit' of which grace would only be the just reward. On the contrary, divine life becomes accessible to man as *a gift which is both gratuitous and common to all the baptized.* That is why Palamas commenting on the First Epistle to the Corinthians (Chapter 12), and the divisions of the church at Corinth in which 'those who had received more grew proud, and those who had received less grew discouraged,' recalls that St. Paul accorded the same dignity to them all 'showing that all were one body, the body of Christ, and that they were all members and parts of a whole, for they had all received the same Spirit.' He then quotes Chrysostom who commented on the same passage in the Epistle, and who considered that 'the coming of the Spirit spoken of here is that which comes about in us through baptism, and before the reception of the mysteries.' [19] It is also baptism which restores the divine 'likeness' lost through sin.[20]

Palamas's thought is perfectly clear on this subject; redeeming, sanctifying and deifying grace is bound up with baptism and the Eucharist. It is completely and objectively present in the Church. Palamas is far from any Messalian tendency in this essential point. 'All those who have been baptized in Christ, who have, according to St. Paul, clothed themselves in Christ (Gal. 3 : 27), while still being children of other men according to nature, supernaturally derive from Christ who has so well conquered the nature in which he himself was incarnate, without sperm, by the Holy Spirit and the Virgin Mary, and has granted to all those who believe on his name the strength and power to become children of God (John 1 : 12).' [21] These passages from the New Testament flow naturally from Palamas's pen to refute those who

---

[17] *Hom.* 57, ed. Oikonomos, pp. 221–2; cf. *Hom.* I, col. 12A.
[18] *Against Akindynos*, V, 23, *Coisl.* 98, *fol.* 138.
[19] ibid., 20, *fol.* 134v–135.
[20] *On the participation to God*, *Coisl.* 99, *fol.* 22.
[21] *Hom.* 57, ed. Oikonomos, p. 121; cf. *Hom.* 1, col. 12AB.

deny the organic and supernatural relations which the Saviour established between himself and the members of the Church; these relations are thus of an essentially mystical type and 'surpass understanding.' So every Christian is called to a conscious intimacy of his whole being with his God who has voluntarily come down from his transcendence to become 'in everything like to us, except for sin.'

An 'obligatory mystique'?

That is the basis of what some have called, with a scornful *nuance,* the 'obligatory mysticism' which the hesychasts, after St. Symeon the New Theologian, inculcated in their disciples, and which Palamas contrasted with the intellectual agnosticism of Barlaam: 'Supra-reasonable knowledge,' he asserts, 'is common to all those who have believed in Christ.' [22] The mysticism here in question is not the exaltation of a natural and uncontrollable sentimentality, the form in which the critics of the hesychasts like to present it, but an affirmation of the supernatural and universal character of the Redemption conferred by baptism. Palamas specifically reproaches his adversaries for considering grace as 'a natural phenomenon, as the 'reason of reasoning beings' and 'the life of the living,' accessible to every creature, and, in fact, spread out through a pantheistic universe: 'If that were so,' writes Palamas, 'all the sons of Adam, good and bad, pious and impious, would form but one body, the body of Christ; according to the words of Paul, they are the very Christ . . . and the unbaptized possess the dignity of those baptized in Christ.' [23] Akindynos's thought, both essentialist and nominalist, did not admit any supernatural and living presence of God himself in man; for him God was an essence, and he could not conceive more than one mode of divine presence—the essential mode—in nature as in deified man. It was this essentially static pantheism, derived from Greek philosophy, which Palamas combated in his adversaries.

'Nature' and 'grace'

He himself provides the precise terminology necessary to understand his thought about nature and about grace. The term 'nature' ($\phi \acute{v} \sigma \iota \varsigma$) applies to all beings created and different from God: 'Every nature,' he writes, 'is as far removed as possible from the divine nature, and is absolutely foreign to him: if God is nature, then all the other beings are not that; and if every being different from God is nature, he is not that, just as he is not a being, if the others are.' [24] According to this

---
[22] *Tr.* II, 3, 66; cf. *Letter to Athanasius, Coisl.* 98, *fol.* 5.
[23] *Against Akindynos,* V, 21, *Coisl.* 98, *fol.* 135v, etc.
[24] *Cap. phys.* 78, col. 1176B.

CHRIST AND DEIFIED HUMANITY

passage, plainly inspired by the Pseudo-Dionysius, nature is determined by its difference from God. As to the term 'grace' (χάρις), Palamas knows that the Greek language gives it various meanings: 'Sometimes,' he writes, 'it is the object given gratuitously which is called grace, but sometimes it is the very act of giving; at other times neither of these senses apply to the word "grace" which designates, so to say, the beauty, the beautiful appearance, the ornament and the glory of each nature, and in that sense we speak of the grace of words and of conversation . . .': hence there is a 'grace of nature' (ἡ χάρις τῆς φύσεως) different from 'deifying grace' (ἡ χάρις ἡ θεοποιός).[25] Palamas therefore accepts the idea of a 'created grace,' but that by no means signifies that he is open to the conception of a 'created supernatural' in the Thomist sense of that term: the 'supernatural' can only designate the reality essentially distinct from the creature, the divine life itself.

What grace is not

The essential peculiarity of Palamas's thought is that for him 'nature' and 'grace' mean *dynamic* and *living* realities; as before the Fall human nature was in dynamic union with God, for that was its true destiny willed by the Creator, so, after Adam's sin, the absence of such a relation characterized his state through the subjection to the Devil and mortality resulting therefrom. That is what Palamas means when he calls grace a 'relation' (σχέσις), making it clear that such relation, when the word applies to grace, is 'supernatural' and therefore not the same as the Aristotelian concept of relation only applicable to a concrete reality; it is therefore relation but no relation (σχέσις ἄσχετος).[26] Taking one step to meet his adversaries who defended the concept of 'created grace,' Palamas tried in abstract fashion to analyse the effects of redemption and to distinguish between a 'created grace,' that is to say the original beauty of created human nature which Christ restored, and 'uncreated deifying grace,' with the provision that the former is non-existent without the latter, and that the latter is reality experienced here below in the Church. The whole time he is defending communion with the living God as the only means of salvation for man, and combating the conception of salvation as an extrinsic justification which leaves man to live independently of God outside the 'supernatural.' That was not God's plan for man, and it was not for that that the Son of God put on flesh and clothed himself in a nature altogether similar to our own; He 'became man that we might become God.' Grace is therefore not a 'thing' which God grants to nature either to 'complete'

[25] *Against Akindynos*, III, 9, *Coisl.* 98, *fol.* 77.
[26] *Tr.* II, *1*, 29.

its deficiencies, or simply to 'justify' it, or to 'add' to it a created supernatural, but it is the divine life itself. It was to live in communion with him that he created us, and it is because we abandoned him that we are subject to corruption and death from which baptism delivers us.[27]

Created grace and uncreated grace

'There is nothing strange,' Palamas writes, 'in using the word "grace" both for the created and the uncreated and in speaking of a created grace distinct from the created.'[28] In what sense can one use the same word 'grace' about fundamentally different realities? We have seen that Palamas was aware of the many meanings of the word; he defines the matter thus : 'All that flows from the Spirit towards those who have been baptized in the Spirit according to the Gospel of grace, and who have been rendered completely spiritual, comes from the Source; it all comes from it, and also remains in it' (ἐξ αὐτῆς τέ ἐστι καὶ ἐν αὐτῇ). So the word is the same because the origin is the same; men 'received by the grace of God, and not through themselves, what they have received, for God alone does not possess his realities through grace; in this context the word "grace" indicates that it was given to them.' 'But,' he continues, 'all is not alike in what God gives us. . . . God has said by the mouth of Ezekiel : "A new heart will I give you, and a new spirit will I put within you; and I will take away your heart of stone, and give you a heart of flesh" (Ezek. 36 : 26), and, "I will put my Spirit into you" (Ezek. 37 : 5). Do you see the difference between the gifts? The new spirit and the new heart are created things : that is what the Apostle also calls "a new creature" (2 Cor. 5 : 17; Gal. 6 : 15), because it was recreated and renewed by the coming in flesh of him who first created it; whereas the Spirit of God given to the new heart is the Holy Spirit.'[29] 'There is a created grace and another grace uncreated,' he writes elsewhere, '. . . but since the gift which the saints receive and by which they are deified, is none other than God himself, how canst thou say that that too is a created grace?'[30] Likewise the risen body of Christ was created,[31] but it is plain that the Divinity which gave him immortality was uncreated.

'Synergy'

All along man's road from his fallen state to union with God, divine grace helps him to overcome corruption, then to surpass himself, and

[27] *Hom.* 45, ed. Oikonomos, p. 40.
[28] *Letter to Athanasius, Coisl.* 98, *fol.* 14.
[29] ibid., *fol.* 12–12v.
[30] *Against Akindynos*, III, 8, *Coisl.* 98, *fol.* 76v.
[31] ibid., V, 23, *Coisl.* 98, *fol.* 138.

finally shows God to him. This 'synergy' of grace and human effort is for Palamas an obvious axiom. The effect of grace is 'to establish the inner powers of soul and body, and make them act in conformity with their nature.'[32] But that is only a secondary aspect of our redemption, the goal of which is to make us contemplate God, that is to say to surpass ourselves. Palamas takes up again the Platonic doctrine that the mind (νοῦς) is the part of the composite human being which is naturally able to surpass itself,[33] but this faculty is not enough to enable it to reach God. The mind must be transformed by grace. Contradicting Barlaam's assertion that the vision of the Saints had no other object than the 'essence of the mind,' he declares, 'In seeing itself, it sees itself other, it does not only contemplate another thing, nor simply its own image, but the glory imprinted in its own image by the grace of God; that glory strengthens the power of the mind to surpass itself, and accomplishes that union with the Best which passes understanding.'[34] Nevertheless, as we have stressed before, it is not the mind alone which receives grace, the whole man being endowed therewith, 'all the faculties and powers of the soul and of the body.'[35] Man then rises to what Gregory calls a 'divine state' (ἕξις θεῖα), the result of collaboration (συνεργία) between grace and human effort manifested in 'the practice of the commandments': 'It is when thou hast in thy soul the divine state, that thou really possessest God within thyself; and the true divine state is love towards God, and it only survives by practice of the divine commandments.'[36]

This 'divine state' of which Palamas speaks is therefore a perpetual progress, for it assumes human collaboration in the world now and, by this latter means, man can never attain perfect conformity with the 'new man' that appeared in us by the grace of baptism. The necessity for 'works' is constantly stressed in Palamas's writings. However he does not so much present this 'practice of the commandments' as a *condition* of grace, but rather as the *necessary* and free *collaboration* of man with the redeeming action of God; the grace of baptism, once received, should, to be effective, become a living reality, and only human goodwill can give it that character. In this way Palamas, following the whole of the great Patristic tradition, avoids the Messalian and Pelagian temptation to consider deification accessible to human effort alone by, in particular, a technique of prayer independent of 'works.' 'Union with God,' Palamas writes, 'is not the result of a cause or an analogy, for

[32] *Tr.* I, 3, 15.
[33] *Tr.* II, 3, 48; cf. *Hom.* 53, ed. Oikonomos, p. 175.
[34] *Tr.* II, 3, 11.
[35] *Tr.* III, 3, 12.
[36] *Tr.* II, 3, 77.

those depend on the activity of the understanding; but is the result of disentanglement, without for all that being itself disentanglement. For if it were simply disentanglement, it would depend on us, and that is the doctrine of the Messalians.'[37] So, 'we cannot speak honestly of our faith and of our adhesion to Christ independently of the power and collaboration which he accords us; and likewise our Lord Jesus Christ cannot speak openly in our favour in the world to come . . . if he has not found in our conduct occasion for such favour,'[38] for 'God has created us free.'[39] One could find no clearer expression of the Greek Fathers' doctrine of *synergy:* Adam was really free when he participated in divine life; 'grace' and 'freedom' do not contradict, but presuppose each other, and true human freedom is being restored in the communion of God in Christ. Baptism therefore is an earnest which we receive in order to make it bear fruit.[40]

Diversity of charisms

Among Western theologians, all more or less dependent on Augustinian writings against Pelagius concerning infant baptism, the doctrine of grace generally has a soteriological and juridical character. Man has need of *grace,* for he cannot save himself. . . . The tradition of the Greek Fathers, with its insistence on the ultimate goal set before the Christian—deification—could not avoid going deeply into the meaning of the passages in St. Paul dealing with the diversity of charisms, while plainly maintaining their soteriological unity. Palamas too, in dealing with grace in relation to man's free effort towards God, recognizes that this effort *never* can be enough, for the *whole amount* of the gifts required for divine life become accessible in Christ. 'What one receives,' he writes, 'is never more than a part of what is given; he who receives the divine *energy* cannot contain the whole of it.'[41] The divine epiphany in Jesus Christ is therefore limited by human capacity to receive it, and also by the infinite variety of the personal paths to God. Its personalist quality is one of the essential characteristics of Palamas's thought : 'The Lord,' he writes, 'dwells in man in many and various ways according to the worth and conduct of those who seek him; he appears in a certain way to the practical man, in another to the contemplative, and in yet another to the man endowed with vision; the zealous receive it in one way, and those who have already become God's in another.'[42] Commenting on the passages concerning the Spirit in the First Epistle to

[37] *Tr.* I, 3, 17.
[38] *Hom.* 25, col. 321D.
[39] *Hom.* 29, col. 369C; *Hom.* 63, ed. Oikonomos, p. 280; *Hom.* 47, ibid., p. 60.
[40] *Hom.* 54, ed. Oikonomos, p. 190.
[41] *Tr.* III, *1*, 9.
[42] *Tr.* III, *1*, 28.

the Corinthians, Palamas writes thus: 'Those who prophesy, those who heal, those who see, and all those in general who have simply received the grace of the divine Spirit, all have charisms, greater or less great, in their own field. Thus Paul thanks God because he speaks languages better than others (1 Cor. 14: 18), but he who has less, also has a gift of God. "Seek," the same Apostle says, "for the greatest charisms" (1 Cor. 12: 31); therefore there must be lesser ones. And indeed . . . one star differs in glory from another (1 Cor. 15: 41) . . . but yet no star is totally devoid of light.' [43]

Unity of God
Does that diversity in the gifts of grace break, to that extent, the unity of salvation? By no means, for salvation essentially consists in contact re-established with the living God present *in completeness* in each charism. Redeeming grace is not a divisible object, but Christ himself who gives himself completely to man. Here is a characteristic passage, which we quote in anticipation of our chapter dealing with Palamas's teaching concerning the divine *energies*: 'Every man worthy of it participates differently in the great gift of the Spirit; this corresponds to the degree of his own purity, mingling with the harmony of that Beauty. But even he who has but little and that little obscure compared to the endowments of others . . . also unites himself to the whole of the very divine light, for it divides without dividing itself after the manner of bodies. . . . That unique light belongs indeed to the unique Christ.' [44] It equally belongs to the Spirit which also appears in completeness in its manifestations.[45] The unity of salvation and the diversity of charisms are thus preserved in a personalist conception of Redemption.

Communion with the uncreated
The man who in baptism receives the firstfruits of the Kingdom of God does not only receive an extrinsic justification, but is grafted on to a new reality, the divine and eternal life of Christ. The uncreated character of this new life seemed all the clearer to Palamas because all the Fathers of the fourth and fifth centuries, at the time of the Christological controversies, had asserted as a basic argument against the Pelagians and Nestorians, that it was impossible to accede to salvation through a created intermediary. In their eyes, the divinity of Christ and the hypostatic union had no other foundation than this soteriological necessity. Palamas's originality lies in his analysis of the state proper to the new man, which emerged from his opposition to the humanism of Barlaam.

[43] *Tr.* II, 2, 11.
[44] *Against Akindynos*, III, 6, *Coisl.* 98, *fol.* 74.
[45] *Hom.* 24, col. 313B.

The real communion of man with God is, for Palamas, the necessary condition of a true knowledge. We have seen above that Palamas's objection to Barlaam turned on the supernatural knowledge accessible to Christians only; such knowledge was but one aspect of the deification of which we receive the firstfruits here below. After the Redemption man is no longer alone in face of God, for God himself has come to put himself within man's reach and accompany him in his ascension towards the Creator: 'The Spirit in person has mingled with our spirit to bear witness that we are the children of God' (Rom. 8: 16) and 'God has sent into our hearts the Spirit of his Son which cries: Abba, Father' (Gal. 4: 6). Hence Christian knowledge of God is essentially different from natural knowledge 'after the creatures.' That is what Palamas means to say when he repeatedly contrasts theology ($\theta\epsilon o\lambda o\gamma\acute{\iota}a$) with vision ($\theta\epsilon\omega\rho\acute{\iota}a$) and with contemplation ($\theta\epsilon o\pi\tau\acute{\iota}a$): 'Theology is as far from the vision of God in light, and as distinct from intimate conversation with God, as knowledge is different from possession; to say something about God is not equivalent to a meeting with God.'[46] True knowledge is therefore distinguished from all external assimilation of the truth; a certain knowledge of God can come from the Scriptures, for by that means one can accept dogmatic truth and confess Orthodoxy,[47] but those are no more than means to attain the immediate and intimate knowledge of God procured for us by baptism. Strictly speaking it is not a knowledge: 'This contemplation is not a knowledge,' Palamas writes, 'it should not be considered as such, nor spoken of as a knowledge; moreover it is not even knowable, unless these words are used in an improper and equivocal sense; or rather, if given their proper meaning, these words acquire a transcendental significance; therefore it is not only wrong to consider it as a knowledge, but it must above all be considered as superior to all knowledge, and to all contemplation depending on knowledge, for nothing can surpass the apparition of God and his dwelling within us, nothing can equal it, nothing can come near to it.'[48] 'Such a union,' he writes elsewhere, 'is beyond all knowledge, although metaphorically we do call it knowledge'[49]; it is also 'by metaphor' or 'by homonymy' that some Fathers have used the word 'intellection' for it.[50] Even less is it a 'sensation.'[51] Only experience will unveil its true nature.[52]

---

[46] *Tr.* I, 3, 42 (text repeated in *Hom.* 53, ed. Oikonomos, pp. 169–170).
[47] cf. *Tr.* II, 3, 18; I, 3, 48; II, 3, 40.
[48] *Tr.* II, 3, 17.
[49] ibid., 33.
[50] *Tr.* II, 3, 39, 47; I, 3, 18; III, 2, 14.
[51] *Tr.* I, 3, 18, 24, 27; II, 3, 24–5; III, 1, 11, 36.
[52] *Tr.* III, 1, 32; III, 3, 3; I, 3, 34.

These are the easily recognized characteristics of the contemplation which, since St. Gregory of Nyssa and the Pseudo-Dionysius, have been adopted by all the mystics of the Christian East. However, with Palamas, this contemplation is understood in a more specifically Christocentric manner, and is expressed with greater care for fidelity to the Bible. In this, as in other respects, Palamas brings Christian theology a step further, surmounting neo-Platonism from within. This new step is particularly in evidence when Palamas speaks of mystical 'apathy.'

The true meaning of disentanglement

Union with God assumes disentanglement—and Palamas often quotes from Dionysius about this—but this disentanglement is not an end in itself: 'The Saints,' Palamas writes, 'reject the error of those who think that . . . after disentanglement from beings, there is nothing but absolute inaction, and not an inaction surpassing all activity.' [53] So Christian spirituality does not lead to *nirvana*, but to a state in which, in union with God, the human person is re-established with all his faculties. Answering Barlaam, who denied the positive mystical experiences of the monks on the ground that 'the passionate part (τὸ παθητικόν) of the soul' must 'die,' Palamas writes: 'The teaching which we have received, oh philosopher, tells us that insensibility does not consist in making the passionate part die, but in moving it from evil to good, and in directing its very being towards divine things. . . . For us the impassive man is one who no longer possesses any evil habits, and is rich in good habits; the man who is distinguished by his virtues, as are men of passion by their evil pleasures; the man who has subjected his appetites of anger and of lust, which two comprise the passionate part of the soul, to his faculties of knowledge, judgment and reason. . . . For it is the ill use of the powers of the soul which engenders abominable passions . . . but if one uses them properly, one will reap knowledge of God from knowledge of beings, for one will grasp the spiritual significance of beings, and will practice the appropriate virtues with the help of the passionate part of the soul acting in conformity with the aim which God set for it, when he created it.' [54] 'Clearly,' Palamas continues, 'we have been ordered to crucify the flesh with its passions and desires' (Gal. 5: 24). However, 'we have not been told this in order to kill ourselves by killing all activity of the body and all power of the soul, but in order to reject all vile desires and acts . . . marching always bravely forward like Lott when he went forth from Sodom. . . . Impassive men have the passionate part of their souls always alive and active to do good, and they do not make it die.' [55]

[53] *Tr.* I, 3, 19.
[54] *Tr.* II, 2, 19; cf. 22–3.
[55] ibid., 23; cf. III, *1*, 36; III, 3, 12, etc.

Such passages are ample to acquit Palamas of any suggestion of quietism! Among the arguments he uses to quash Barlaam's taste for profane philosophers, is that which stresses the missionary power imparted to those who receive the Holy Spirit. 'The Apostolic wisdom of but few men possessed of the Holy Spirit in a short time drew the whole world to heaven, binding it by the links of the Gospel; but now all the wise men together, whatsoever be their pertinacity and their zeal, do not avail to draw the smallest part of the world from the abyss of impiety.' [56] At the same time, union with the divine, though fundamentally different from 'knowledge of beings,' is in no way opposed to the latter, but rather gives it a new value: 'Spiritual contemplation . . . is also a true and genuine knowledge of beings . . . and is the only means of distinguishing what is really good and useful from what is not.' [57] For Palamas, therefore, search for deification in no way implies a rejection of the world; rather does it imply a detachment which enables the Christian to understand the world better, and to conquer it for the law of Christ.

Faith

For Palamas divine union, being different from all knowledge and from all natural intellectual processes, is equivalent to St. Paul's conception of 'faith.' 'It is faith,' Palamas writes, 'which is above all demonstration, and is, as it were, the undemonstrated principle of the holy demonstration.' [58] It was by faith too that the Apostles saw the divinity of Christ on Mount Tabor.[59] In the *Triads* there are long passages devoted to faith,[60] and in them the profoundly Biblical character of Palamas's thought comes out, and he makes an even clearer identification of 'vision' and 'faith': 'Our holy faith,' he writes, 'is . . . a vision of our hearts which goes beyond all sensation and all understanding, for it transcends all the intellectual faculties of our souls. How is it that by vision we see what is promised for us in the time without end which is to come? By the senses? But faith is a firm assurance of our hopes; that is why the Apostle also called it "evidence of things not seen" (Hebrews 11 : 1). Is there no intellectual faculty to see the things we hope for? But how could that be, since they have never entered into the heart of man (1 Cor. 2 : 9)? Let us again dwell on the faith, on the holy and joyous contemplation which it supplies; the faith, pillar of the power of the Gospel, life of the Apostles,

[56] *Tr.* II, 1, 7.
[57] *Tr.* I, 3, 42; cf. *Tr.* II, 1, 8; II, 3, 17, 72.
[58] *Against Akindynos*, VI, 1, *Coisl.* 98, *fol.* 149v.
[59] ibid., V, 9, *fol.* 123v.
[60] *Tr.* II, 3, 40–3.

justification of Abraham; faith, the beginning and the end of all justice, by which the just shall live (Rom. 1 : 17) . . . faith which continually frees mankind from error; establishes us in truth, and truth in us; that truth which no one shall ever take from us. . . . What is that faith? Is it a natural faculty, or a supernatural one? Surely supernatural. That is why no one can go to the Father except through the Son (Matt. 11 : 27; John 6 : 44, 65) who has lifted us above ourselves, granted us the deifying simplicity, and brought us back to unity with the Father.'

Hence knowledge of God, become accessible in Jesus Christ, is a unique reality. 'Whatever name we give it—union, sensation, knowledge, intellection, illumination—cannot properly be applied to it, or rather can properly be applied to it alone.' [61] The Biblical term 'faith' is therefore the only one which Palamas dares to apply to it unreservedly. To describe it he also uses concepts which the Bible and the Eastern Fathers before him had rendered familiar; the 'vision of the heart,' and the 'divine eye,' and the 'holy sensation.' For Palamas those are different ways of expressing a single reality, that of the supernatural faculty possessed by all Christians to know God, a faculty developed by the Saints through prayer and the 'practice of the commandments.' The element of originality in Palamas lies in his rejection of any spiritualizing or dualistic interpretation of the 'spiritual senses' : in the whole tradition deriving from Evagrius these senses were essentially a faculty of the intelligence, as opposed to the body. Now, as we have seen in the last chapter, Palamas takes the essential points in his teaching concerning man from the Pseudo-Macarius, and he regards man as one living and indivisible unity; supernatural grace is granted to the whole man, and not to the mind only. If, as we have seen, the 'spiritual senses' are neither 'sensation' nor 'intellection,' they assume an active state of man, and are the opposite of a negative 'impassivity.' Man possesses intelligence and senses which, transformed by grace, also participate in the supreme drama for which man was created, that is to say union with God.

The 'intelligible' and the 'spiritual'

As for the mind it goes without saying that its true function is to unite with 'the primal Mind,' and that, in regenerate man, it returns to the destiny intended for it by God.[62] But deification of the Christian does not only consist in salvation of the intelligence. One of the temptations besetting all Neo-Platonic Christian writers was to confuse the Platonic *nous* (νοῦς) with the spirit (πνεῦμα) of the New Testament, of St. Paul

[61] *Tr.* II, 3, 33.
[62] *Hom.* 3, col. 40B.

and of St. John, which is not contrasted with matter (ὕλη) but with the 'flesh' (σάρξ), that is to say with the whole fallen creation. One of Palamas's great virtues was that he clearly established the perspective and even the terminology of the Bible in a field in which Platonic dualism had, since Origen, caused many misunderstandings; for him spirit (πνεῦμα) and spiritual (πνευματικός) are terms signifying, not the immaterial, but the supernatural and the revealed, whereas mind (νοῦς) and mental refer to the intellectual faculties of the natural man. Thus speaking of St. Stephen's vision—a subject which St. Gregory of Nyssa had introduced into Christian mystical literature—Palamas asks, 'In what manner did the First Martyr have this vision, if he saw neither through his mind, nor through his senses, nor by negation, and if he did not conceive holy things either by deduction or by analogy? I dare assert that he saw spiritually (πνευματικῶς), just as I have said of those who saw the pure light, by revelation.'[63] The 'spirit' and not the mind provides the only means of seeing God: 'No one, neither man nor Angel, has seen God (John 1: 18), nor will ever see him,' he writes elsewhere, 'because we only see by our senses and by our mind, and this is true of Angels as of men; but he who has become Spirit and sees in Spirit, how should he not contemplate that which resembles his mode of contemplation?'[64] Here is another equally clear passage: 'The sensual and intellectual faculties constitute means of knowing beings; they are limited to beings, and manifest the Divine through these beings. But those who possess not only powers of sensation and intellection, but have also attained spiritual and supernatural grace, are not limited by beings in their knowledge, but know also spiritually, above sense and intelligence, that God is Spirit, for in their entirety they become God, and know God in God.'[65] So the coming of grace assumes a transformation in the human being, his communion with the divine life, his deification; the supernatural is not only the object of the vision, it is also the means thereof. 'Spiritual light,' Palamas writes, 'is not only the object of vision; it is also the faculty enabling us to see; this is neither sensation nor intellection, but a spiritual power distinct, in its transcendence, from all created cognitive faculties.'[66]

Transformation of the faculties of sense

In this sense the word 'spirit' (πνεῦμα) is connected, not with the immaterial, but with supernatural deification; it is contrasted with the intelligence as well as with created matter. However, inversely, in so

[63] *Tr.* I, 3, 30.
[64] *Tr.* II, 3, 31.
[65] ibid., 68.
[66] *Tr.* III, 2, 14; cf. *Against Akindynos*, VII, 10, Coisl. 98, fol. 189v–190.

far as grace is granted to the mind as much as to the body, spiritual vision will be as much intellectual as bodily, in that both mind and body are transformed by the Spirit. The whole man shares in the divine light. 'He who has received the divine *energy* . . . is, as it were, completely light.'[67] This completeness of the composite human being includes body as well as senses. From this results that astounding mystery of which the Transfiguration of Christ described in the Bible is an example; the vision of an uncreated light by created eyes. 'That light,' Palamas writes, 'is not a light apparent to the senses, though the Apostles were thought worthy to perceive it with their eyes'; and he adds this qualification, 'thanks to another power which was not that of the senses.'[68] This vision occurred, Gregory says quoting St. Maximus, 'through a transformation of the activity of the senses, brought about in them by the Spirit.'[69] In that we see the distinction between Palamas's thought and Messalianism, for he was not asserting that it was possible to have 'a vision of God with bodily eyes,' in so far as the latter are limited by their natural powers; nevertheless he refused to use a dualistic and Platonic doctrine concerning man as an argument against the Messalians, and to restrict the activity of grace to the intelligence alone. Would not the body rise again on the Last Day? Why should it be refused participation in vision here below?[70]

Emphatically Palamas always defends the reality of the Incarnation, and all his thought about deification turns on doctrine about the Church, the Body of Christ. Created faculties, whether bodily or intellectual, are not enough for man to see God; for that we need His own peculiar faculties, his life and his *energy*. The Son of God came expressly to unite, in his Person, human to divine *energy* to enable man to return to the Father. That is why, as we shall see in the next chapter, the dogmatic decisions of 1351 were presented as 'a development' of the definitions of the Sixth Oecumenical Council concerning the *energies* or wills of Christ; the Christology of St. Maximus the Confessor gave a solid Patristic foundation to Palamas's thought.

The Light: means and object of vision

As we have already noted from several quotations, Palamas's teaching about the knowledge of God assumes the deification of man, granted as 'firstfruits' from the day of baptism, and brought to more perfect realization in the spiritual life. To see God, we must acquire 'a divine eye' and let God see himself in us. Palamas once more quotes

---
[67] *Hom.* 53, ed. Oikonomos, p. 177; cf. *Hom.* 34, col. 432C.
[68] *Tr.* I, 3, 28.
[69] *Tr.* II, 3, 22; Maximus, *Ambigua*, *P.G.* XCI, 1125D–1128A.
[70] *Against Akindynos*, IV, 2, Coisl. 98, *fol.* 71.

St. Maximus: 'The soul becomes God by sharing in the divine grace, after it has itself halted all activity of the spirit and of the senses, as well as all the natural *energies* of the body, for the body becomes divine at the same time... Then God alone appears in the soul and in the body...'; and he comments, 'God is invisible to creatures, but is not invisible to himself,' and it is he 'who will see not only through the soul which is in us, but also through our body.' [71] Speaking of the supernatural faculty to see God granted to us by the presence of the Holy Spirit in us, Palamas continues: 'As this faculty has no other means of acting, having quitted all other beings, it becomes itself nothing but light, and grows like that which it sees; it unites with it without mixture, being light. If it looks at itself, it sees the light; if it looks at the object of its vision, that again is light, and if it looks at the means it employs in seeing, that too is light; it is there that there is union; all that is one, so that he who sees can distinguish neither the means, nor the end, nor the essence, but is only conscious of being light, and of seeing a light distinct from any created thing.' [72] The Saints are thus 'transformed by the power of the Spirit; they receive a power which they did not possess before; they become Spirit and see in Spirit.' [73] Here one clearly sees that the Biblical idea that the new birth of baptism gives man power 'to be Spirit' (John 3: 6) fits in perfectly with the 'luminous vision,' which also comes in the Bible, though more commonly used in the mystical vocabulary of the Neo-Platonic tradition. For Palamas, both terminologies refer to a single and unique reality, that of the divine-human union made accessible in Christ. To describe the state of deified man, he, following St. Maximus, refers to the mystical experience of the Apostle Paul (2 Cor. 12: 2ff.): 'The great Paul,' he writes, 'after this extraordinary ecstasy, declares that he did not know what it was. Surely he saw himself. How?... By the spirit that accomplished the ecstasy. But what was he himself...? He was certainly that to which he was united, that through which he knew himself, and that through which he had left all things. ... So Paul was Light and Spirit.' [74] Nonetheless this vision and this deification is never a way of 'possessing' God, of containing him, and submitting him to the laws of creatures: while manifesting himself, he yet dwells in mystery. After speaking of the vision of Moses, Palamas asks: 'Can one then no longer say that the divine is in mystery? Why not? He does not come forth from mystery, but communicates it to

---

[71] *Tr.* I, 3, 37; Maximus, *Cent.* II, 88, P.G. XC, 1168A.
[72] *Tr.* II, 3, 36.
[73] *Against Akindynos,* IV, 16, *Coisl.* 98, *fol.* 109; cf. *Cap. phys.* 75, col. 1173BC.
[74] *Tr.* II, 3, 37.

others, concealing them beneath the divine shade.' [75] 'This,' he writes elsewhere, 'is the most divine and extraordinary fact; the Saints, possessing understanding of God, possess it in an incomprehensible way.' [76]

It is the supernatural character of deifying grace that Palamas wishes to stress; it is the divine way itself, infinite and uncreated, which appears to us, and *really becomes ours*. This divine mystery into which God allows us to penetrate, this union which he makes accessible to us, is the Mystery of the Church, the Body of Christ. There is no other way of 'knowing God in God' but to be grafted by the new birth of baptism on to the Body of the Incarnate Word. The Saints are those 'who are born of God by the Word through grace in the Spirit and who keep the likeness to God, their Father.' They are in truth 'God,' 'since in all birth that which is begotten is identical with the begetter; that which is born of the flesh is flesh, and that which is born of the Spirit is Spirit' (John 3 : 6).[77]

Real deification

Palamas expressed this 'identity with the Father' in striking phrases which shocked his adversaries. However his essential thought is borrowed from St. Maximus : man 'becomes by participation ($\mu\epsilon\theta\acute{\epsilon}\xi\epsilon\iota$) that which the Archetype is as cause' ($\kappa\alpha\tau'$ $\alpha\grave{\iota}\tau\acute{\iota}\alpha\nu$ or $\phi\acute{\upsilon}\sigma\epsilon\iota$) [78]; he becomes 'God by grace' ($\chi\acute{\alpha}\rho\iota\tau\iota$ or $\theta\acute{\epsilon}\sigma\epsilon\iota$).[79] As a result the life of God becomes his life, and God's existence his existence. Hence St. Maximus had written, 'God and the Saints had one and the same *energy*.' Not only did they themselves rejoice in the presence of God, but that presence was manifested to others through them. So deification is not only an individual gift of God, but constitutes a means of manifesting him to the world. 'The Saints participate in God; not only do they participate, but they also communicate him. . . . They not only live, but also bring to life, and that is not the attribute of a created faculty.' [80] In the same way he writes of the divine light that it is 'a gift of deification . . . a grace of the Holy Spirit, a grace by which God alone shines through the intermediary of the soul and body of those who are truly worthy of this.' [81] The true likeness to God consists in making him appear through oneself, and accomplishing the works which are

---

[75] ibid., 56; cf. 66.
[76] *Tr.* I, 3, 17; *Hom.* 14, col. 168B.
[77] *Apology*, Coisl. 99, fol. 13r-v.
[78] *Tr.* I, 3, 39; Maximus, *Opusc. theol. et pol.*, P.G. XCL, 33C; *Amb.*, 1084C, 1345D, etc.
[79] *Tr.* II, 3, 52, 68; *Tr.* III, 1, 25; *Theophanes*, col. 948C, etc.
[80] *On participation to God*, Coisl. 99, fol. 26; *Tr.* III, 1, 33; Maximus, *Opusc.*, 12B, 33A; *Amb.*, 1076BC.
[81] *Against Akindynos*, IV, 22, Coisl. 98, fol. 113.

his. The divine life, which becomes the inheritance of their whole being, does not leave the Saints at the moment of death, but continues to be manifest in their bodies. That is the very foundation of the veneration of relics : 'Glorify the holy tombs of the Saints,' Palamas teaches, 'and, if they are there, the relics of their bones, for the grace of God has not abandoned them, just as the Divinity has not passed from the worshipped Body of Christ after his death which brought life.' [82] Grace is also manifest in their images, as in that of Christ.[83] The Saints are, as it were, the substance which is consumed by the fire of grace; God needs them to manifest himself, as a fire needs fuel to burn brightly.[84] 'The soul united to the light of the heavenly image,' Palamas writes quoting Macarius, 'is initiated from that moment, in its hypostasis, in knowledge of the mysteries; then on the great day of the Resurrection the body too will be illuminated by the same heavenly image of glory.' 'He said, "in its hypostasis," ' Palamas comments, 'lest any one should suppose that that illumination comes from knowledge and from concepts. In other words, the hypostasis of the spiritual man is composed of three parts; the grace of the heavenly Spirit, the rational soul, and the earthly body.' [85] The word 'hypostasis' is clearly used here in a general sense to designate the very existence of man into which grace penetrates. We have seen that Palamas rejected any idea of deification 'by nature' (φύσει) which should make us consubstantial with God; he simply wanted to say that grace becomes the permanent quality of deified man who, as we have seen, contemplates God from within himself. In this way he again avoids Messalian dualism by contrasting the power of Christ, which may become intrinsic to man, with that of the Devil which cannot in any final way attach itself to his being.[86]

'Uncreated by grace'

The miraculous power of the Saints, which in potentiality belongs to all the baptized, is an *uncreated* power, otherwise it would not be divine but only a simple natural manifestation : 'All that which flows from the Spirit towards those who are baptized in him according to the Gospel of grace and who have become spiritual men, still remains attached to its source; from Thence it comes and Therein it dwells in its present and its past existence.' [87] Divine grace is not distinct from God, but is divine life granted to man; that is the basis of Palamas's

[82] *Decalogue*, 1093A.
[83] *ibid..* 1092; *Hom.* 25, col. 325A.
[84] *Tr.* I, 3, 8; III, 1, 20.
[85] *Tr.* I, 3, 43; Macarius, *De libertate mentis*, 23-4, P.G. XXIV, 957B.
[86] *Tr.* I, 2, 1; I, 3, 2; II, 3, 13.
[87] *Letter to Athanasius, Coisl.* 98, *fol.* 12.

teaching about the 'inseparability' of essence and *energies*. It is therefore an uncreated life which man receives in Jesus Christ: 'Those who share in the *energies* and act in conformity with them, are by God made gods without beginning or end through grace.'[88] The idea that deified man becomes 'uncreated through grace' is frequent in Palamas's writings; it constitutes one of the essential proofs of the uncreated character of the *energies*: 'The gifts which lead us to be one single body—the Body of Christ—and one spirit with the Lord (cf. 1 Cor. 6: 15–17) are not created.'[89] In Christ and in the baptized there is *one sole* indivisible Spirit and, in him, all distinction between created and uncreated is inadmissible.

'Concorporality'

Palamas's theological formulas are basically just an expression of the Christocentric and sacramental mysticism which, as we have seen, was the main justification of hesychast spirituality. For this reason the Archbishop of Thessalonica, when preaching about the Mysteries with the Eucharist specially in mind, developed the conception of St. Paul and of the Fathers about the *concorporality* (σύσσωμοι) of Christians with Christ; he does this in language showing a profound intimacy with the writings of the New Testament, and also a true mystical emotion. In calling his flock to communion, he reminds them that 'they must be with Christ not only one Spirit, but also one Body,' that they are 'flesh of his flesh and bone of his bone,' and that 'such is the union that has been granted to us by this Bread.' 'Christ,' he continues, 'has become our brother, by sharing our flesh and blood and so becoming assimilated to us. . . . He has joined and bound us to himself, as a husband his wife, by becoming one single flesh with us through the communion of his blood; he has also become our father by divine baptism which renders us like unto him, and he nourishes us at his own breast as a tender mother nourishes her babies. . . . Come, (Christ) says, eat my Body, drink my Blood . . . so that you be not only made after God's image, but become gods and kings, eternal and heavenly, in me clothing yourselves with me, King and God.'[90]

Participation in the divine nature

It is not by their own efforts that Christians become 'eternal' and 'uncreated'; it is the divine life, which they only possess through grace, which gives them that character. One sees here clearly that the word

---

[88] *Apology*, Coisl. 99, *fol.* 13.
[89] *Against Akindynos*, V, 24, Coisl. 98, *fol.* 142.
[90] *Hom.* 56, ed. Oikonomos, pp. 206–8.

'uncreated' signifies the whole field of the 'supernatural'; so to be 'uncreated' does not mean that one ceases to be a creature, but that one is transported into a different state, and that one gratuitously acquires a condition fundamentally foreign to that of nature, and that condition is the divine life. That is the point Palamas is making every time when, speaking of deification, he makes it clear that men cannot become 'gods' except through grace (θέσει or χάριτι) and not through nature (φύσει). Clearly he was not unmindful of the famous passage in the Second Epistle of Peter (1 : 4): 'Exceeding great promises have been given to us, that you may thus become *participants in the divine nature*' (θείας κοινωνοὶ φύσεως)—and his adversaries did not fail to quote that text against him. But Palamas rightly answers that there is no question of identifying the word 'nature' (φύσις) as used in the New Testament with the Patristic conception of 'nature'; all that the Apostle wished to express was the *reality* of our participation in the *very* life of God; he himself speaks of the promises 'given'; therefore by 'nature' he means sanctifying and deifying grace,[91] and some of the Fathers have occasionally followed his example in this; 'Theologians,' Palamas writes, 'have been accustomed to use the words "nature" and "essence" not only of that anonymous superessentiality which passes beyond all names, but also of the productive power of essence and of all the natural properties of God.'[92]

Palamas's adversaries also often quoted those passages in which he speaks of the Saints as 'uncreated through grace,' and have taken them as proof of his heterodoxy. But, in fact, even in his use of words, Palamas was no innovator; he used phrases of St. Maximus about Melchisedek, become 'without beginning,' and about St. Paul who lived 'by the divine and eternal life of the Word dwelling in him.'[93] In quoting the great seventh century Mystic, Palamas simply wanted to express the full reality of salvation and deification accomplished in Christ; one cannot truly understand his thought without constant reference to the Christological context in which it was expressed. Taken out of context, his phrases are clearly inexact and can give rise to misunderstandings. Moreover we shall see that Palamas often protested against the judgments of his adversaries based on certain verbal expressions which could easily be given an inaccurate interpretation. In any case Palamas's statements about the 'uncreated' character of the Saints did not appear in the Synodal decisions which approved his doctrine as a whole.

[91] *Theophanes*, 933B; cf. V. Lossky, *The Mystical Theology*, London, 1957, pp. 67-8.
[92] *Against Akindynos*, II, 14, *Coisl.* 98, *fol.* 59v.
[93] *Amb.*, *P.G.* XCI, 1144BC; *Cent.* V, 85, *P.G.* XC, 1384D.

The Church

As we have seen, it was by reference to the mystery of the Body of Christ that Palamas justified the bodily method of prayer, and it is also in ecclesiology that he finds the basis for his teaching about deification. It is in the Church that Christ enters into such intimate relations with us that they cover and transcend all human relations, even those that are closest; Jesus is Bridegroom, Brother, Father and Mother . . . The Christian no longer has any life of his own, but acquires that of Christ, the divine and uncreated life. That possesses his whole being, and controls all his activity. Gregory conceives the Church as a real and visible community; in that, as in all else, spiritualizing tendencies are foreign to him. Baptism obliges us to see Christ not in ourselves only, but in our brothers.[94] By carrying Christ within himself each Christian also bears all his brothers; when one does good to a brother, one does it to Christ and to the whole Church, for 'who shall divide those that are one, in accordance with the Master's prayer (John 17 : 21), and united to the one God, by the one Word in the one Spirit?'[95] The teaching which he stresses concerning the Church as a community, following Theoleptus of Philadelphia, turns his teaching towards sacramental realism; it is by taking part in the Sunday Liturgy, and therein sharing in the Holy Mysteries, that man in very fact renews his nature.[96] It is also the community of the Church which is the guardian of revealed truth; God 'wishes that we who have been born in him through grace should remain inseparable from him and from one another. . . . Just as our own tongue, being one of our members, does not tell us that sweet is bitter, or that bitterness is sweet . . . so each one of us, who call ourselves Christians, is a member of the whole Church; therefore we must not proclaim anything that is not the fact, nor recognize it as being true; otherwise a man is a deceiver and an enemy, not a member.'[97]

Its truth

Sin separates us from the Church, and only repentance reconciles us with it; and sin against the truth is the worst of all. Bishops themselves, invested with the *magisterium* of truth, are not exempt from this rule; if they are faithful to tradition and act in accord with the whole Church, and if they dwell in their dioceses, then they dwell in truth. But if they abandon Orthodoxy, then they lose not only their *magisterium*, but their

---

[94] *Hom.* 1, col. 9A–12B; *Hom.* 57, ed. Oikonomos, pp. 217–22.
[95] *Letter to Dionysius, Coisl.* 98, *fol.* 207; *Hom.* 53, ed. Oikonomos, p. 180.
[96] *Decalogue*, 1093C–1096A.
[97] *Hom.* 54, ed. Oikonomos, p. 187.

very status as Christians, and their anathemas have no value.[98] Not bishops only, but whole local churches may stray from the path of truth. Palamas recalls that in the course of history all churches have so strayed, but only the Latin Church has not yet returned to Orthodoxy, 'although it is the greatest and the first, and includes the most exalted of all the patriarchal thrones.'[99] The Church, pillar and foundation of truth, 'nonetheless stands firm and unshaken, resting solidly on those who maintain the truth; and, as a fact, those who belong to the Church of Christ, dwell in the truth, and those who have once for all abandoned truth, have also left the Church.'[100] The miracle of ecclesiastical infallibility is thus realized in the whole ecclesiastical body, that is to say that it finally remains the exclusive privilege of Christ, head of the Church, who, while granting to men the charisms of the Spirit—the Apostolic *magisterium* in particular—of which all may prove unworthy, continues to live and to manifest himself in the whole Body. This Church, the Body of Christ, is not just a sociological or geographical entity, of which only the living form part; it equally includes the Angels and the just of all times. This 'recapitulation' of the whole creation is one of the consequences of the Incarnation.[101]

The Christological problem

Palamas's doctrine of deification led him to pose a Christological problem about which he was in conflict with his adversaries. If the Saints possess 'one single *energy*' with Christ, if they 'become uncreated' and receive the divine life, if their bodies and their souls produce works which, in our Lord's own words, are 'greater' than those which he himself accomplished (John 14: 12), one may ask whether the Saints do not identify themselves entirely with God, and whether their created humanity is not absorbed by the divine life. That is the objection which his adversaries raised against him, though they themselves found no other solution than the participation of man in the divine essence, which, for Palamas, did signify total absorption of the human by the divine. That is a problem in Gregory's theology to which we shall return. For the moment it is enough to state the essential Christological assumptions which determined Palamas's thought about deification.

To defend the nominalist positions which he had inherited from Barlaam, Akindynos had recourse to a Christological argument. How,

---

[98] *Refutation of the Patriarch of Antioch, Coisl.* 99, *fol.* 144; *To Xene,* 1045BC.
[99] *Apodictic Treatise,* II, *Coisl.* 100, *fol.* 34.
[100] *Against Akindynos,* I, 10, *Coisl.* 98, *fol.* 41v.
[101] *Against Gregoras,* II, *Coisl.* 100, *fol.* 244v; III, *fol.* 272.

he asks, can one say that participation in Christ confers an uncreated grace, when the humanity of Jesus—in which we participate—was itself created? To assert the contrary would be Monophysite heresy. For Akindynos, the concept of 'nature' was a static notion, and the uncreated character properly belonging to the divine nature could not, clearly, be communicated even by participation. 'The Lord, One of the Holy Trinity,' he writes in an important Christological passage inspired by the Council of Chalcedon, 'having become man, has preserved inalienable and invisible his own divinity; he did not transform his own nature into ours with which he united, nor did he transform the nature in which he clothed himself into his own, although he deified it; on the contrary, after the union, the one remained uncreated as before, and the other created, and the two together constituted the incarnate Son of God, man and God; but if such a transformation was to take place, should it not have occurred in him? *A fortiori* (in dwelling) in all the others, he preserved the inalienability of his dignity; and just as, being incorruptible, he could submit himself to corruption . . . so, when he lets himself be seen by the bodily eyes of the holy contemplatives . . . he takes on a certain aspect of such visible (created) beings.' [102] This exposition, though verbally accurate, is however incomplete in so far as it does not take into account the 'communication of the idioms' as defined by Leontius of Byzantium and St. Maximus the Confessor, and in that it does not allow any real content to the two references it makes to that communication, 'although he deified it' and 'both together constitute the Son of God.' But the very basis of Palamas's conception of deification was formed from the doctrine of St. Cyril of Alexandria concerning the 'appropriation' of the flesh by the Son of God, and from the ideas of St. Maximus about the 'communication of idioms.' On the other hand Barlaam's, and the other fourteenth century humanists' nominalist thought led to a return towards Nestorianism: humanity and divinity, inalienable natures impermeable one by the other, are in a purely external relation of juxtaposition; deification and grace are created entities, for that reason essentially different from the divine nature, and belonging to the domain of symbols; the participation in God through essence which they sometimes allowed in order to answer Palamas's arguments, leads them on the other hand necessarily to Monophysitism. So it is the Orthodox position, situated at an equal distance away from the two main Christological heresies, that Palamas studies to defend, expressing this doctrine in terms which are almost always borrowed from St. Maximus the Confessor.

[102] *Against Palamas*, II, *Monac. gr.* 223, *fol.* 163-163v.

There are two main points which he stresses:
1. Humanity and divinity are *united in the hypostasis* of Christ, Son of God.
2. Sanctifying and deifying grace does really reach us by virtue of the 'communication of idioms' starting from the *humanity* of Christ, 'source of deification,' and not only from his divinity.

Hypostatic union and divine energies

The 'hypostatic union' of divinity and humanity in Jesus Christ is the very foundation of salvation, and therefore of deification: in Christ, humanity has already participated in the uncreated life of God, because the 'flesh' has truly become 'the flesh of God.' Akindynos, 'in wishing to show that deification is something created,' 'has dared to cite as an example the deification of (the humanity) put on by the Master and to declare that it too was created.'[103] Did not the life of that humanity of Christ come from the hypostasis of the Son to which it belonged *as his own*? That is the whole argument of St. Cyril against Nestorius: 'The Son of God,' Palamas writes, '*is one* with the humanity which he put on, for in his hypostasis he is united with the firstfruits of humanity; that is why we apply to him appellations which derive from humanity, and he grants his appellations to humanity: however, he is not one with every man who receives grace, as he is one with his own humanity: with each (Christian) he is united through *energy* and by grace, and not by the hypostasis; that is why there is only one Christ, because there is only one sole and indivisible hypostasis of the Word of God....'[104] It is therefore the *life of the Word* which deifies the human nature of Christ, and it is *that very life* which, in Christ, is accessible to us, for otherwise our salvation would not have been realized. 'What connection should we have with Christ, if he had made a temple in the firstfruits taken from men, without making us temples of his divinity?'[105] 'God in his completeness was incarnate, even though all the divine hypostases were not incarnate; he has united one of the three hypostases with our "mixture" ($\tau\tilde{\omega}$ $\dot{\eta}\mu\epsilon\tau\dot{\epsilon}\rho\omega$ $\varphi\nu\rho\dot{\alpha}\mu\alpha\tau\iota$), not through essence, but by the hypostasis; thus God in his completeness deifies those who are worthy of this, by uniting himself with them not through the hypostasis—that belonged to Christ alone—nor through the essence, but through a small part of the uncreated *energies* and the uncreated divinity ... while yet being entirely present in each.'[106]

[103] *Letter to Athanasius, Coisl.* 98, *fol.* 13.
[104] *Against Akindynos*, III, 6, *Coisl.* 98, *fol.* 73v; cf. *Tr.* II, 3, 21.
[105] *Against Akindynos*, ibid., *fol.* 74v.
[106] ibid., V, 26, *fol.* 145v.

Palamas indignantly rejects the imputation that he had said that the *humanity* of Christ was uncreated; that would be to disregard the difference between hypostatic union and essential union; the latter assumes a 'mixture' ($\varphi\upsilon\rho\mu\acute{o}\nu$) of the two natures in Christ, and the participation of all in the essence of the divinity: 'If the deifying gift, the deification accorded to the saints ... is the divine essence and hypostasis, all the Saints are equal to Christ,' and the deity becomes 'polyhypostatic' ($\mu\upsilon\rho\iota\upsilon\pi\acute{o}\sigma\tau\alpha\tau\sigma\varsigma$).[107] Thus, the humanity proper to Christ 'became heavenly not by nature but by dignity, and because of its hypostatic union with the Word of God.'[108] So, in Palamite terminology, we have here a clear distinction between the concepts of 'essential union,' 'hypostatic union' and union through the *energies;* for him, these three modes of union are simply established on traditional Chalcedonian and post-Chalcedonian Christology, and on the doctrine of the *communication of idioms*.

The 'Body of God'

Though Christ alone united *in his hypostasis* divinity and humanity, he communicates to all Christians the *divine energy*—in other words, sanctifying grace—of which he is the source. This he can do in that he has made himself like to men by making *his* their whole nature; therefore it is as Son of God become man that he communicates the divine life. Palamas expresses that soteriological reality in his mystical doctrine of the Body of Christ which, because it is truly the 'Body of God,' can communicate the divine life: 'The Lord, even as man, had received and possessed the divine *energy* and grace.'[109] His deified flesh had received and communicates the eternal glory of the Deity; that is what is represented on the Icons and worshipped in so far as it manifests the Divinity of Christ,[110] and it is that too which is offered to us in the sacrament of the Eucharist. 'This bread,' Palamas writes, 'is as a veil between us and the mystery of Divinity (Heb. 10 : 20), and by this flesh our community is raised to heaven; that is where this Bread truly dwells (cf. John 6 : 36ff.); and we enter into the Holy of Holies by the pure offering of the Body of Christ.'[111]

So Palamas's doctrine of deification is only one aspect of his christology and ecclesiology. It avoids the snags on which the Messalians —the Pelagians of the East—struck, and those other snags on which the humanists were wrecked. While uniting himself fully with man,

---
[107] *Against Gregoras*, IV, *Coisl.* 100, *fol.* 285; *Theophanes*, 941A.
[108] *Against Akindynos*, III, 5, *Coisl.* 98, *fol.* 72v.
[109] ibid., III, 7, *fol.* 75.
[110] *Decalogue*, 1092.
[111] *Hom.* 56, ed. Oikonomos, p. 205.

God remained inapproachable in his essence; the union of the two *natures* without mixture is only accomplished in the hypostasis of the Son of God become man; but, by grafting themselves sacramentally on to his Person, men can participate in the divine life in a way that is both real and distinct from the union of essences; essential union would make them 'equal to Christ,' multiply indefinitely the number of the divine hypostases, abolish all distance between the Creator and created beings, transform a voluntary act (ἐνέργεια) of the living God into the inevitable property of an impersonal essence, and finally absorb all activity proper to man in the divine Absolute.

CHAPTER IV

A THEOLOGY OF HISTORY: SYMBOLS AND REALITIES

Linear time and cyclical time
We have seen already that Palamas's thought concerning man was based on a doctrine sharply opposed to Platonic dualism; for him, supernatural life was accessible to the whole man; such life entailed the re-establishment of the original hierarchy with the spirit exercising sovereignty over the flesh, but it was not a disincarnation. This doctrine concerning man which Palamas defended, was in fact Biblical and closely linked with the scriptural conception of history and of time. 'We must start from the fundamental truth,' O. Cullmann writes, 'that for primitive Christianity, as for Judaism and the Persian religion, the symbol representing time is an *ascending line,* whereas for Hellenism it is a *circle.* . . . The Greeks could not conceive that deliverance could result from a divine act accomplished in temporal history. For them, deliverance depends on passing from our existence here below, linked to the circle of time, into the beyond, which is exempt from time and always accessible. So for the Greeks felicity is represented in spatial terms of contrast between 'here-below' and 'there-beyond'; time, and the contrast between present and future, do not come into the picture. . . . Contrariwise, in primitive Christian preaching the conception of salvation is strictly temporal and fits in with a linear conception of time such as we find in the Bible.'[1] This Biblical conception of time underlies all Palamas's thought, not forgetting that, for him, the eschatalogical *future* stands for an *already present* reality, fully anticipated in the Church and, therefore, in the spiritual experience of Christians.

The intervention of God in history
In returning to the fundamental principles of Classical philosophy, Palamas's adversaries, the Byzantine humanists, had adopted, in part at least, the Greek conception of a closed universe. The Incarnation did not have any real place in this scheme of thought, and they tended to interpret its consequences—the sacraments of the Church and knowledge of God—in a *symbolical sense.* As we shall see, they found some arguments in favour of this thesis in the thought of one whom Palamas

[1] *Christ et le temps,* Neuchatel, Paris, 1947, p. 36–7.

himself could not fail to call 'the Great Dionysius.' The whole of Palamas's teaching, however, was dominated by the essential affirmation of the intervention of God in history through the Incarnation of his Son; it was therefore no longer possible, after that, to speak in any absolute way of the 'unknowability' of God and one was forced to take into account the *change* which God himself has brought into his relations with man by revealing himself to him by an act of his almighty power. It was that fundamental change which the 'philosopher' Barlaam rejected by limiting knowledge of God only to indirect comprehension 'through created things'; 'the philosopher,' Palamas writes in this context 'has taught us . . . that he considers knowledge coming from created things as the most perfect vision of God, saying that all men possess this in superabundance if they know all the visible parts of the world and all the secret powers.' Therefore it is enough for man to deepen his 'scientific' knowledge of created things to see God. Hence this vision depends on simple human effort and is not due to grace: 'but we have all known the Son through the Voice of the Father who has announced this teaching to us from on high (Matt. 3: 16–17) and the Holy Spirit itself, the indescribable light itself, has shown us that here assuredly is the Beloved one of the Father; and the Son himself has manifested to use the name of his Father and has promised, ascending to Heaven, to send down to us the Holy Spirit that it may dwell with us for ever (John 14: 16); and the Holy Spirit itself has descended and dwelt in us, and has announced and taught us the whole truth (cf. John 16: 30).' [2] 'If deification,' Palamas writes elsewhere, 'is only a state of our rational nature . . . Christ, coming into the world, has not given the power to become children of God to those only who believe in his name (John 1: 12). Hence Deification would belong as of right to all peoples even before his coming.' [3] 'Before the incarnation of the Word of God,' he proclaims in his *Physical Chapters*, 'the Kingdom of Heaven was as far from us as the sky is from the earth (cf. Psalm 103: 11); but when the King of Heaven came to dwell amongst us, when he was pleased to unite himself with us, then the Kingdom of Heaven came close to all of us.' [4] To say, after the Incarnation, that God remains unknown to man, or to say that his acts do not put us in contact with the very reality of his uncreated life, is to abolish the Christian mystery, 'to reject the Kingdom which then, on the day of the Transfiguration, came down in power according to the word of the Lord' (Mark 9: 1).[5]

[2] *Tr.* II, 3, 67.
[3] *Tr.* III, 1, 30.
[4] *Cap. phys.* 56, col. 1161C.
[5] *Against Akindynos*, II, 15, *Coisl.* 98, *fol.* 61.

Barlaam's symbolism

This Christian reality founded on a historical fact which overthrew the natural condition of knowledge of God, is Palamas's essential argument against the nominalism of his adversary. We have seen above that the controversy with Barlaam originated from the latter's unreadiness to accept any supernatural conception of knowledge of God; such knowledge, in his view, could not be fundamentally distinct from the natural *intellection* of beings. As a result, to know God, man must contemplate the creation and, by the path of deduction, reach the First Cause; but Barlaam and his disciples could not have long passed as true Orthodox at Byzantium, if they had not admitted that the coming of Christ and the reality of the Church had furnished new means of knowledge; so they freely recognized that the sacraments of the Church, the mystical experience of the saints, and the miraculous theophanies connected with the Incarnation, had put us in contact with divine realities, but *only as intelligible symbols*. They could, moreover, refer, specially as concerning the Eucharist, to the authority of the Pseudo-Dionysius. who also had 'gone beyond the horizons of sacramental realism and made of this very realism the symbol of the intelligible union which it should arouse and promote.' [6] Barlaam, though he seems never to have tackled the question of the sacraments directly, held firmly to the Platonic conception that the faculty of imagination (τὸ φανταστικόν) was the only possible link between the divine and the body,[7] and that union with God could not, in the last resort, be anything but *intellective* or symbolical. So the light which the disciples saw on Tabor would be 'a light sensible and visible through the intermediary of the air, which then appeared to arouse their astonishment and immediately vanished, and which one calls divine in that it was a symbol of divinity' [8]; if one rejects that too material interpretation, Barlaam sees no other possibility but to consider the light as 'imaginary' (φανταστόν) and in that event it would have been a vision inferior to *intellection* (χείρων νοήσεως). Barlaam saw in the liturgy of the church no more than a symbolical means of acceding to the 'immaterial archetypes.' [9] In all this Barlaam was a disciple of the Pseudo-Dionysius, whom he quotes abundantly, and when Palamas reproaches him for borrowing his symbolism from 'Hellenic sciences,' he was really complaining about the Areopagite himself. We shall see later in what sense Palamas was prepared to use the word 'symbol' and to apply it to Christian realities.

---

[6] R. Roques, *L'univers dionysien*, p. 270.
[7] *Epist.* IV, ed. Schirò, p. 315.
[8] *Against the Messalians*, quoted by Palamas in *Tr.* III, 1, 10.
[9] cf. texts of Barlaam quoted in *Tr.* II, 3, 61; I, 3, 6; II, 1, 6, 58.

Shadows and 'bodily types'

The later anti-Palamites, Akindynos and Nicephorus Gregoras, adopted Barlaam's symbolism. For Akindynos, every vision of the Apostles and of the Prophets was necessarily symbolical; Angels themselves, in the Old Testament and in the New, could only be seen symbolically; as to the visions of God of which the Gospel speaks, they could only have taken place through a bodily intermediary, in the form of a symbolical type or apparition such as fire, light, cloud or a dove. These symbols and types, are manifestly created, Akindynos asserted, and Palamas and his disciples were adoring created things.[10] The same ideas appear in Nicephorus Gregoras's writings: 'This is a universal dogma of the Church,' he writes, 'which we have received from our God and Saviour Jesus Christ and his disciples: it is absolutely impossible to see God except through the intermediary of symbols and bodily types.' The light on Tabor was, in his view, 'a typological and symbolical apparition of the uncreated Divinity.' The vision face to face could only be glimpsed as a shadow or as an enigmatic promise.[11]

We have only dwelt on these anti-Palamite quotations, whose number could easily be multiplied, to bring out the danger which Byzantine Christianity ran from nominalist theology; its influence was at that time brought to bear on the most diverse aspects of religious and intellectual life. In the field of art, as in that of religious thought, there developed a taste for symbolism which, though it was one of the essential features of the 'Renaissance of the Palaeologi,' nonetheless undermined the traditional—and realist—doctrine concerning holy images; the council *in Trullo* (Canon 82) had formerly forbidden the representation of Christ in the form of a lamb; Christians, it had proclaimed, have no need since the Incarnation for symbols and 'shadows,' as the Reality itself has appeared to them; but symbolism flourished to such an extent in Byzantine art of the thirteenth and fourteenth centuries that one cannot fail to see this as a result of the humanist Renaissance.[12] There were some theologians who pressed to their ultimate conclusions the premises laid down by the Pseudo-Dionysius, and ended by writing whole treatises to demonstrate the purely symbolical character of the Eucharist.[13] So this was a movement very like that stirred up in the West by the thought of William of Ockham, one of the results of which was the Protestant Reformation.

[10] *Against Palamas*, II, *Monac. gr.* 223, *fol.* 107; IV, *fol.* 108, 109, 183, 185, etc.
[11] *Hist.* XXVIII, P.G. CXLIX, 357AB, 373C, 377BC, 381B.
[12] cf. our article *La Sagesse divine dans l'art de tradition byzantine* in *Cahiers archéologiques*, X, 1959.
[13] This is the case of Theophanes of Nicea whose works are preserved in Paris gr. 1249.

The Pseudo-Dionysius

This was the type of thought that Palamas opposed, refusing to conceive divine-human relations, after the Incarnation, in the framework of a dualistic universe, in which there was a 'there-beyond' which remained 'spatially' unapproachable from a material 'here-below,' and which could only reveal itself below through the intermediary of created symbols. However Palamas was constantly stumbling on quotations from the Pseudo-Dionysius which his adversaries brought up against him. . . . He himself made constant use of the Areopagite, applying, as St. Maximus had done, a Christocentric corrective to his thought; nonetheless he came into such clear opposition to Dionysius that he had to resort to a forced and artificial exegesis of his thought, in order to avoid a direct attack on so venerable an authority: actually Palamas's Christological corrective completely changes the structure of Dionysius's thought. That is especially the case in his doctrine of hierarchies.[14] One knows that for Dionysius the order of the hierarchies constituted a necessary and universal intermediary for the transmission of the divine outpouring (πρόοδος)[15]; 'Jesus himself, the supernatural Cause of the essences that dwell beyond the sky, having condescended without change in his own nature to take on our human form, in no way abolished the excellent order which he himself had instituted and chosen for the human race, but quietly submitted himself to the forms transmitted by the Angels from God the Father'; as examples of this 'submission,' Dionysius quotes the apparitions of the Archangel Gabriel to Zacharias, to the Virgin Mary and to Joseph, to prove by this that 'the Angels first received initiation into the divine mystery of the love of Jesus for men.'[16] So the Incarnation left the hierarchic universe perfectly intangible, and granted no immediate communion with divine life, but only established an 'ecclesiastical' hierarchy, image of the 'celestial' hierarchy, Christ being *in different capacities* the head of both—there as God, here as man.

A single quotation from Palamas is enough to show that he differs from Dionysius on just the point indicated by O. Cullmann; for Dionysius's closed and 'anagogic' universe he substitutes a theology of history. Dionysius's hierarchies are retained—for Palamas could not dismiss the views of one whom he, and all his contemporaries, considered as a disciple of St. Paul and one of the greatest Fathers of the Church—but only in the natural order, Christ having brought *immediate*

---

[14] cf. J. Meyendorff, *Notes sur l'influence dionysienne en Orient*, in *Studia Patristica*, II (*Texte und Untersuchungen*, 64), Berlin, 1957, p. 550-2.
[15] R. Roques, op. cit., pp. 101-11.
[16] *Celestial Hierarchy*, IV, 4, *P.G.* III, 181C; cf. R. Roques, op. cit., pp. 319-29.

vision of God. Answering Barlaam who relied on Dionysius, Palamas writes, 'If by the Spirit, in the light of the Father, we see the Son as light, an immediate union with God, and a gift of the light which comes from him are accessible to us, and this does not depend on the mediation of Angels, even though the philosopher Barlaam does not agree and thinks that his view was taught by the great Dionysius . . .' There follows a rather arbitrary exegesis of the Areopagite's thought, which takes away the universal character from his *Celestial Hierarchy*: 'In disclosing the origin of the names of Angels,' Palamas writes, 'Dionysius tells us that many visions appear to us through their mediation, but he does not say that *all* those that manifest themselves, and *all* union, and *all* glory come through them.' After quoting passages in which Dionysius mentions illuminations without specifically referring to the hierarchies, he cites the case of Mary 'who was told by an Angel of the manner in which she should conceive God and give him birth according to the flesh,[17] but it was not the mediation of an Angel which realized the union of God with her.' Finally Palamas draws this conclusion, which in fact contradicts Dionysius, especially in the case of Gabriel: 'The Lord of Lords is not subject to the laws of creation. That is why, according to the holy traditions, Gabriel, first and alone, was initiated into the inexpressible condescension of the Word, although he did not belong to the first rank of Angels in the immediate presence of God. It must therefore be that the beginning of the new creation was itself new, for he who in his condescension came down to us (Phil. 2 : 7) has made all things new (Rev. 21 : 5). That is why, when he ascended to Heaven, as St. Cyril says, it was the Angels of lower rank nearer to the world, who were sent to bring illumination and initiation to the superior hosts; it was the lower Angels who ordained and revealed to their chiefs the necessity to lift up the eternal gates (Psalm 24 : 7), that he might enter and rise to be enthroned above all principalities and dominions (Eph. 1 : 21), he who put on the flesh in his ineffable love for men. For he is the Lord of powers, and the King of glory (Psalm 24 : 10) who possesses all power, even that of raising the last above the first when he so desires. But after the apparition of God in the flesh, nothing of such sort was taught us by Angels, nor by the Prophets, except for those who by anticipation described the grace to come; *and now that it has appeared, there is no more need that it should be accomplished by intermediaries.* And this we find in the great Paul too: "Now the manifold wisdom of God has been revealed through the Church to principalities and dominions" (Eph. 3 : 10). And in St. Peter, the leader of the band of the Apostles: "By those who

---

[17] *Celestial Hierarchy,* IV, 4, col. 181.

preached the Gospel in the Holy Spirit sent from heaven, these things have been announced to us which the Angels desire to see" (1 Peter 1 : 12). *The least having thus become greatest* by the action of grace, good order is re-established to remain intangible and wonderful.' [18]

Vision face to face

Here we see the true meaning of that superiority of men over Angels, to which we referred earlier; the hierarchies of Angels are neither the objects of nor the chief actors in the economy of salvation; they were created to serve man,[19] and occupy *a secondary position in the Biblical theology of history*. In fact Palamas, without being fully conscious of the Neo-Platonic character of Dionysius's system, has relegated it to the station appropriate to profane philosophy in Christian thought, that is to say to the domain of nature; but that domain, he asserts, was utterly overthrown by the intervention of a *historical* and *essentially new* fact, the Incarnation of the Word. In the natural order of things Angels are superior to men,[20] but the Incarnation reverses that order and raises humanity above the skies. Contrary to Dionysius, who considers that the hierarchies of Angels, though in continual progress towards a more perfect illumination, have attained purity,[21] Palamas asserts that they lack such absolute purity, whereas it has been granted in Christ to man. 'Heaven itself, that is to say the Angels therein, is not pure in the face of the God of heaven, for, being in a process of eternal purification and illumination through the fact of the sublime and mighty hierarchy, it does not yet possess the absolute purity of that hierarchy. Whereas our nature in Christ, *God-hypostasized* and absolutely like to God (θεοϋπόστατός τε οὖσα καὶ ὁμόθεος ὑπερτελῆ), acquires purity and receives, so to say, all the glory, all the light, power and energy of the divine Spirit.' [22] So we see that, for Palamas, deification is always a grace, granted in full freedom by the almighty power of a living God, and not a divine emanation linked to the place in creation occupied by created beings in a pre-established hierarchy; it is in Jesus Christ, by a historic act, that this grace has been granted, and the economy of history takes precedence over the natural order of the universe in which Dionysius's categories remain acceptable. 'If the Emperor wanted to give a soldier the honour of speaking to him personally,' Palamas writes, 'the latter would not immediately become a general, and because at that moment this soldier was the man nearest the Emperor, he would

---

[18] *Tr.* II, 3, 28–30.
[19] *Hom.* 3, col. 33BC.
[20] *Cap. phys.* 43, col. 1152B.
[21] R. Roques, op. cit., pp. 164–6.
[22] *Hom.* 62, ed. Oikonomos, p. 252.

not assume the dignity of commander-in-chief.'[23] But Barlaam continued to rely on Dionysius, and to assert the intangible character of the hierarchy: 'Man cannot meet God,' he wrote in his treatise *Against the Messalians*, 'except by the mediation of an Angel, for we are subject to the Angelic hierarchy.' 'What doest thou, man?' Palamas answers. 'Dost thou make subject to necessities the Master of necessities, who can abolish them, when he wishes, and sometimes transforms them utterly? Tell me, who was the Angel who said to Moses, "I am that I am, the God of Abraham, of Isaac, and of Jacob" (Exod. 3 : 6), if not the Son of God, as the great Basil told us?[24] What is the meaning of the words written in the book of the *Exodus* of Israel : "The Lord spoke to Moses face to face, as a man speaketh unto his friend" (Exod. 33 : 11)? And he who spoke to Abraham and swore by himself (Gen. 22 : 16), if he was but an Angel, how could the Apostle say that he could not swear by any one greater than himself (Heb. 6 : 13)? But if God has been pleased himself to speak to the Fathers in the shadow of the Law, how should he not manifest himself through himself to the Saints now that the truth has appeared, and the law of grace is manifest, that Law by which the Lord himself, and no Angel and no man, has saved us (Isa. 63 : 9), and the very Spirit of God has taught us the truth (John 16 : 13)? Has he not borne for us the cross and death, while we were yet unbelievers (Rom. 5 : 6) according to the Apostle? Would he not deign to make his dwelling in man, to appear to him, and to speak to him without intermediary, now that this man has become not only believing, but sanctified, purified in anticipation, in his body and in his spirit, by keeping the divine commandments, and being thus transformed into a vehicle and an instrument suitable to receive the almighty Spirit?'[25]

Typology of historical realities

A realistic explanation of the words of the Bible is clearly the main inspiration for Palamas, and the hierarchic universe of Dionysius has practically no place in his conception of the Church, the Body of Christ and 'place' of deification.

In the long passage we have just quoted one can already see the importance attached by Palamas to the theology of the Biblical account of salvation as it is found in the Greek Fathers. The theophanies of the Old Testament are interpreted as apparitions of the *Son of God;* they, therefore, all anticipate his Incarnation, and have no other end but to

---

[23] *Tr.* III, 3, 5.
[24] *Contra Eunom.* II, 18, *P.G.* XXIX, 609B.
[25] *Tr.* III, 3, 5.

prepare for it. The Old Testament preparation for the Gospel is one of the favourite themes of Gregory's sermons; *Homily 11*, for instance, gives us a whole series of typological similes of the cross taken from the traditional Patristic exegesis. Salvation is thus conceived in a temporal perspective, and the realist interpretation of the Theophanies —true apparitions of God himself—does not contradict the equally Scriptural assertion mentioned before, according to which contact with God, before the coming of Christ, was realized through the mediation of Angels; for Palamas, the Theophanies themselves were only extraordinary means of preparing for a future act, the Incarnation, and manifested the One who was to come, the Son of God.

The Incarnation, at the centre of the divine economy and of all history, determines the Palamite conception of the spiritual life. We have seen that Gregory regarded it as the essential justification of the hesychast method of prayer; for him the whole of Christian spirituality takes its bearings from the *history* of salvation; what the Christian seeks in spiritual life is not a spatial or material 'beyond,' but a *future,* the Kingdom of God, already present in the sacramental mystery. Christ himself, by his Resurrection, has become 'the firstfruits of those that were asleep' (1 Cor. 15 : 20, 23) and 'Father of the time to come'; thus he has let us enter into the new time, of which the 'paschal time' of the Liturgy is a symbol; this time is dominated by the essentially eschatological number 8, whereas the present time, that of the Creation, is under the sign of the number 7 (ἑβδοματικὸς γάρ ἐστιν ὁ αἰὼν οὗτος).[26] Baptism, by which we share in the Resurrection, is therefore also 'firstfruits of the blessedness to come'[27]; its significance is essentially eschatological, as 'the resurrection of the soul' which it accords to us, is only an anticipation of the bodily resurrection in the time to come.[28] The Christ whom the hesychast seeks and finds within himself is thus the King of the future, and the divine light which he sees is the 'light of the time to come'; all Christian spirituality can have no other foundation but this eschatological reality, anticipated in the sacraments, and progressively assimilated in the spiritual life.

Eschatology

This eschatological meaning is one of the keys which enable us to see the inner link between the various aspects of Palamas's thought. One might, for instance, ask why those who claimed to see God within themselves should see him in the shape of light, and why they likened that

[26] *Hom.* 19, col. 219; the symbolism of members goes back to Basil, *On the Holy Spirit,* 27, *P.G.* XXXII, 192AB.
[27] *Hom.* 16, col. 216A.
[28] *Tr.* II, 3, 4.

light to a particular Theophany, that on Mount Tabor. Palamas gives that question an exact answer; on Tabor, and in the hearts of the Saints, appeared an *identical* reality, the Kingdom of God, and that is the *unique* wealth to which Christians aspire. This eschatological interpretation of the Transfiguration is traditional in Patristic literature, and from the purely Biblical point of view it is correct. As for the luminous vision with which the Saints are blessed, it is enough to quote some passages at random from Palamas to show that that too was a reality no different from the 'firstfruits of resurrection' which all Christians receive at baptism.

For instance in the second *Triad* he writes : 'That supernatural knowledge is common to all who have believed in Christ'; and, when he has pointed out the link between this supernatural knowledge and the sanctifying grace of Christ in glory, he goes on : 'It is in the glory of the Father that Christ will come and . . . the just will shine as the sun (Matt. 13 : 43); they will be light and will see the light, a delightful and holy sight belonging only to the purified heart; this light now shines in part, as an earnest for those who, by impassivity, have passed beyond all that is accursed and, by pure and immaterial prayer, all that is impure; but on that day it will, in manifest fashion, deify the children of the resurrection (Luke 20 : 36), who will enjoy eternity and glory, in communion with him who has given to our nature divine glory and brilliance.' [29] 'Is it not clear,' he writes elsewhere, 'that the divine light is always one and the same, whether it be that which the Apostles saw on Tabor, or that which purified spirits now see, or that of the very reality of eternal blessedness to come? That is why the great Basil called the light which blazed on Tabor at the Transfiguration of our Lord, a prelude to the glory of Christ in his second coming.' [30]

The passages in which Palamas speaks of the eschatological nature of the light are extremely numerous. They leave no doubt about his thought and his eschatological view of spirituality. This throws much light on his argument with Barlaam and his disciples; for Palamas, it was a question of knowing whether the Kingdom of God was already present in the Church, whether the New Alliance was really different from the Old, and whether the present period in the history of salvation, inaugurated by the Resurrection of Christ, was indeed the Reign of Christ, a Reign hidden under sacramental veils but true and fully real for believers. To use a modern theological vocabulary, Palamas was defending a *realized eschatology* against the attempts of nominalist thought to relegate the reality even of the Incarnation to the future

---

[29] *Tr.* II, 3, 66.
[30] *Tr.* I, 3, 43; Basil, *In Ps.* XLIV, P.G. XXIX, 400CD.

only, and to deny its efficacity in the present. Palamas's insistence on the importance of the sacramental life, his realism concerning the Eucharist, his doctrine of sanctifying grace affecting the whole man, soul and body, thereby anticipating the bodily resurrection on the Last Day, are only different aspects of a realist and Biblical conception of Christianity. In some ways the crux of the controversy between him and his adversaries was similar to that which opposed Reformers and Counter-Reformers from the sixteenth century onwards in the West. The essential difference is that, in the East, the defenders of sacramental realism were unaware of the philosophical categories inherited from scholasticism, and only used traditional Biblical and Patristic formulas to counter their adversaries.

Palamas opposed the symbolism of his adversaries by maintaining the essential identity between the spiritual experience of the hesychasts and eschatological reality. He was in no doubt that a nominalist conception of *present* spiritual realities implied an equally nominalist attitude to *future* realities, for the life of the Church and the Christian experience *consist* in a veiled but real anticipation here below of the Kingdom of God. Palamas's objection to symbolism is fundamentally linked to his theology of history.

Beyond symbolism

The categories of symbolism can be applied to the Old Testament,[31] though even then certain isolated elect, such as Moses, did perceive the divine light itself in its reality and without symbolical intermediaries. Thus the Mosaic tabernacle was a symbol and 'showed by anticipation' that the 'hypostasized power of God would one day permit itself to be lodged in a tabernacle, and that the superessential and formless Word would attach itself to a form and to an essence. . . . These visible symbols, the tabernacle and all the attributes of the tabernacle, the priesthood and all pertaining thereto, were veils covering the visions seen by Moses through the darkness, but these visions themselves were not symbols.'[32] Now, after the Incarnation, that 'supernatural knowledge' with which of old only Moses was blessed 'is common to all those who have believed in Christ,'[33] on condition, clearly, that they cultivate the fruits of their baptism by 'the practice of the commandments' and prayer. Christ is really present in them, and is accessible without symbolical intermediaries; just as all the Theophanies of the Old Testament announced the coming of Christ,

[31] *Tr.* I, 3, 6; II, 3, 70.
[32] *Tr.* II, 3, 55.
[33] ibid., 66.

and now, when he was already come, his real, and not symbolical, presence anticipates his eschatological Kingdom, with which it is identical, for there is only one Christ. 'For us,' Palamas writes, 'God in his future Kingdom will replace all things, according to the words of the Apostles and the Fathers (cf. Col. 3: 11). . . . How should we still have symbols of this sort, still mirrors, still enigmas, and how could the vision face to face still remain a hope for the future? Or rather, if there are still symbols here below, mirrors and enigmas—oh ruse and betrayal—we have been deceived in our hopes and fooled by sophisms; thinking that the promise would lead us to acquire Divinity, we do not accede even to the vision of Divinity.' [34] Throughout his works Palamas protests against a symbolical interpretation of the light on Tabor and of Christian experience, for such symbolism seemed to him both a negation of the Incarnation and a rejection of the eschatological Kingdom, 'of the foundation and beauty of the age to come.' [35] The Theophanies might have been symbolical, but not the Incarnation; it was thus that the Holy Spirit appeared, but was not incarnate; the dove which manifested it was a symbol, but 'the body of Christ is truly Body of God and not a symbol.' [36] Palamas fights the symbolical interpretation of Scripture advanced by his adversaries. 'What then?' he asks about the Transfiguration which Akindynos regarded as a symbolical apparition, 'neither Elijah nor Moses were really there, as they too served as symbols . . . and the mountain was not really a mountain, because it also was a symbol of elevation in virtue . . . ? Moreover symbolism was known to Greek philosophers: in what is Christian knowledge different from theirs?' [37]

Realistic symbolism

But in a particular sense, and following St. Maximus, Palamas does allow the word 'symbol' to be applied to the light on Tabor; just as the apparitions of God in the Old Testament were symbols and types of the Theophany on Tabor, so 'the brilliance which blazed from the Saviour on the mountain is a prelude and a symbol of the glory of God which must be revealed in the future.' [38] So symbolism is admissible when it has its place in the history of salvation, and does not deprive it of its Christocentric meaning. For instance, Palamas does not refuse to

---

[34] *Tr.* III, *1*, 11; inspired by Chrysostom, *Ad. Theod. lapsum*, I, 11, P.G. XLVII, 292.
[35] *Tr.* II, 3, 38, etc.
[36] *Against Akindynos*, VII, 15, *Coisl.* 98, *fol.* 195v–196; cf. *Letter to Athanasius*, ibid., *fol.* 7.
[37] *Against Akindynos*, IV, 5, 18, *Coisl.* 98, *fol.* 100v, 110v.
[38] ibid., V, 8, *fol.* 123v.

interpret historical facts symbolically, if to do so seems useful as an aid to 'contemplation,' provided that these facts fully preserve their original meaning and place in history. Certain expressions of St. Maximus the Confessor were hotly debated between Palamas and his adversaries: 'In an analogical and spiritual Theophany,' he writes in this context, 'objects having an existence of their own become also symbols by *homonymy*'; it is in this sense that Maximus calls this light a 'symbol'; that is why he overtly gave his treatises the title of 'contemplation.' [39] He makes 'Moses the symbol of judgment, and Elijah of foresight! [40] Were those men therefore not really present, and had they too been devised symbolically? And Peter . . . could he not become a symbol of faith, James of hope, and John of love? . . .' [41] In such a passage one sees Palamas's remarkable and characteristic power of making distinctions; while allowing all the authority which tradition ascribed to St. Maximus, he places some aspects of his thought in their true context; allegory and symbol, inevitable in some types of reasoning, could never purely and simply replace the Gospel story. Elsewhere in the *Triads* he comes back to the symbolism of Maximus, especially a passage concerned with 'the Body of the Master, raised on the cross, become a symbol of our body nailed to the passions,' and another concerning the light on Tabor being 'a symbol of cataphatic and apophatic theologies' [42]; he notes that Barlaam used these passages as a pretext to affirm that the luminous vision itself was no more than 'a hallucination and a simulacrum.' To get out of this difficulty Palamas distinguishes several types of symbol; he finds three [43]:

1. The natural symbol ($\sigma\acute{\nu}\mu\beta o\lambda o\nu\ \phi\nu\sigma\iota\kappa\acute{o}\nu$) which 'derives from the nature of the object of which it is a symbol': heat for example 'is the natural symbol of the caustic power of fire,' or, in other words, its natural attribute.

2. The symbol which has its own existence, but signifies a nature different from its own and which 'nothing prevents from existing before and after' the thing it signifies; Palamas gives as an example the fires of an army ready to attack, which clearly only signify the army in those given circumstances.

3. 'The symbol which has no existence of its own, and does not

---

[39] Maximus wrote several $\theta\epsilon\omega\rho\acute{\iota}\alpha\iota$ on the Transfiguration (*Amb.*, P.G. XCI, 1128A, 1160C).
[40] In fact, in Maximus (col. 1168C) the symbolism is reversed, Elijah designating judgment and Moses foresight. Palamas corrects his error in *Tr.* III, 1, 13 by quoting Maximus exactly.
[41] *Tr.* II, 3, 22.
[42] *Amb.*, col. 1376CD, 1165BC.
[43] *Tr.* III, 1, 13-14.

exist before or after'; 'such are the signs which the Prophets showed in visible fashion, and in the form of a simple figure; the roll of Zechariah (Zech. 5 : 1–2), the axes of Ezekiel (Ezek. 9 : 2) . . .'

It is clear that the light on Tabor, if it is at all a symbol, could only belong to the first category, for it did not possess an existence of its own, and, on the other hand, it could not be a simple hallucination; the Fathers unanimously call it 'Divinity' and identify it with the Kingdom of God to come. Moreover St. Maximus himself points out the way in which the word 'symbol' may be applied to Christ; 'By love of man,' he writes, 'he had become his own symbol' ($\sigma\acute{u}\mu\beta o\lambda o\nu$ $\dot{\epsilon}\alpha\nu\tau o\tilde{u}$),[44] that is to say he manifested himself in a way perceptible to the disciples who, till then, had not seen the Divinity. Christ, Palamas writes, 'is also a symbol, in so far as he manifests himself'[45] In this way a symbol is no longer considered as an intermediary between the subject and object of the vision : 'He who contemplates God not through the medium of a foreign symbol, but through a natural symbol, *has seen God.*'[46] Akindynos counters the Palamite theory of the natural symbol by the doctrine of divine simplicity—God, a simple being, possesses no 'natural symbol,'[47] but was he not thereby contradicting St. Maximus himself?

Monasticism: a prophetic ministry

By integrating the whole of spiritual life into a Christian theology of history, Palamas also supplies an eschatological foundation for the monastic life. The grace of baptism accords us the firstfruits of the Kingdom, and the whole of Christian life is only a realization of these firstfruits, and as full an anticipation as possible of the glory of the time to come; monastic life is a particular form of this anticipation, a means which Scripture[48] and ecclesiastical tradition recommend better to realize the grace of baptism, and to manifest the Kingdom to come here below. This eschatological interpretation of the monastic life and of holiness is expressed most clearly in the most solemn document ever written by Palamas, the exordium of his *Hagioretic Tome:* 'Doctrines which are now a common heritage, known to all and openly proclaimed, were under the Mosaic Law still mysteries, accessible by anticipation only in the visions of the Prophets. Moreover the blessings which the Saints announce for the time to come, are mysteries for our Evangelical

---

[44] *Amb.*, 1165D, quoted in *Tr.* III, 1, 20.
[45] *Against Akindynos*, IV, 21, *fol.* 112v.
[46] *Tr.* III, 1, 35.
[47] *Against Palamas*, II, *Monac, gr.* 223, *fol.* 107v.
[48] Palamas often quotes in this connection 1 Cor. 7: 29, 31; cf. *Hom.* 63, ed. Oikonomos, p. 286.

society, for the Spirit has made the Saints worthy of the vision, and they receive these blessings and see them by anticipation as firstfruits . . .' Who are these Saints? 'All those,' Palamas writes, 'who have relinquished the enjoyment of material goods, human glory and the evil pleasures of the body, choosing instead the Evangelical life, and, moreover, asserting this relinquishment of the world by obedience to those who have reached adult fulfilment according to Christ.' [49]

Palamas sees the monastic life as a form of the prophetic ministry known to the early Church; in contrast to prophecy in the Old Testament, which consisted in illuminations granted to individuals, that of the New Alliance is based on the 'firstfruits' of the Kingdom belonging to all Christians; the Christian prophets are, above all, the *Saints* who have realized in themselves, in a manner more complete than others, the potential holiness granted to all by baptism; so far from being opposed to the sacramental and hierarchic nature of the Church, the mysticism of the monks is a fruit thereof. 'Monastic society,' Palamas writes, 'is better suited than any other Orthodox community to the divine nature.' [50]

The prophetic quality of the monastic life gives it a very particular responsibility towards the whole Church, and not only for the individual salvation of the monks. Without becoming substitutes for the hierarchic ministry, and without pretending to infallibility, the monks are able to mitigate the human weaknesses of the bishops in the defence of Orthodoxy; the history of the Eastern Church is rich in examples of those who have played this part. It was his conception of the *ecclesial* function of monasticism and its prophetic role in the history of salvation which made Palamas leave his retreat on Athos, plunge into dogmatic controversies, and play an active part in the social and political life of his time.

Monastic detachment

The very basis of the monastic state is complete detachment from the goods of this world. While using expressions borrowed from the Pseudo-Dionysius, Palamas always tries, when speaking of this detachment, to refer to Scripture: 'They were constantly in the temple, persevering in prayer and supplication (Acts 1 : 14), in prefiguration and practical realization of monastic life which is truly high and sacred; for we have the promise, if we follow that way, to pass above the middle way (i.e. that of Christians in the world); we detach our-

---

[49] *P.G.* CL, 1225A–1228C, inspired by Maximus, *Cent. gnost.* 29, *P.G.* XC, 1137CD; *Amb., P.G.* XCI, 1256BC.
[50] *Discourse to John and Theodore*, ed. Oikonomos, p. 291.

selves from all distinction, all life, all imagination, to raise ourselves after the manner of true monks by observing the unifying commandments . . . to find a sacred fulfilment in the very holy Monad.'[51] The detachment which monks should attain is not limited to superfluous things, but extends even to those the world considers useful. Several times Palamas indicates that profane studies are totally forbidden to monks [52]; anticipating an objection of his adversaries, he writes: 'The Lord has not expressly forbidden literary studies. True, but he has also not forbidden marriage, the eating of meat or the cohabitation with married people. . . . There are many things done by the generality of Christians, without incurring condemnation, though they are strictly forbidden to monks because of their particular way of life.'[53] The Fathers advise novices to abstain from lengthy reading even of holy books and to give themselves to prayer alone; that by no means signifies that reading is an evil thing, but that it may distract one from contemplation.[54] Moreover, the hesychasts, when they have acquired the gift of perpetual prayer, devote themselves assiduously to reading: 'We know of no hesychast among us who, if he knows how to read, does not apply himself to study the Scriptures; while those who cannot read may be taken as living books, for they recite the greater part of the scriptures by heart.' But emphatically, 'It is the practice, and not the knowledge of the Scriptures, that brings salvation.'[55] So Palamas is not advocating ignorance on principle, but is putting up against the humanists, who sought for perfection in knowledge, the ideal of the monk who wishes to possess in himself the living God, Christ 'who is Wisdom-in-itself and contains all true knowledge in himself': 'The man who possesses him himself by observation of the divine commandments will not then have any more need to study the Scriptures, but will know them all exactly without study.' In this context he cites the example of St. John the Baptist and of St. Anthony of Egypt; according to St. Athanasius, the latter, when he was a child, refused to study, but later he refuted the Greek philosophers.[56]

While he frequently refers, following St. Gregory of Nyssa, to Moses, Elijah and Stephen as models of the mystical life, Palamas often reminds the hesychasts of the figure of St. John the Baptist to whom 'all those who abandon the world look as their first model.'[57] John, in fact, 'was not only the precursor of Christ, but also of his

[51] *Tr.* II, 1, 34; cf. Ps.-Dionysius, *Eccl. Hier.* VI, 3, col. 533A.
[52] *Tr.* I, 1, 12; 11, 1, 33.
[53] *Tr.* II, 1, 35.
[54] *Tr.* I, 3, 2.
[55] *Tr.* II, 1, 11.
[56] ibid., 43, cf. Athanasius, *Life of Anthony*, P.G. XXVI, 841A, 944sq.
[57] *Tr.* I, 1, 4.

Church, and especially, my brothers, of our monastic society.'[58] Just as the Baptist announced the approaching coming of the Messiah to the world, so do monks announce the imminence of the *Parousia* . . .

The 'great scheme'

While exalting the prophetic ministry of monks, Gregory saw matters clearly enough to oppose its abuses, especially the division of monastic orders into a 'little scheme' and a 'great scheme,' which, by his time, had been long in existence. This hierarchy among the monks adds nothing, in Gregory's view, to the basis of monastic life; unknown in the beginning, it was invented by doctors of more recent date who, unable to establish a real distinction between the two rites, could only make candidates of the 'great habit' undertake the same renouncements and the same vows. Relying on the authority of St. Theodore the Studite, Palamas in a letter to Paul Asen condemns this new practice; 'some people,' he writes, 'study not to go out from their dwellings and not to be seen by the crowd, passing the greater part of their lives in a sort of sanctuary, so as to appear as great men who live an exceptional type of life.' Palamas urges his correspondent 'to learn by the grace of Christ usefully to better his way of life, and not to change his garments.'[59]

In Palamas's view, if the monastic life was truly to accomplish its prophetic mission, and keep its place in the history of salvation, it must keep free from all Pharisaism and stay faithful to Evangelical simplicity. This is another illustration of what we have noted several times before; Byzantine hesychasm of the fourteenth century was not an unhealthy, esoteric movement, but a spiritual revival which helped to restore the most authentic traditions of the Christian East.

---

[58] *Hom.* 40, col. 509B.
[59] *Paris gr.* 1239, *fol.* 286–7.

CHAPTER V

AN EXISTENTIAL THEOLOGY: ESSENCE AND ENERGY

PALAMAS'S doctrine about the distinction between essence and *energies* in God is the best known part of his thought, but it has by no means always been correctly understood. The distinction is found in most of Gregory's published works, to which both critics and apologists have had to confine themselves; unfortunately these were basically occasional and polemical treatises—such is particularly the case with the *Theophanes* and the *Physical Chapters*—which give no real picture of the whole thought of Palamas. Writers bred in the Scholastic tradition have been at pains to refute formulas manifestly incompatible with their philosophic presuppositions, without concerning themselves with the religious content which Palamas was striving to defend, and without indicating how that content could have been differently expressed from the way in which Gregory did so in the concrete historical situation of his time. Some of these writers moreover look in Palamas's work for analogies with this or that view condemned in the West, or with some of Duns Scotus's propositions.[1] We shall be at pains here not to follow them into this ground, which would be outside the scope of our study; besides, it seems to us these comparisons with writers from a completely different background of spiritual thought and philosophical method, are altogether premature while Palamas's own works are still so little known. So we shall try briefly to analyse this thought against its proper background, sometimes referring to the Greek Fathers who were for Palamas the only doctrinal authority, and we will leave others to undertake a comparative study, which must be based on Palamas's writings as a whole, and may lead to some unexpected conclusions.

When it comes to those Orthodox writers who have analysed the Palamite system and related it to the generality of the Eastern Christian tradition, they too have had at their disposal only a relatively limited selection of Palamas's works, all dating from a time when the Palamite formulation was established, and in which his thought could no longer be seen in its whole Christological and Biblical context. Our

---

[1] The late V. Lossky has made a remarkable survey of the origins of Western opposition to Palamism; cf. *Le problème de la 'Vision face a face' et la tradition partristique de Byzance,* in *Studia Patristica,* II (*Texte und Untersuchungen,* 64), Berlin, 1957, pp. 512-37; also *Vision of God,* London, 1963, pp. 9-20.

short 'introduction' to Gregory Palamas's theology may complete those writers in just this respect, that we have tried to bring it back into that context. Without resolving all the difficulties which Western Christian thought finds in understanding Palamas, the integration of his theology in a Christocentric synthesis, free from any pre-established metaphysic, may contribute, we hope, to make him more accessible to Western readers.

The hidden God

Most accounts of Palamas's thought begin with an indication of his place in the history of what in the East is called 'apophatic theology.' Two currents are distinguished therein; the first, directly dependent on Neo-Platonism, conceives the transcendence and unknowability of God as a consequence of the *limitations of the created mind;* it is enough 'to go beyond oneself,' to 'become detached from created things,' and to 'unify oneself,' to accede to knowledge of the divine Being. But the second, while keeping the universally accepted Neo-Platonic vocabulary, asserts divine transcendence as a *property of God,* and one which no detachment and no surpassing oneself could make vanish; the God of the Bible is a 'hidden God' who only reveals himself when he so desires and on conditions which he himself fixes. Palamism—and Orthodox theology in general—has rightly been seen as an expression of this second current.[2] So the problem of 'apophatic' theology is at the source of the Byzantine theological controversies of the fourteenth century, for all Palamas's adversaries undoubtedly defended, each with particular nuances, the *first* conception of divine unknowability. Barlaam, for his part, adopted an extreme apophatic position entirely dependent on Greek philosophy; God cannot be known by the human intellect, for our intellect has only limited possibilities, so God remains unknown to us. Apophatic theology, granted Barlaam's philosophic presuppositions, led to a kind of vague agnosticism. On the other hand Akindynos and Nicephorus Gregoras had adopted a purely defensive position in face of Palamism, in that differing from Barlaam. They went no further than a refusal to recognize the formulations which Palamas opposed to Barlaam, and advanced no particular theory of the knowledge of God; in practice they wavered between agnosticism and an affirmation of the possibility of knowing the divine essence itself. Thus Akindynos could at the same time assert that every Theophany was only 'a sign' of a God 'symbolically polymorphous,' known only

[2] I. V. Popov, *Lichnost' i uchenie ll. Avgustina, I,* Sergiev-Posad, 1917, pp. 361–70; V. Lossky, *Mystical Theology,* pp. 28–9; Kiprian, *Antropologiia sv. Grigoriia Palamy,* Paris, 1950, pp. 276–80.

through his works like a simple essence whose properties are only nominally distinguished from one another (πολυωνύμως, οὐ πραγματικῶς), and that the divine is 'as a whole able to be shared essentially by created beings,' since it is the 'essence of all essences.'[3]

In spite of their apparent divergencies, Palamas's adversaries had in common an intellectual conception of knowledge of God, and an essentialist philosophy as the foundation of their theology. It would be easy to point a parallel in this between their conception of God and that of St. Thomas, and it is not surprising that several anti-Palamites ended their days in the West, having embraced the Roman faith, but it is important to stress once more that neither Barlaam, nor Akindynos, nor Nicephorus Gregoras were directly influenced by Latin thought; what drew them near to the latter was essentially common philosophic notions, borrowed from the same Aristotelian or Neo-Platonic sources and given validity by the same authority, that of the Pseudo-Dionysius.

Two exegeses of Dionysius

We cannot here get to the bottom of the problem concerning Dionysius the Areopagite, nor even decide *which* of the interpretations, Thomist or Palamite, of his works is correct. However we must note that the two interpretations coexisted for a certain time, in the East as in the West; on the one hand an Irishman, John Scotus Erigena, could read Dionysius with the eyes of an Easterner, but without possessing the theological education and the Christocentric spirituality which enabled Palamas to integrate Dionysius into an authentic Christian synthesis [4]; on the other hand, real Easterners, such as Akindynos and Gregoras, could interpret the Areopagite in the Western way clearly without possessing the philosophic genius of a St. Thomas. So the problem of the exegesis of Dionysius was at the centre of the argument in the Byzantine controversies of the fourteenth century.

Barlaam, in his interpretation of the Areopagite, strove to prove that the vision of God of which the latter spoke was only a sort of *created habitus* and not a contact with the divine Being. For instance he quoted that passage in the *Ecclesiastical Hierarchy* in which Dionysius spoke of the 'aim of the *Hierarchy*' both as a 'continual love of God' and as a 'knowledge of beings as they are,' a 'vision' and a 'science of the holy

---

[3] *Against Palamas*, II, *Monac gr.* 223, *fol.* 102v, 122v–123; III, *fol.* 188, V, *fol.* 304, 309v; cf. Gregoras, *Hist.* XXX, *P.G.* CXLIX, 256B, 277D; XXXII, col. 357AB; XXXIII, col. 373A, 381A.

[4] See an Orthodox appreciation of Erigena's work in A. Brilliantov, *Vlianie vostochnago bogosloviia na zapadnoe v proizvedeniiakh Ioanna Skota Erigeny*, St. Petersburg, 1898.

truth' and a 'divine participation in the unifying perfection,'[5] and Barlaam drew from that this conclusion: 'The best gift which God has given us is the hierarchy, its end is the knowledge of beings; as the words of Dionysius teach us, knowledge of beings, that is to say philosophy, is the best thing we possess.'[6] This intellectualism of Barlaam in his theory of the knowledge of God led him to some conclusions of a metaphysical sort, all in the context of an exegesis of Dionysius. The latter wrote: 'The providential powers produced by the imparticipable God are Being-in-itself, Life-in-itself and Deity-in-itself; in so far as beings share therein according to the manner proper to them, one says that they are beings, living beings and divine beings . . .' And Barlaam commented: 'The Deity-in-itself and the other realities which the Great Dionysius has here clearly called powers are not eternal, for the Good has given them existence. . . . There is the imparticipable glory of God, eternal reality, therefore identical with the essence; there is participable glory, different from the essence of God; it is therefore not eternal, for the universal Cause gives existence to it too.'[7] Akindynos too interprets Dionysius in the same way: the deification which God grants to men does not make them participate in the unique Deity, but confers on them 'what is called the divinity of men' (ἡ οὕτω λεγομένη τῶν ἀνθρώπων θεότης), which, being created, does not impair the divine unity and simplicity.[8] Finally, Gregoras also interprets Dionysius's *processions* (πρόοδοι) as created things, in so far as they are 'analogically' participable.[9]

Thus we see that, for the adversaries of Palamas, the passages in Dionysius about deification were not enough to take away its absolute character from divine transcendence: God remained imparticipable even for 'deified men'; the apophatic theology of Dionysius served to justify their negation of real deification; it allowed them to give a nominal or symbolical meaning to Scriptural or Patristic passages—especially those of Dionysius himself—which speak of the participation of men in the 'divine nature.' Finally, under their pens, the system of the Areopagite neutralized itself, and at the same time neutralized Revelation.

Insufficiency of the negative way
As for Palamas, we have already seen that, in the context of Dionysius's

[5] *Eccl. Hier.* I, 3, *P.G.* III, 376A.
[6] Quoted in *Tr.* II, 3, 73.
[7] *Divine Names* XI, 6, col. 953D–956A; Barlaam, *Against the Messalians*, in *Tr.* III, 2, 13.
[8] *Against Palamas*, I, *Monac gr.* 223, *fol.* 22, referring to Dionysius, *Ep.* II, *P.G.* III, 1068–1069A.
[9] *Hist.* XXX, *P.G.* CXLIX, 296BC.

doctrine of hierarchies, he applied to the Areopagite a fundamental Christological corrective which relegated Dionysius's universe to the field of 'natural' cosmology anterior to the Incarnation. This proceeding affected not only the system of hierarchies, but equally 'apophatic theology.' The 'negative way,' Palamas writes, 'belongs to the first comer who desires it; it does not transform the soul to give it angelic dignity; it frees the reason in relation to other beings, but it cannot, by itself, procure union with transcendental things.' [10] So, as far as apophatic theology is concerned, Palamas agrees with Barlaam who wrote to him in his first letter: 'I cannot refrain from admiring the profane philosophers who have so nobly recognized human weakness and divine transcendence.' [11] The philosophers too had been aware of apophatic theology which, in fact, belongs to the domain of natural thought; it is by contemplating beings that one perceives their relativity and arrives at the conception of an Absolute and of a Creator. Having enumerated the wonders of creation, Palamas asks: 'What man, appreciating all that in his mind, would not think of him who has so well put each thing in its place . . . ? What man, having thus known God, would confound him with one of those created beings of which he is the cause, or one of those things which are his image? He too would thus possess negative knowledge of God.' [12] The negative way is not enough, because it is limited to *comparing* beings to God in order to recognize the unknowability of God, and is not itself the result of more than a *knowledge of beings*. 'Those men who only venerate apophatic contemplation, and who do not believe in the existence of any activity, or any vision beyond that . . . do not see at all, strictly speaking, nor do they know anything, but are deprived of knowledge as of vision.' [13] 'Negation by itself is not enough for the intelligence,' he writes elsewhere, 'to reach supra-intelligible things; elevation by negation is actually only an intellection of that which appears different from God; it does not bring the image of inexpressible contemplation; it is not by itself that fulfilment.' [14]

Although the negative way 'draws closer to the Deity than positive theology,' [15] it remains a detachment *from beings* and so is by no means sufficient to know God. The Transcendent remains unknown to us, not because we are too weak to attain to it, but because It is Itself unknown by nature: 'It is not only a God who surpasses beings, but more-than-

[10] *Tr.* I, 3, 21.
[11] Ed. Schirò, pp. 261–2.
[12] *Tr.* II, 3, 44.
[13] *Tr.* II, 3, 53.
[14] *Tr.* I, 3, 19.
[15] *Cap. phys,* 106, col. 1192D.

God; the excellence of him who surpasses all things is not only above all affirmation, but also above all negation; it surpasses all excellence which could enter into the mind.' [16] True contemplation 'is the product of detachment, without for that reason being itself detachment; for if it was simply detachment, it would depend on us, and that is the doctrine of the Messalians. Contemplation therefore is not only detachment and negation; it is a union and a divinisation which happens mystically and inexpressibly by the grace of God after detachment.' [17] Hence the true vision comes from a *positive gift* of God, and itself constitutes a *positive experience*. But, for all that, it does not express itself in terms of a *positive* or cataphatic *theology;* it constitutes an encounter with a God who is by nature transcendent. 'For those who have been purified by *hesychia* know that the Divine surpasses these contemplations and these initiations, and so possesses that grace supra-intelligible and super-additional in a way that surpasses us; they possess it not because they do not see after the fashion of those who practise negative theology, but because there is in the very vision which they know something which surpasses vision, by undergoing negation and not by conceiving it. *Just as the act of undergoing and seeing divine things differs from cataphatic theology and is superior to it, so does the act of undergoing negation in spiritual vision, negation linked to the transcendence of the Object, differ from negative theology and is superior to it.'* [18]

Positive vision of the Invisible

In thus neutralizing the absolute conception of apophatism which Barlaam championed, Palamas was coming back to another aspect of Dionysius's thought: that of the divine darkness conceived as a *positive* experience of God. As we have seen in our previous quotations, Palamas refused to apply to this experience of the Transcendent the term 'apophatic theology,' because, in his time, 'theology' had come necessarily to mean expression and conceptualization: 'The mark made on the mind by the divine and mysterious signs of the Spirit is very different from apophatic theology . . . theology is as far from the vision of God in light, and as distinct from intimate conversation with God, as knowledge is different from possession.' [19] This possession 'is not acquired by the mind only by raising itself by negation. . . . Beyond detachment from beings . . . there is an ignorance, but it is more than a knowledge; there is a cloud, but it is more than brilliant; and in this

---

[16] *Tr.* II, 3, 8.
[17] *Tr.* I, 3, 17; cf. Dionysius, *Myst. Theol.* I, 2, *P.G.* III, 1000B; V, 1048B.
[18] *Tr.* II, 3, 26.
[19] *Tr.* I, 3, 42.

cloud more than brilliant, according to the Great Dionysius, divine things are given to the Saints; thus the very perfect contemplation of God and of divine things is not simply a detachment, but also, beyond the detachment, a participation in divine things, a gift and a possession more than a detachment.' [20] When the Saints receive the vision they enter into direct contact with God himself, who remains totally transcendent though revealing himself to them. Palamas thus describes a vision of St. Benedict according to the old Greek version of his *Life;* St. Benedict 'saw the whole universe as though enveloped by a single ray of this intelligible sun, though he too had not seen the essence and the measure of what he saw, but only the measure to which he had been able to make himself receptive . . . he has not learnt what that light was by nature, but he has learnt that it really existed (ὅτι ἐστὶν ὡς ἀληθῶς), that it was supernatural and superessential, that it was different from all beings, that its being was absolute and unique and that in itself it mysteriously comprehended all beings.' [21] Let us analyse Gregory's words : the Saint perceived the 'existence' of God and some properties of his Being without however knowing his 'essence' . . . the better one perceived that existence and the better one recognized those properties, the more clearly did the transcendence of God stand out. 'He who has become Spirit, and who sees in Spirit, how should he not see that which resembles his mode of seeing. . . . However, in spiritual vision itself *the transcendent light of God only appears the more completely hidden.'* [22] So it is just when one acquires 'true' vision and true knowledge, when one 'is united with God' and when one 'sees God through God,' after 'passing beyond all cognitive activity,' that one sees the transcendence of God. 'Those who by revelation see the divine light' see in God a mystery much better than we who try to understand the incomprehensibility of the divine nature, as incomprehensibility, by symbol or by symbolical concepts or by negation. He who is united with God 'glorifies God not only above the simple intellectual faculty of his mind, that human faculty which many created beings themselves surpass, but also above that supernatural union.' [23]

Revelatory function of Christ

Thus Palamas, who does not recoil from the most realistic expressions when he is speaking of deification—did he not say that the Saints were 'uncreated through grace'?—asserts with equally strong emphasis the transcendence of God. These two poles of Christian reality and of

[20] *Tr.* I, 3, 18; cf. Dionysius, *Ep.* V, *P.G.* III, 1073A.
[21] *Tr.* I, 3, 22; cf. Gregory the Great, *Life of Benedict,* P.L. LXVI, 197B.
[22] *Tr.* II, 3, 31.
[23] ibid., 52, 57.

true religious experience are for him correlatives, in spite of their character as antinomies. By depriving first one, and then the other, of its value, and by rejecting the antinomy, his adversaries threatened an essential point of Christian doctrine.[24] Fully to understand his thought on this point, in what he agrees and in what he differs from the Pseudo-Dionysius, one must again turn to his Christology for, in his view, it is in Christ that man finds the way of Deification and of true knowledge of God. Indeed it is the absence of all Christology which gives its ambivalent character to the *Corpus Areopagiticum* and makes it possible for both nominalists and realists to make use of it. In stressing that the antinomy of transcendence and union had a purely religious foundation, independent of all apophatic or cataphatic 'theology' and so of all philosophic conceptions, Palamas simply wanted to assert a fundamental revealed assumption: 'no man has ever seen God; the only Son, who is in the bosom of the Father, has made him known' (John 1 : 18). In other words, Revelation always remains a free and sovereign act of God, by which the Transcendent comes down from his transcendence and the Unknowable makes himself known; therefore the knowledge that we have of him is always the knowledge 'through grace' ($\chi \acute{a} \rho \iota \tau \iota$), subject to his will ($\theta \epsilon \lambda \acute{\eta} \sigma \epsilon \iota$), and dependent on an *act* ($\dot{\epsilon} \nu \epsilon \rho \epsilon \acute{\iota}_{\wp}$) of condescension ($\sigma \upsilon \gamma \kappa \alpha \tau \alpha \beta \acute{a} \sigma \epsilon \iota$) of Almighty God. 'God, by a superabundance of goodness towards us, being transcendent over all things, incomprehensible and inexpressible, consents to become participable to our intelligence and invisibly visible in his superessential and inseparable power.' [25] The Angels themselves have need of this divine condescension, without which they could not see God; therefore, they too do not see God except through grace, and not by essence.[26]

Thus, the cataphatic and apophatic 'theologies' are relegated by Palamas to the domain of natural thought in so far as they depend on an 'intellection' and only bring a knowledge of God 'through beings.' So by using the vocabulary of Dionysius, he is able to free this notion from all the philosophic conceptions: 'He is being and not being; he is everywhere and nowhere; he has many names and cannot be named; he is both in perpetual movement and immovable; he is absolutely everything and nothing of that which is.' [27] In face of this reality, such concepts as 'the essence' or 'God'—used in the philosophic

---

[24] *Theophanes*, 917AB, 932D; *Cap. phys.* 123, col. 1205D–1208B; cf. V. Lossky, *Mystical Theology*, p. 67. The antinomy has also been seen by Maximus (cf. P. Sherwood, *Maximus and Origenism*, in *Berichte zum XI Byzantinisten-Kongress*, Munich, 1958, pp. 25–6).
[25] *Tr.* I, 3, 10.
[26] ibid., 47; cf. *Against Gregoras*, IV, *Coisl.* 100, *fol.* 281, 284.
[27] *Apology*, *Coisl.* 99, *fol.* 2.

sense of First Cause—lose their meaning, for the God of the Bible is 'superessential' (ὑπερούσιος) and more-than-God (ὑπέρθεος).[28] His superessentiality cannot be assimilated to an essence *sui generis*, since God would be transcendent to this superessentiality [29]; the divine Being is absolutely unique and inexpressible; 'If God is nature, the other beings are not nature; and if the other beings are nature, God is not; in the same way, he is not a being, if the others are beings.' [30] But why then was Palamas opposed to Barlaam's agnosticism? He answers this question in his *Apology* immediately after asserting the divine transcendence: 'But there is one fact which stands distinct with reference to this transcendence: the complete and unadulterated existence in us of Jesus.' [31] The presence of God in us is therefore a personal existence and it excludes all definition of the divine Being in the context of an essentialist philosophy.

Divine existence 'ad extra'

After enumerating Aristotle's ten categories of existence, Palamas defines God as 'a superessential essence in which one can only see the categories of relation and of action' (τὸ πρός τί τε καὶ τὸ ποιεῖν); further, these two categories only define God provided that one does not introduce into him any 'confusion,' [32] that is to say in a way different from other beings. In striving thus—very imperfectly—to define the divine Being in Aristotelian terms more accessible to his adversaries than the Biblical or Patristic expressions, Palamas selected two categories which, for Aristotle, meant the manifestation *ad extra* of the being, and his reservations further limit the meaning of the words. For Palamas, God is above all a living God, the God of the Bible, whom no philosophical conception can define. To those who blamed the lack of philosophic strictness in his writings, he answered: 'We think that the true opinion is not that found in words and reasonings, but that which is shown by works and by life. . . . Every word, it is said, clashes with another word, but what word can clash with life?' [33] The existentialist attitude which he adopted in theology, led him to start, not from arguments, but from actual and historical assumptions, not from abstract concepts. The nominalist agnosticism of Barlaam was repugnant to him because it deprived men of a personal and active God: 'Therefore we must,' he writes, 'look for a God who not only possesses his own end within

---

[28] *Tr.* I, 3, 23; II, 3, 8; *Theophanes*, 937A.
[29] *Against Akindynos*, IV, 7, *Coisl.* 98, *fol.* 102.
[30] *Cap. phys.* 78, col. 1176B.
[31] *Coisl.* 99, *fol.* 2v.
[32] *Cap. phys.* 134, col. 1213D–1216A.
[33] *Tr.* I, 3, 13.

himself, his own *energy* and his own deification, but who is a good God—for so it will not be enough for him just to exist in the contemplation of himself—not only perfect, but surpassing all fullness; so when he wishes to do good, he can; he will not only be immobile, but will set himself in motion; thus he will be present for all in his manifestations and his creative and providential energies.'[34] It is the real experience of God which is the best 'proof' of his existence, for it touches that existence itself: 'Contemplation surpassing intellectual activities is the only means, the plainest means, the means *par excellence* to show the real existence of God and the fact that he transcends beings. For how could the essence of God not exist, since the glory of that divine nature makes itself seen by men?'[35] 'Indeed, it is only through his energies,' he writes elsewhere, 'that one knows that God exists; hence, he who rejects the divine energies . . . must necessarily be ignorant of the existence of God.'[36] In this one sees very clearly that it is Christian existentialism that Palamas opposes to the nominalist essentialism of his adversaries, while sharing with them—at least with Barlaam—the doctrine of the essential unknowability of God, he sees no other means of maintaining Biblical and Patristic realism except to affirm existentially the revelation of the unknowable God by free acts (or 'energies') of his almighty power.

St. Maximus

This proof of the existence of God through his manifestations, leads us to the main traditional argument which Palamas used against his adversaries, and which provided the essential element in his terminology: the Christology of St. Maximus the Confessor confirmed by the Sixth Oecumenical Council. Did not monotheletism deny that all nature was defined *ad extra* by an *energy*? Maximus, in his doctrine of the two energies or wills in Christ, has, on the contrary, affirmed that without an energy every nature, whether divine or human, does not possess a real existence, and that consequently Christ must necessarily possess two energies manifesting the full reality of his two natures. References to this doctrine of St. Maximus are frequent throughout Gregory's writings. For instance, in the *Third Triad* he writes: 'Either God does not possess natural and essential energies, and he who speaks thus is a godless man (that in fact amounts to openly denying the existence of God, for the holy Fathers say clearly, according to the divine Maximus,[37]

[34] *Tr.* III, 2, 24.
[35] *Tr.* II, 3, 38.
[36] *Dialogue, Coisl.* 99, *fol.* 48v; cf. *Cap. phys.* 141, col. 1220A.
[37] *Ep. ad Nicandr., P.G.* XCI, 96B; *Opusc.*, col. 200C, etc.; cf. also Basil, *Ep.* 189, 6-7, *P.G.* XXXII, 692-6; *Gregory of Nyssa, Ad Ablabium,* passim; more patristic references on this terminology in Lossky, *Vision of God,* pp. 67-72, 106-10, etc.

that no nature can either exist or be known without its essential energy), or the divine energies would be neither essential nor natural, and hence would not be God, or alternatively, if they are divine *energies,* natural and essential, but created, the essence of God which possesses them would be equally created.'[38] Moreover, one recalls that the dogmatic definition of the council of 1351 described itself as a 'development' (ἀνάπτυξις) of the decisions of the Sixth Oecumenical Council, and that the *Tome* made a long reference to the debates of 681. It is clear that, if the doctrine of the two natures confirmed by the Council of Chalcedon needed a complement concerning the 'two energies' of Christ, that was because ecclesiastical tradition refused to interpret the Christological problem in the terms of an abstract essentialism: every essence, in fact, remains an abstraction, if it does not manifest itself really and existentially in action [39]: 'God appears because he acts' (φανεροῦται ἐκ τοῦ ἐνεργεῖν), Palamas was to say.[40]

Personalism

The problem which seems to present the greatest difficulty in the synthesis of St. Maximus is that of the person or hypostasis. Indeed one knows that his monothelite adversaries could not bring themselves to admit that Christ could have possessed a human 'will' without being a human hypostasis, and claimed that the logical conclusion of Maximus's orthodoxy was Nestorianism or the assertion of two hypostases in Christ. To maintain the full reality of the humanity of Jesus, Maximus affirmed, following the Cappadocians and in the terms used by Leontius of Byzantium, the autonomous existence of the divine person, *source and not product of nature:* human nature and 'energy' could have been *'enhypostasized'* in the person of the Logos, because the latter is not an emanation or an internal irradiation of the divine essence, but the Person of the living God, possessing a unique mode of existence and receiving the divine nature from the hypostasis of the Father. In this Maximus is a faithful disciple of the Cappadocians who had defined the 'consubstantial' by starting from the three concrete realities of the Deity, the Father, the Son and the Spirit, to reach thence the community of the essence.[41] If Maximus developed the doctrine of the Cappadocians, it was by treating the essence as more abstract, the hypostasis becoming the concrete reality of all experience and all theology.[42] Theological personalism is the fundamental feature of the

---
[38] *Tr.* III, 3, 6, etc.
[39] H. Urs v. Balthasar, *Liturgie cosmique,* Paris, 1947, pp. 98–9.
[40] *Letter to Damian, Coisl.* 98, *fol.* 202.
[41] cf. G. L. Prestige, *God in Patristic thought,* pp. 233–9, 242ff.
[42] cf. G. L. Prestige, op. cit., pp. 277–81.

tradition to which Palamas belonged; in that we shall find the key to the understanding of his doctrine of the divine energies.

In his argument with Barlaam who put before him an essentialist conception of God, Palamas expresses his view clearly. He writes: 'It is through his essence, Barlaam would say, that one says of God that he possesses in himself, in a unique and unifying fashion, all these powers. But, in the first place, one must call that "God," for that is the word we have received from the Church to designate it. God, when he was speaking with Moses, did not say: "I am the essence," but "I am that I am" (Exod. 3 : 14). It is not therefore He-that-is who comes from the essence, but it is the essence which comes from He-that-is, for He-that-is embraces in himself all the Being.'[43] Formally, Palamas refuses to identify all being with the essence: 'The essence,' he writes, 'is necessarily being, but being is not necessarily essence.'[44] Hence God can manifest himself in his very being, while remaining imparticipable in his essence : that is the real significance of what is called 'Palamism.' Here we shall first examine some passages of Palamas about the manifestation of God and then see the terminological consequences which he derives therefrom.

An 'Inferior Divinity'?

As we have noted several times before, Palamas's logic always takes as its point of departure experience of the life in Christ and the deification accessible in the Church; and there—there can be no doubt of this—it is the living God who *in his very wholeness* appears to the Christian. 'Grace,' he writes, paraphrasing St. Maximus, 'accomplishes the mysterious union . . . God in all fullness comes to dwell in the complete being of those who are worthy of it, and the saints fully dwell with their complete being in the whole God by drawing to themselves the whole God, and not receiving any other reward but God himself for the ascent accomplished towards him; he attaches himself to them as the soul is attached to the body, as to his own members.'[45] It is therefore an *immediate* communion: 'God lets himself be seen face to face, and not through enigmas . . . he unites himself to them to the extent of coming to dwell in his entirety in their entireties, so that, on their side, they dwell completely in him and, through the Son, the spirit spreads in abundance over them (Titus 3 : 6) . . . you do not however consider that God lets himself be seen in his superessential essence, but according to the deifying gift and according to his energy, according

[43] *Tr.* III, 2, 12 (cf. *Gregory of Naz., Hom.* XLV, 3, *P.G.* XXXVI, 625C; Dionysius, *Div. Names* V, 4, col. 817C).
[44] *Against Akindynos*, II, 10, *Coisl.* 98, *fol.* 78; cf. *Tr.* III, 2, 7.
[45] *Tr.* III, *1*, 27; cf. Maximus, *Amb. P.G.* XCI, 1088BC, 1320B.

to the grace of adoption, uncreated deification, and the direct hypostasized glory.'[46] In this we see how inaccurate it is to consider the energies as a sort of inferior divinity distinct from God himself. The ancient and modern critics of Palamism could not have reached this conclusion except as a result of their own philosophic presuppositions about the identity of God with his essence; these presuppositions clearly could not be reconciled with the living God of Palamas, a God essentially inaccessible and existentially present, through his almighty power, in the created universe.

The whole of God in the energies

One could quote many passages to leave no doubt about Palamas's thought on this point: 'Neither the uncreated goodness, nor the eternal glory, nor the life and all such things are simply the superessential essence of God, for God, as Cause, transcends them; nevertheless we say that he is Life, Goodness and other such things. . . . As God complete is present in each of the divine energies, each serves as his name.'[47] 'That which is manifest, that which makes itself accessible to intellection or participation, is not a part of God, for God is not thus subject to partition for our benefit; complete he manifests himself and does not manifest himself, complete he is conceived and is inconceivable by the intelligence, complete he is shared and is imparticipable.'[48] Hence each divine power and each energy is God himself (ἑκάστη δύναμις ἢ ἐνέργεια αὐτός ἐστιν ὁ θεός)[49]; 'They do not compose,' Palamas writes, 'the being of God,' for that is not a composite entity, and 'it is he who gives them their existence, without taking his existence from them; indeed it is not the realities which surround God (τὰ περὶ θεόν) which are the essence of God, but he is their essence.'[50] So one sees that it is as living God that God *acts,* that is to say possesses energies. We are thus led to consider Palamas's view of the person or hypostasis.

The sole Actor

As already noted Palamas is in the tradition of the great Cappadocians in conceiving the divine hypostases as 'supports' of the divine Being, 'in which' the essence is manifest, and not only as internal relations or hypostatic characters identical with that essence: 'The hypostatic charac-

---

[46] *Tr.* III, *1,* 29; cf. *Tr.* II, *3,* 26, 37.
[47] *Tr.* II, 2, 7; cf. *Tr.* III, 3, 6.
[48] *On participation to God,* Coisl. 99, *fol.* 22; cf. *Letter to Damian, Coisl.* 98, *fol.* 202.
[49] *Letter to Gabras,* Coisl. 99, *fol.* 84, etc., cf. *Theophanes,* col. 936; *Cap. phys.* 72, col. 1172A.
[50] *Tr.* III, 2, 25.

ters are not the hypostasis, but they are characteristics of the hypostasis.'[51] If the hypostases were only manifestations of the essence, the Son and the Holy Spirit would not be hypostases, for the Father, considered as the source of the essence, would be the Sole divine hypostasis. So, when for instance one speaks of the Son as the Power of the Wisdom of the Father, it is necessary to bear in mind that he is the 'autohypostasized Wisdom,' for, in another sense, he is not Wisdom, but possesses the same wisdom and the same power as the Father and the Spirit, since wisdom and power are operations or energies of the divine Being.[52] With great clearness Palamas proclaims that the origin of the divine Essence is the *hypostasis* of the Father, for if that were not so, Christian personalism would give place to the essentialism of the Greek philosophers: 'The essence of God would produce itself, and God would be his own Father, as the boasting of men famous among the Hellenes formerly proclaimed: in fact God himself exists, and to him belong the divine essence and the divine energy.'[53] From this personalist conception of God it results that what is called the divine 'simplicity' does not manifest itself in the identity of the whole divine Being with the essence—which, for the Greek tradition, would be an abstract and philosophical conception of that simplicity—but in the fact that there is only one sole God living and acting in the imparticipable essence as in the energies. The holy Fathers, Palamas writes, 'did not say that all this (essence and energies) is one sole thing, but that it belonged to one sole God. . . .'[54] Therefore divine activity remains 'simple,' because God is the sole Actor within all the energies. Each of them really signifies a distinct divine property, but they do not constitute different realities, for all are the acts of a unique living God.[55]

'Perichoresis'

In the created world every personal act is of necessity particular to one sole acting hypostasis: in this human acts are like each other, but are not identical. It is not so with God: the three divine hypostases in fact possess *one sole energy,* and every divine act is of necessity the act of the Father, the Son and the Holy Spirit, because of their consubstantiality. Therefore the common divine essence is the cause (αἰτία) of the energies, but these energies remain personal acts, for consubstantiality does not suppress the personal element in God, but establishes a 'copenetration' (περιχώρησις) between the hypostases which is

---

[51] *Letter to Daniel, Coisl.* 99, *fol.* 95v.
[52] *Against Akindynos,* VI, 23, 25, *Coisl.* 98, *fol.* 177, 181.
[53] *Against Gregoras,* II, *Coisl.* 100, *fol.* 254.
[54] *Against Akindynos,* V, 13, *Coisl.* 98, *fol.* 128v.
[55] *Apology, Coisl.* 99, *fol.* 6v, 8.

manifest in just this common energy: 'God is always like himself, for the three divine hypostases possess one another naturally, totally, eternally and indivisibly, but also without mixture or confusion, and they "copenetrate" each other in such a way that they only possess one energy.'[56] Thus the Mystery of the Trinity is conceived by Palamas as the union of three hypostases who each keep, in a real way, their personal identity, but who are not 'parts' of God, for the fullness of the Deity lives in each of them.

There is no essence without energy

This real distinction between essence and hypostases, for which modern adversaries of Palamism blame him, but which can be traced back in a straight line to the Greek conception of the Trinity as already expressed in the fourth century at the end of the Arian dispute, appeared to Palamas all the more necessary because the common nature of the hypostases was, for him, a 'superessential essence,' an unknowable entity, whereas all his theological activity was in the direction of establishing the reality of the Revelation of the living God manifesting himself in his acts or energies. The Trinity itself is totally present in the divine energies, and there is no question of the emanations of Plotinus or of beings distinct from God. On every suitable occasion Palamas stresses the fact that the energies have neither hypostasis nor existence of their own, but result from the divine hypostases and constitute for us signs of the existence of God. For, as we have seen, it is impossible for us to prove that existence unless God manifests himself outside his unknowable essence. 'Since these energies,' he writes, 'have no hypostasis of their own, but are powers which express the existence of God, one cannot, because of them, say that there is another God, or a second God! Those who do not accept them are completely ignorant even that God exists.'[57] So Palamas is defending against his adversaries a living God who manifests himself in concrete Persons and by concrete acts: 'The divine and unknowable essence, if it did not possess an energy distinct from itself, would be totally non-existent and would only have been a product of imagination.'[58]

'Enhypostasized' energies

Although they do not exist outside the divine hypostases and have no hypostases of their own, the energies can be called 'enhypostasized'

[56] *Cap. phys.* 112, col. 1197BC; for the passage of the doctrine of 'copenetration' from christology to triadology, see G. L. Prestige, *God in patristic thought*, pp. 291–99.
[57] *Apology, Coisl.* 99, *fol.* 13.
[58] *Cap. phys.* 136, col. 1216D.

AN EXISTENTIAL THEOLOGY

(ἐνυπόστατοι or ὑποστατικαί) provided these words both keep their etymological meaning of a real and permanent existence, and the particular meaning which they have taken on in Christian theology, i.e. a personalized existence.[59] Palamas several times quotes passages from the Pseudo-Macarius—in its mediaeval paraphrase by Symeon Metaphrastes—which speak of 'an illumination of the Spirit which is not only like a revelation of thoughts, but a sure continuous illumination of the *hypostatic light* in souls.'[60] Here clearly the point is to stress the real character of communion with God. In other passages the term 'enhypostasized' (ἐνυπόστατος) expresses both the personal character of the divine 'acts' and their immanence in the nature of the actor.[61] Moreover one knows that in Christology, after Leontius of Byzantium, the term 'enhypostasized' was used to designate the human nature 'appropriated' by the hypostasis of the Logos; it thus applies to a reality transmissible from one hypostasis to another; what before had only been 'enhypostasized' in a human hypostasis, has been 'enhypostasized' in the hypostasis of the Son.... Thus, according to Palamas, the divine life, naturally 'enhypostasized' in the divine hypostases, is granted to human hypostases, and so is 'enhypostasized' in them. We will here quote a characteristic passage well illustrating how the doctrine of deification fits into Gregory's terminological system : 'The divine and heavenly life which belongs to those who live in a way pleasing to God ... does not exist in the actual nature of the Spirit.... It is "enhypostasized," not because it possesses a hypostasis of its own, but in so far as the Spirit sends it from one hypostasis into another; it is in the latter that it may be seen.'[62] The divine life—which is deifying grace when it is granted to man—therefore belongs to the divine nature even when men benefit from it (by grace and not by nature); hence it constitutes the means of a communion both personal and real with God, a communion which does not involve the impossible confusion of the natures. It is therefore just the opposite to an 'intermediary' between God and man; that would be the case with a created grace, for then it would be an intermediate nature, neither divine nor human. Whatever name one gives them—grace, divine life, light, illumination—the energies or divine acts belong to the existence of God himself; they represent his existence *for us*. It is therefore not only justified but necessary to apply thereto the

---

[59] cf. the terminology of St. Maximus, H. U. v. Balthasar, op. cit., pp. 170–1.
[60] *De libertate mentis*, 22, *P.G.* XXXIV, 956D, quoted in *Tr.* I, 3, 7; II, 3, 6; IV, 2, 1.
[61] Maximus, *Ep.* 15, *P.G.* XCI, 557D, quoted in *Against Akindynos* VI, 19, *Coisl.* 98, *fol.* 174.
[62] *Tr.* III, *1*, 9, paraphrasing Ps-Basil, *Against Eunomius*, V, *P.G.* XXIX, 772C.

attributes proper to the divine Being; they are God (θεός) and Deity (θεότης), as the Council of 1351 formulated it.[63]

The essence 'cause' of the energies

Manifesting the personal Being of God the divine energies reflect the unity of the divine essence. By virtue of their 'Perichoresis' the three hypostases have only 'one sole energy' and in this sense the divine essence is the 'cause' of the divine acts. The Father, the Son and the Spirit act not only in mutual 'accord,' but in the unity of their essence. In so far as it is the cause of the energies, this unknowable Essence remains 'transcendental' with respect to them and the energies are 'inferior' (ὑφειμέναι) in relation to the essence; the same God reveals himself and remains transcendent to his own revelation. Thus the extreme realism of Palamas in his doctrine concerning deification does not lead him to assert a more or less pantheistic fusion of the human and the divine; even while uniting himself in his completeness to man, God remains transcendent to him. Commenting on John 1: 16 ('For of his fulness we have all received'), Gregory asks: 'How should the fullness not be transcendent to that which comes from the fullness? In Christ we all have communion with God, but God remains transcendent even to that communion.'[64] This transcendence of the essence-cause in relation to the caused energies does not, according to Palamas, break the unity of God, since the 'superiority' of the Father in relation to the Son does not blemish it either. Christ could say: 'The Father and I are one' (John 10: 30); but he also said: 'The Father is greater than I' (John 14: 28). This last quotation from the Gospel applies not only to the humanity of Christ, but affirms the eternal superiority of the Father—source and cause of Divinity—in relation to the Son. Palamas refers to the theology of the Cappadocians in asserting that this 'inferiority of the Son,' avoiding the Sabellian reef, by no means implies that the Son was created, as the Arians would have it.[65]

The terms 'transcendent essence' (ὑπερκειμένη οὐσία) and 'downgoing divinity' (ὑφειμένη θεότης) had been used by the Pseudo-Dionysius and taken up again by Barlaam in a sense that, for Palamas, had an Arian meaning; for Barlaam the passages in Dionysius's *Letter to Gaius* in which it is said that 'He-who-is-more-than-God' (ὑπέρθεος) transcends the participable Deity, signified that the latter was a created Deity.

---

[63] According to the Cappadocian Fathers, the word 'God' designates not the unknowable essence, but the energy (*Gregory of Naz., Hom.* XXX, 18, *P.G.* XXXVI, 128A; Basil, *Ep.* 189, *P.G.* XXXII, 696, etc.).
[64] *Apology*, Coisl. 99, *fol.* 12v–13; cf. *fol.* 8; *Against Akindynos*, II, 9, Coisl. 98, *fol.* 52v–53, VII, 11, *fol.* 191v; *Theophanes*, 945D, 935A.
[65] *Theophanes*, 917BD, etc.

According to Palamas, Dionysius was only speaking in this passage of the distinction between the essence and the energy in the bosom of one unique God; to speak of a 'created Deity' was to fall into dytheism.[66] 'There is a transcendent reality,' he writes, 'in relation to the energies and to the natural powers, because it is their cause, the trihypostatic essence; and in the trihypostatic essence there is a transcendent cause, the Deity-Source,' that is to say the Father.[67] In neither the one case nor the other is the simplicity of the divine nature found to have been broken.

The energies and the Trinity

Moreover, the anti-Palamites recognized that the concept of 'energy' involved the idea of dependence in relation to a cause and, in so much as they also accepted that the divine energies were uncreated, they identified the latter with the Son and the Spirit: 'It is the Son and the Spirit,' so Akindynos writes, 'who are the natural and essential powers of God the Father.'[68] In fact they were thus going back to a theology current before the Council of Nicaea, which considered the Father as the inaccessible element in God, while the Son and the Spirit were the organs of revelation; without ceasing to be correct that doctrine was complemented, after the Arian controversies, by the doctrine of 'consubstantiality'; according to the Great Cappadocians, the Son and the Spirit share in the incommunicable essence of the Father. Hence Palamas accepts that the Son and the Spirit should also be called 'energies' of the Father, but 'hypostatic energies' (ἐν ἰδίᾳ ὑποστάσει) distinct from the non-hypostatic ones (οὐκ αὐθυπόστατοι) which constitute the existence of God *ad extra* and which belong to the three divine hypostases. By not making this reservation, his adversaries, in his view, risked falling into subordinationism. Their error once more consisted in identifying essence with existence; thus Arius and Eunomius had identified a hypostatic property of the Father—the unbegotten character—with the uncreated essence, and from this resulted their view that the Son, begotten of the Father, was neither consubstantial nor uncreated.[69] Palamas in his *Against Akindynos* gives a precise account of his conception of the hypostases and of the *energies* of God; this account is an example of the somewhat scholastic form which Palamism tended to take in the

---

[66] Dionysius, *Letter to Gaius*, P.G. III, 1068–9; Palamas, *Third Letter to Akindynos*, ed. Meyendorff, in *Theologia*, XXIV, 1953, p. 577.
[67] *Against Akindynos*, I, 7, Coisl. 98, fol. 36; cf. Ps. Dionysius, *Divine Names*, II, 5, P.G. III, 641D.
[68] *Against Palamas*, II, Monac. gr. 223, fol. 91, etc.
[69] *Letter to Paul Asen*, Coisl. 99, fol. 119v; *Against Gregoras*, I, Coisl. 100, fol. 243.

course of the controversy, but its precision, comparable to the formulations of the Cappadocian Fathers concerning the essence and the hypostases, is useful, provided we appreciate to what realities in Palamas's thought it corresponds: 'The proper appellations of the divine hypostases are common to the energies, whereas appellations common to the hypostases are particular to each of the divine energies. Thus life is a common appellation of the Father, the Son and the Spirit, but foreknowledge is not called life, nor is simplicity, nor unchangeableness, nor any other energy. Thus each of these realities which we have enumerated belongs at the same time to the Father, the Son and the Spirit; but they only belong to one energy, and not to all; each reality in fact has only one signification. Inversely, Father is the proper appellation of one sole hypostasis, but it is manifest in all the energies . . . and the same is true of the appellations Son and Spirit. . . . Thus since God in his wholeness is wholly incarnated, he has unchangeably united to the whole of me . . . the divine nature and all its power and energy in one of the divine hypostases. Thus, also, through each of his energies one shares in the whole of God . . . the Father, the Son and the Holy Spirit . . .'[70] Hence God appears complete in the total simplicity of his personal being and the real diversity of his providential and redemptive activity.

Multiplication of the 'Indivisible'

In the course of his polemics against Akindynos, Palamas achieved a final formulation of his theology based on a triple distinction: 'Three elements belong to God,' he writes, 'essence, energy and the Triad of the divine hypostases.'[71] We have seen that the personal nature—trihypostatic—of the divine Being represented its simplicity, whereas the essence and the *energies* designated the antinomian poles of the Unknowable making itself known, the One multiplying itself, and the sole Existent making creatures share in its existence. These distinctions are necessary for Palamas to show 'how God, while letting himself be contained by creatures in a limited fashion, could be shared in his completeness and contained' without dividing himself, for 'Goodness, Wisdom, Majesty or Providence are not parts of God, but he himself is wholly Goodness, Wisdom, Providence and Majesty; for, being unique, he does not divide himself, but he possesses as his own each of these energies and manifests himself fully by his presence and his

---

[70] *Against Akindynos*, V, 27, *Coisl.* 98, *fol.* 146–146v; cf. *Cap. phys.* 91, col. 1185CD.
[71] *Cap. phys.* 75, col. 1173B; cf. on that point S. Verkhovskoy, *Bog i chelovek*, New York, 1956, pp. 238–46.

action in each of these in a unified, simple and indivisible fashion.'[72] It is possible and justified, according to Palamas, to consider the divine essence itself as Goodness, Wisdom and Majesty, but, as this essence is imparticipable, these appellations in fact apply to it alone and all signify the same thing[73]; now we can also state that God is the 'source' of Goodness, of Wisdom and of real deification[74]; these are existential manifestations or energies. 'In a word,' Palamas writes, 'we must seek a God who can be shared in one way or another, so that each of us by participating therein receives, in the way most proper to him and by analogy of participation, being, life and deification.'[75]

All presence and all real action of God in the multiple universe involve a divine existence which 'multiplies itself.' Palamas makes use of an expression often employed by St. Maximus concerning this 'multiplication of God.'[76] He writes: 'There is therefore a reality between creatures and the imparticipable superessentiality; not one sole reality, but as many as the objects which share therein; I want to speak about these mediating realities; they are powers of the Superessentiality which, in a unique and unifying way, possesses by anticipation and resumes in itself all the multitude of the participable realities; because of this multitude, it multiplies itself ($\pi o \lambda \lambda a \pi \lambda a \sigma \iota \acute{a} \zeta \epsilon \tau a \iota$) in its manifestations and all creatures share in it, although it remains indivisibly within its imparticipability and unity.'[77] In that sense too one can say that God possesses fullness, though remaining, through essence, above all fullness.[78]

The Creation

The distribution between the divine essence and the energies, which is especially manifest in this 'multiple' existence of God in the universe, is particularly important for an understanding of the Palamite conception of the Creation. Gregory knew the accepted axiom of Patristic literature that 'to beget is the property of nature, and to create that of energy.'[79] The Son and the Spirit, eternal and consubstantial results of the 'natural' act of the Father, are not creatures produced by the free

[72] *Dialogue*, Coisl. 99, *fol.* 55.
[73] *Against Gregóras*, II, *Coisl.* 100, *fol.* 261; cf. *Cap. phys.* 34, *col.* 1141C–1141A.
[74] *Cap. phys.* 35, col. 1144B.
[75] *Tr.* III, 2, 24.
[76] Maximus, *De charitate*, I, 100, *P.G.* XC, 985A; *Amb.*, *P.G.* XCI, col. 1289A.
[77] *Tr.* III, 2, 25; cf. *Tr.* III, 1, 19; *Theophanes*, col. 941CD; *Hom.* 8, col. 101A; *Hom.* 33, col. 420C, etc.
[78] *About union and distinction*, Coisl. 98, *fol.* 27.
[79] Cyril, *Thesaurus*, 18, *P.G.* LXXV, 312C; John of Damascus, *De fide orth.*, I, 8, *P.G.* XCIV, 813A, etc.

will or energy of God. Thus we see that, from Palamas's viewpoint, the distinction between essence and energies is indissolubly linked with the polemics of the Fathers against Eunomius in one direction, and Sabellianism in the other; the essentialist philosophy lurking behind both these heresies is incapable of distinguishing in God between the act of begetting and the act of creating, and ends either in pantheism—the creation is an essential act, hence coeternal with God—or in the Arian negation of the divinity of the Son and of the Spirit who are reduced to the status of creatures. It is against this philosophy, and especially against the danger of pantheism, that Palamas raises his voice when arguing against Akindynos and Gregoras in particular; if there were in God no distinction between will and nature, creatures would belong 'by nature to God' [80]; hence, either Akindynos considers that creatures are beings begotten and consubstantial with God the begetter, or else he thinks that the Son and the Holy Spirit are creatures.[81] Therefore he is opposed to Nicaean Orthodoxy, according to which the begetting of the Son is an act of the essence of the Father distinct from the creation which is an act of the divine will.[82]

As noted before à propos of deification, the created being is defined by its 'essential' difference from God, and by the impossibility for it to communicate with the uncreated 'Essence'; so Palamas asks: 'Is the Wisdom of God which manifests itself in creatures, the essence of God? But the latter is always imparticipable and simple, whereas the divine Wisdom allows itself to be shared by those who show themselves wise and, in its providence towards them, it sometimes appears to them as infinite in resources (Eph. 3: 10); I speak now of the Wisdom seen in the Father, Son and Holy Spirit.' [83] This quotation brings out clearly the points of contact and the differences between Palamism and modern Russian 'sophiology,' to which it has sometimes been compared. Palamas, in his polemics against Akindynos, was led to envisage the divine Wisdom not only in its traditional Christological aspect which identifies it with the Logos, but also as an essential divine attribute, in so much as the three hypostases share in the creative act; however he is careful not to identify it with the divine essence itself, as do the Russian 'sophiologists,' and he accuses his adversaries of that error which leads to pantheism.[84] If the creation actually is an 'essential' act and independent of the divine will, the creatures are

---

[80] *Against Akindynos*, I, 7, Coisl. 98, fol. 33v.
[81] *Letter to Gabras*, Coisl. 99, fol. 85v.
[82] *Against Akindynos*, V, 11, Coisl. 98, fol. 124v.
[83] *Apology*, Coisl. 99, fol. 14.
[84] The identification is formally made by Gregoras, *Hist.* XXX, P.G. CXLIX, 294CD.

necessarily coeternal with the divine essence; that is exactly the conception of God formed by the Greek philosophers. But the God of the Bible 'created when he wished'; before time, he only possessed the power to create.[85]

The creative act is a mystery perfectly inaccessible to human reason,[86] and could only take place in as much as the divine Being was not totally identified with his inaccessible essence, but 'came out from it' to act outside himself: 'it is in fact his will'—not his essence—'which is the origin of beings.' [87] Therefore God is Creator in an absolutely unique fashion, for the creation leaves his essence unchanged in the sense that he had *no* need of the creation and does not suffer (οὐδὲ πάσχει) any limit in his power, for such a need and such a limit would be both weakness and 'complexity' in the Being of God.[88] If he were only essence, God could not be at the same time supremely free, impassive and active; if he were not himself at the same time both essence and energy, he could not *naturally possess* the creative power, and *begin* to create: 'Because God began and ended creating when he wished, we will not say that he does not naturally possess the creative faculty, that is to say that energy which allows him to create. . . .' [89] The distinction between essence and energies thus makes it possible to avoid the snag on which Origen struck, namely the argument that God, if he began to create in time, must have undergone a change in his nature; Origen's mistake consisted just in this, that he identified God with an essence, and did not know that unchangeableness and movement, unknowability and revelation, supratemporality and action in time, could really coexist, united in the simplicity and mystery of the personal Being of God.[90]

It is in the general context of a specifically personalist conception that one must envisage Palamas's view of the problem of the *logoi* of beings which existed in God before the creation and which, disseminated through the universe, lead natural thought to the Creator. He often comes back to the idea that creatures participate in the divine *energies,* and that it is possible to know God through his providence.[91] For him, these uncreated and eternal energies are the thoughts of God, who is himself present in each of them; however they are not the

---

[85] *Against Akindynos,* IV, 13, *Coisl.* 98, *fol.* 106v; *Letter to Gabras, Coisl.* 99, *fol.* 90.
[86] *Tr.* II, 3, 42, 65.
[87] *Cap. phys.* 91, col. 1185C.
[88] ibid., 133, col. 1213CD.
[89] *Against Akindynos,* VI, 20, *Coisl.* 98, *fol.* 174v.
[90] ibid., cf. II, 12, *fol.* 57v; *Letter to Daniel, Coisl.* 99, *fol.* 96.
[91] *Theophanes,* 956A; *Cap. phys.* 140, col. 1217D–1220A; *Against Akindynos,* IV, 11–12, *Coisl.* 98, *fol.* 105–6.

essence of God, for in that case the creation would have been a necessity for God, but are powers which his sovereign will transforms into temporal acts. 'How could the manifold divine thoughts, and the images of beings to come which these thoughts reflect . . . be themselves the essence? In fact through them God is in relation with beings, whereas, by essence, he is outside all relation.'[92] So it is a living God—but transcendent in his essence—who, before the creation, thinks the world and thereafter remains active in it through his providence.

Terminological misunderstandings

In the context of the Creation, as in that of sanctifying and deifying communion, a problem arises in connection with the nature of the distinctions within God made by Palamas. Before dealing with this subject, it is as well to eliminate some misunderstandings, for Palamas has been blamed for expressions which he did not use. For instance the use of the word 'Divinities' in the plural, which is nowhere found in Palamas's work, except perhaps in a doubtful passage of the *Letter to Arsenius*, a passage, incidentally, never quoted by the anti-Palamites: 'Even if one says,' following the Saints, 'that there are several divinities, it is only a question of the energies of the unique God.'[93] As we have seen, the doctrine of divinities actually derives from *interpretations* or *paraphrases* of Palamas's works by his adversaries, who often present such paraphrases as if they were verbatim quotations from Gregory. The latter frequently protested against these falsifications[94]: 'It is not Palamas, but Barlaam, who says,' he writes, 'that there are two divinities, one transcendent, the other inferior; his own writings bear inescapable witness to this, as well as most of those who heard him.'[95] There would indeed be several divinities, if the *energies* were objects or 'things'; but that is not at all the case, even if one says that God 'possesses' them, for they are not 'essences' and so do not prevent there being one sole Divinity; 'quite the contrary, they greatly contribute to that unity' because all manifest the same God.[96] If one admitted that the *energies* are essences or hypostases, one would fall into Platonism; equally, if the *energies* were created, there would be two Gods, one created and the other uncreated, or perhaps a God simultaneously created and uncreated (κτιστοάκτιστος).[97]

[92] *On union and distinction*, Coisl. 98, fol. 23; cf. *Against Gregoras*, II, Coisl. 100, fol. 254.
[93] Coisl. 99, fol. 123.
[94] *Hagioretic Tome*, col. 1228D, etc.; cf. Philotheus, *Against Gregoras*, VIII, P.G. CLI, 989AB; IX, col. 995B, 1009B, etc.
[95] cf. *supra*, pp. 60–2.
[96] *Refutation of Calecas*, Coisl. 99, fol. 161–161v; *Tr.* III, 2, 5.
[97] *Dialogue*, Coisl. 99, fol. 41; cf. *Letter to Athanasius*, Coisl. 98, fol. 15; *Against Gregoras*, II, Coisl. 100, fol. 245.

Nature of the Palamite distinctions

What then are the *energies,* and how different from the essence? In this field Palamas hesitates much in his use of words, for the theological vocabulary in use was too dependent on the essentialist categories of Greek thought adequately to express the existential reality of the living Being. From one point of view Palamas maintains that the divine acts are 'real things' ($\pi\rho\acute{\alpha}\gamma\mu\alpha\tau\alpha$) in the sense that the nouns denoting them— Goodness, Life, Deification—are not just 'empty noise of words'; that would be the case if these names claimed to refer to the superessential essence; but they are 'real things,' although not essences; so the expression 'real things' will only pass provided we remember they have no self-sufficient existence.[98] Similarly, one cannot simply say that they are 'accidents' ($\sigma\upsilon\mu\beta\epsilon\beta\eta\kappa\acute{o}\tau\alpha$) of the essence, for they belong to it as its own by nature[99]; nevertheless, unlike creatures which can never be considered as 'accidents' of God, the *energies* are 'in one sense accidents' ($\sigma\upsilon\mu\beta\epsilon\beta\eta\kappa\acute{o}\varsigma\ \pi\omega\varsigma$),[100] but that conception can only be applied to them in so far as the whole Being of God cannot be identified with the essence; energy 'is neither essence, nor accident, and if some theologians have used the word "accident" that was only to show that everything in God is not essence.'[101] Nothing shows Palamas's main preoccupation better than these hesitations; that preoccupation was to free theology from Aristotle's philosophic categories which were clearly inadequate worthily to express the Mystery. Thinking along the same lines, he refuses to call the *energies* 'qualities' of God, for there may be no freedom about a quality, whereas the energies are the expression of the sovereign divine will; wisdom is the necessary quality which a master must possess to teach his pupil, but God only possesses wisdom as energy, for he only grants it according to his will.[102] The energies are inseparable from the essence, but not identical with it: 'In a certain sense,' Palamas writes, 'essence and energy are identical in God, but, in another sense, they are different.'[103] They are 'something other' than the Holy Spirit, but are not the divine essence. They involve a certain 'distinction' ($\delta\iota\alpha\sigma\tau o\lambda\acute{\eta}$) in the divine Being, but they do not divide it ($o\dot{\upsilon}\ \mu\epsilon\rho\iota\sigma\mu\acute{o}\varsigma$).[104]

---

[98] *Against Gregoras,* I, Coisl. 100, fol. 238v; II, fol. 250.
[99] *Against Akindynos,* VI, 21, Coisl. 98, fol. 175v.
[100] ibid., 19, fol. 174.
[101] *Cap. phys.* 127, col. 1209C; 135, col. 1216BC.
[102] *Against Gregoras,* II, Coisl. 100, fol. 259.
[103] *Letter to Daniel,* Coisl. 99, fol. 95.
[104] *Against Akindynos,* II, 17, Coisl. 98, fol. 64v; *Theophanes,* 940C.

God in action

Palamas's thought becomes clearer when he speaks of God as an active agent; then he feels closer to reality than when he is trying, with more or less felicity, to mould his thought in Aristotelian terms. As noted before, he says the divine simplicity expresses itself in the divine Persons : 'In essence and *energy* there is one unique Divinity of God; not only unique, but simple; for what synthesis could there be of the thing moved and movement?'[105] However, the action or *energy* of created beings necessarily involves a certain 'synthesis'; human intelligence, for instance, in order to think needs to 'undergo' an experience; but the divine act is pure action foreign to all passivity ($\dot{\epsilon}\nu\epsilon\rho\gamma\epsilon\tilde{\iota}$ $\mu\acute{o}\nu o\nu$, $\dot{a}\lambda\lambda'$ $o\dot{v}$ $\pi\acute{a}\sigma\chi\epsilon\iota$),[106] and so does not blemish the simplicity of the personal Being of God; so, for God, the *energies* are not an 'object' or a Platonic 'ideal world,' or a 'Sophia' in Bulgakov's sense which, while identifying itself with the divine essence, is yet an object of love for God. This absence in God of 'passion' caused by the energies explains how Palamas could both write that the energies 'divide themselves' and deny that this doctrine introduces 'division' in God.[107] In fact this division *is not imposed on him, but he, in his almighty power and voluntary condescension, imposes on himself a really diversified mode of existence:* 'God,' Palamas writes, 'by an excess of goodness towards us, being transcendent to all things, incomprehensible and inexpressible, consents to become participable by our intelligence and invisibly visible in his superessential and inseparable power.'[108]

E. von Ivanka has recently introduced a new element into the discussion by opposing Palamas to the modern Palamites : according to Palamas himself, 'the difference between the substance and the energies of God' would be a 'metaphysical statement,' whereas most modern Orthodox theologians only see it as 'a necessity of our understanding,' which would make their explanation more acceptable, but would in no way justify Palamas.[109] Really the problem is not one of opposition between metaphysics and a speculative necessity, but lies in the impossibility of reconciling essentialist metaphysics, derived from Greek philosophy, with the personalist and existentialist metaphysics which Palamas had inherited from the Bible and the Fathers.

It is also unprofitable to do as M. Jugie does, and contrast Palamas

---

[105] *On union and distinction, Coisl.* 98, *fol.* 24v.
[106] *Cap. phys.* 128, 134, 145, col. 1212A; 1216A; 1221C, etc.
[107] *Theophanes,* 944A, 940C.
[108] *Tr.* I, 3, 10.
[109] *Le fondement patristique de la doctrine palamite,* in *Actes du IXe Congrès International des Etudes byzantines,* II, 1956, pp. 127-8.

with some of his immediate disciples who are said to have promoted a 'mitigated Palamism'; the reservations which are said to have been made by such as John Cantacuzene about Palamas's views,[110] are actually already found in Palamas himself who never did teach the 'multitude of divinities.' If there is a certain difference of stress in Cantacuzene's explanation when compared to Palamas's works, the reason is that he was pursuing a specific aim, namely to make Palamism more comprehensible to the Papal Legate, Archbishop Paul; for all that he did not betray its essential elements. As for Philotheus, presented by M. Jugie as the most faithful of Palamas's followers—*palamaticas theses omnes retinet et copiosiori stylo explicat et propugnat* [111]—he does several times state, as E. von Ivanka would have it, that the distinction between the essence and the energies is only established 'through our understanding' (διακεκριμένον ἐπινοίᾳ),[112] which does not mean that he wanted to identify the divine being with the essence, but that, like Palamas himself, he refused to admit that the existential diversity of the energies introduces confusion into the divine Being itself.

---

[110] M. Jugie, *Theologia dogmatica*, II, pp. 114–16.
[111] ibid., p. 118.
[112] *Against Gregoras*, V, P.G. CLI, 878C, 880D; VIII, col. 983AB, 994C.

CHAPTER VI

TWO PARTICULAR PROBLEMS: PROCESSION OF THE HOLY SPIRIT AND MARIOLOGY

THERE is no Byzantine theologian of the Middle Ages who has not, in one way or another, taken part in the endless controversy about the Procession of the Holy Spirit. As is well known, the problem of the *'Filioque'* clause was first raised by the Frankish theologians at the Court of Charlemagne who reproached the Greeks for suppressing(!) this word in the Creed; it was taken up again by Photius in connection with the activity of German missionaries in Bulgaria. Greek theology and Latin theology which, in spite of their 'essential difference,'[1] had nonetheless till then formed two poles of a common dogmatic development thus clashed openly, and the conflict was all the harder to solve when the West, after the adoption of the *Filioque* at Rome in the eleventh century and the decision of the Council of Lyons about the Procession *tanquam ab uno principio,* had definitely set out on its own road and would find it difficult to go back to the situation before the controversy arose.

Echoes of the Arian controversies

The discussion between the Greeks and the Latins after the schism covered essentially the same ground as the disputes about the essence and the hypostases in the fourth century. The Greeks continued to defend the primacy of the hypostases in relation to the essence and, particularly, to assert that the Father, as hypostasis, is the Source of all Divinity; it is as Father that he begat the Son and sent forth the Holy Spirit.[2] The synthesis on the Trinity formulated by the Church when it condemned Arianism had, in the East, preserved a personalist character, while in the West it had been moulded to the shape of St. Augustine's essentialist philosophy. The Easterners had never been able to efface the suspicion of tritheism which had been brought against St. Basil, and which the Latins continued instinctively to nourish against them; but to the Greeks the Latins appeared suspect of Sabellianism with their

[1] G. L. Prestige, op. cit., p. 236.
[2] On the present state of the controversy between Orthodox and Roman Catholics on the question of the *Filioque,* see *Eastern Churches Quarterly,* VII, 1948, 5, and *Russie et Chrétienté,* 1950, Nos. 3–4.

doctrine of the unique 'substance' of the Divinity. So, when Photius was faced by the Latins who, on the basis of their own theology, arbitrarily modified the wording of the common Creed, the reproach of heresy came readily to his pen. He clearly saw the weak point of his adversary; if one admits the doctrine of Procession *ab utroque,* he wrote, 'the name of "Father" is deprived of meaning and sense; the property characterized by that word no longer belongs exclusively to him, and two divine hypostases are confused in one sole person. That is the view of Sabellius, or rather of some other half-Sabellian monster.' [3]

This theme was to be taken up again by all the later Greek writers who, down to the thirteenth century, introduced no new aspect into the debate. It was the Patriarch of Constantinople, Gregory of Cyprus, of whom we have spoken before, who was the first to try to discover an element in the Eastern Patristic tradition which would give an answer to the legitimate worries in the minds of the Latins, while preserving the personalism of Greek theology; that element was the distinction between the divine essence and the eternal uncreated energies. Whereas Photius, accepting the distinction between essence and *energies* in God and applying it to his conception of the gifts of the Spirit,[4] in his anti-Latin polemics always opposed the *eternal* procession of the Spirit from the Father to its *temporal* emission from the Son, the latter being considered solely as a consequence of the Incarnation,[5] Gregory of Cyprus spoke of an *eternal* illumination of the Spirit from the Son. That, as noted before, was the Palamite thesis, and Akindynos did not fail to take exception to Gregory of Cyprus as a forerunner of Palamas, while making constant reference to the 'very wise and zealous Photius.' [6]

In his attitude to the *Filioque* question, as in many other matters, Palamas was on the side of those who, not satisfied with the sterile repetition of hoary arguments, had a lively reaction to the problems of their own day. Conversely, as usual, the adversaries of Palamism urged a formalistic scholasticism, refractory to any attempt to smooth out Greco-Latin misunderstandings. Palamas was fiercely faithful to doctrinal Orthodoxy, but he was not systematically anti-Latin, as is proved by his attempts, and those of his followers, to explain his point of view to any Westerners whom he could reach, the Genoese of Galata, the Hospitalers of Rhodes and, later, the Legate of Urban V.

---

[3] *Mystagogy,* 9, *P.G.* CII, 289AB.
[4] *Amphil.,* 181, *P.G.* CIII, 892AB.
[5] *Mystagogy,* 30, col. 312B.
[6] *Against Palamas,* VI, *Monac. gr.* 223, *fol.* 283v; Barlaam also liked to quote Photius in his anti-Latin treatises (*Paris, gr.* 1278, *fol.* 108, etc.).

Personalism

The anti-Latin polemics to which he contributed in his correspondence with Akindynos and Barlaam between 1337 and 1339, and especially in his two *Apodictic Treatises,* were in his case essentially founded on the traditional argument of the supremacy of the hypostases over the essence; moreover his thought was completely personalist, and he could not help regarding the doctrine of the 'double Procession' as a threat to the attributes of the hypostases.[7] The Latins 'have no answer to those who blame them for introducing two origins for the Spirit,' because the Father and the Son, as hypostases, are *two* and not one, and because the procession is a hypostatic act of the Father. . . . They are one by nature, but the Spirit equally possesses that unique nature and should proceed from itself if procession was conceived as an act of nature. . . . The hypostasis of the Father is the active principle of the divine unity : 'God is one,' writes Palamas, 'not only because his nature is one, but also because the persons who proceed go back to one unique person.'[8] That is a paraphrase of St. Gregory Nazianzen : 'The nature is one in the Three; it is God; but that which makes their unity is the Father' (ἕνωσις δὲ ὁ πατήρ).[9] In God, 'the origin is hypostatic,'[10] and if the Latins accept that the Father and the Son constitute but one sole origin of the Spirit, they must equally recognize that the Son is 'homohypostatic' (ὁμουπόστατος) with the Father.[11] This theme is developed throughout the *Apodictic Treatises,* but the novelty therein consists in bringing into the debate the argument put forward by Gregory of Cyprus and approved officially by the Council of 1385.

Palamas explains in this sense those passages from the Fathers, St. Cyril of Alexandria especially, in which it is asserted that the Spirit comes 'from the two' (ἐξ ἀμφοῖν), or 'from the Son,' or again 'through the Son.' 'When you understand,' Palamas writes, 'that the Holy Spirit proceeds from the Two, because it comes essentially from the Father through the Son, you should understand this teaching in this sense : it is the powers and essential energies of God which pour out, not the divine hypostasis of the Spirit.'[12] 'The hypostasis of the All Holy Spirit does not come from the Son; it is not given or received by anybody; it is only the divine grace and energy which are received.'[13] He notes that the passages in the Fathers which appear to

---

[7] cf. our introduction to the text of the *First letter to Akindynos*, in *Theologia*, XXV, 1954, pp. 610–12.
[8] *Apodictic Treatise*, I, *Coisl.* 100, *fol.* 29v (ed. Constantinople, 1627, p. 38).
[9] *Hom.* 42, 15, *P.G.* XXXVI, 476B; quoted by Palamas, ibid., *fol.* 23 (p. 24).
[10] *Apodictic Treatise*, II, *fol.* 46v (p. 76).
[11] ibid., *fol.* 58 (p. 100).
[12] ibid., *fol.* 41 (p. 63). [13] ibid., *fol.* 51 (p. 86).

favour the Latin doctrine, do not say that the Spirit proceeds from the hypostasis of the Son, but 'from the nature of the Son,' that 'it comes naturally ($\varphi\upsilon\sigma\iota\kappa\tilde{\omega}\varsigma$) from him.' [14] Now, that which comes by nature is the energy, not the hypostasis. There is no doubt that all these disputed passages from the Fathers tend, in their contexts, to prove the *divinity of the Son* by a soteriological argument: only God can grant the gift of the Spirit; therefore Christ is God; he has a *common* nature with the Father. Moreover, the Western *Filioque* clause was first proclaimed by the Spanish Councils of the sixth and seventh centuries as an argument against the Arians. Palamas deduces from this that, since the 'spreading' of the Spirit from the Father and the Son is a proof of 'consubstantiality,' only an energy and not a divine hypostasis could proceed from this common substance, for the hypostasis of the Spirit itself shares therein and cannot proceed from itself.[15] The hypostasis of the Spirit does not manifest itself, or incarnate itself like that of the Son, but it manifests the Son. To prove, in his writings against Barlaam and Akindynos, that the *energy* is quite distinct from the essence, Palamas tries to show that the charisms of the Spirit which are granted by grace are not the very hypostasis of the Spirit; the latter was communicated neither at Pentecost, nor in the spiritual gifts of which the New Testament speaks. In this context, Palamas distinguishes between those passages of the New Testament which speak of 'the Spirit' ($\tau\grave{o}$ $\pi\nu\epsilon\tilde{\upsilon}\mu\alpha$) with the definite article, and those which speak of spirit ($\pi\nu\epsilon\tilde{\upsilon}\mu\alpha$) without the article; the latter signify gifts or spiritual energies, and naturally proceed from the Father and the Son, but also from the Spirit itself, for the whole essence of God is the 'cause' of the *energies* . . . [16] In any case the Son is the only channel for the outpouring *towards us* of sanctifying grace, for it was he alone who was Incarnate. So Palamas summarizes his thought in these terms: 'The Holy Spirit belongs to Christ by essence and by energy, because Christ is God; nevertheless, according to essence and hypostasis it belongs but does not proceed, whereas, according to energy, it belongs and proceeds.' [17]

Openings

The distinction between essence and *energy* allows Palamas to adopt a much more tolerant attitude than other Greek theologians towards the Latin formulations: as *energy*, 'the Spirit pours itself out from the Father through the Son and, if you like, from the Son over all those worthy thereof'; this 'pouring out' may moreover also be called 'pro-

[14] ibid., *fol.* 57 (p. 99).
[15] ibid., *fol.* 62v (p. 110).
[16] ibid., *fol.* 36, 40 (pp. 54–5, 62).
[17] ibid., *fol.* 44v (p. 71).

cession' (ἐκπόρευσις): 'We must not behave in unseemly fashion vainly quarrelling about words. . . .'[18] That is the Orthodox meaning which can be given to the Latin *Filioque* clause; while preserving the personalism of the Fathers and the traditional Byzantine position concerning the 'economic' procession of the Spirit from the Son, Palamas, because he considers the divine energies as uncreated and eternal, does not limit that 'economy' to temporal existence. On the other hand it is true that the distinction between essence and energy makes it impossible to pass by induction from the 'economic' order, subject to the divine will, to the essential order which does not involve the action of the energies of God; even if, by reason of 'consubstantiality,' the Father and the Son have only one energy which is called 'Spirit' and which is distinct from the third hypostasis, we still have no means of drawing any conclusions from that about the eternal relations of the divine Persons. However in his *Physical Chapters* Palamas does a little unveil his conception of these relations, and it is somewhat surprising to find there a psychological simile rather like that used by St. Augustine. After referring to the traditional Patristic scheme of the Word (λόγος) and the Breath (πνεῦμα), he goes on, 'This Spirit of the Word from on high is like a mysterious love (οἷόν τις ἔρως ἀπόρρητος) of the Father towards the Word mysteriously begotten; it is the same love as that possessed by the Word and the well-beloved Son of the Father towards him who begat him; this he does in so far as he comes from the Father conjointly with this love, and this love rests naturally on him.'[19] It seems unlikely that one could find another passage similar to this in Byzantine theological literature.

This short account of some of Palamas's ideas about the procession of the Holy Spirit is by no means a complete analysis of his doctrine on this point. We have limited ourselves to stressing certain points which seem important to give direction to future researches, and which show that, in spite of the difficulties that remain and the manifestly unfinished character of Palamas's thought, one finds his mind much more open towards the West than was the case with many of his contemporaries. In any case his attitude is much more worth studying than are the political or humanist interests which led some of his adversaries to capitulate unconditionally before Latin thought.

The Mother of God

Gregory's thought concerning Mary is inspired by an extremely realist view of the divine Maternity, expressed by the dogma of Ephesus; the

[18] *Apodictic Treatise*, I, ibid., *fol.* 24 (p. 26).
[19] *Cap. phys.* 36, col. 1144D–1145A.

Incarnation of the Word was brought about in her and by her; the person of Christ is therefore inseparable from that of his Mother. When Palamas, following the tradition of the Fathers and, even more, the Liturgy, applies to Mary adjectives which, biblically, seem reserved for Christ, he is not thinking of the person of Mary taken by itself and, so to say, statically, but of 'Her who begat God.' For him, as for the whole tradition of the Church, 'Mariology' is one particular and necessary aspect of orthodox Christology which asserts both the full divinity and the full humanity of Christ: without Mary, this union could not have been realized in the person of Jesus. . . .

Thus the Mother of God is 'the source and root of the race of liberty' [20]; her body—temple of God—is 'the medicine which saves our race' [21]; 'alone, placing herself between God and the whole human race, she made of God a son of man and transformed men into sons of God' [22]; 'the Virgin Mother alone dwells on the frontier between created and uncreated natures, and those who know God recognize also in her the habitation of the infinite' [23]; it is from her that 'the Saints receive all their sanctity' [24]: 'no one can come to God except through her . . . for it is only through her mediation that he has come to us, that he appeared on earth and dwelt among men' [25]; being thus at the centre of the story of salvation the Virgin is 'the cause of events before her time, the leader in the sequence of events thereafter, and the distributor of eternal blessings; she is the thought of the Prophets, the chief of the Apostles, the prop of the Martyrs, and the foundation of the Doctors . . . she is the summit of the achievement of all that is holy' [26]; 'all divinely inspired Scripture was written for the sake of the Virgin who begat God.' [27] She enjoyed the particular privilege of being the first to see the risen Jesus.[28] . . . The temple at Jerusalem was the 'type' of Mary, for she is the true 'place of God,' [29] the true throne of the Lord, 'for there where the King sits, there is his throne' [30]; she is

---

[20] *Hom.* 14, col. 169C
[21] *Hom.* 37, col. 464D.
[22] ibid., col. 465A; cf. *Hom.* 53, ed. Oikonomos, p. 136.
[23] *Hom.* 14, col. 177A; cf. *Hom.* 53, ed. Oikonomos, pp. 156, 162; *Hom.* 37, col. 473A.
[24] *Hom.* 37, col. 461A.
[25] ibid., col. 472BC.
[26] *Hom.* 53, ed. Oikonomos, p. 162.
[27] *Hom.* 57, ed. Oikonomos, p. 216.
[28] *Hom.* 18, col. 237AB, 241BC; *Hom.* 20, col. 269C; on this ancient tradition, see Kiprian (Kern), *Iavlenia voskresshago Gospoda Bogomateri*, in *Pravoslavnaia Mysl'*, VIII, Paris, 1951, pp. 86–112; C. Gianelli, *Témoignages patristiques grecs en faveur d'une apparition du Christ ressuscité à la Vierge Marie*, in *Revue des é byzantines*, XI, 1953 (Mélanges Jugie), pp. 106–19.
[29] *Hom.* 53, ed. Oikonomos, pp. 145–6.
[30] ibid., p. 157.

the receptacle of the treasure which God granted to men,[31] the tongs which the Seraphim used to take up the live coal which touched the mouth of the prophet Isaiah, prefiguring the Incarnation.[32] . . . These epithets applied to Mary, for all their rhetorical and lyrical quality, all refer to her part in the Incarnation; therefore they do not infringe on the worship due to God alone, but rather bear witness to an extremely Christocentric form of piety and conception of history; worship of the Mother is indeed addressed to the God-Man whom she bore. It is only when one considers that worship outside the precise concept of divine Maternity, that one strays beyond the biblical and traditional domain.

The pure Virgin

Naturally Palamas is aware that, to play her part in the economy of salvation, Mary was the subject of a particular choice: 'God, before time was, chose her for himself,' he proclaimed '. . . and thought her worthy of a grace more abundant than that granted to other humans; he made her holy of the holy even before her wondrous child-bearing.'[33] 'It was necessary,' he writes, 'that she, who was to bear the fairest among the children of men (Psalm 45 : 2), should herself be incomparable in all things and prepared to receive that beauty: a wondrous beauty since it came from her Child who in all things resembled her exactly.'[34] 'That is the one thing that would be impossible for God,' we read elsewhere, 'to unite himself to something impure, before it had been purified in anticipation of that union; so it was necessary that it should be a Virgin free from all blemish and perfectly pure, who should bear and engender him who loves and bestows purity.'[35] It is understandable that passages of this sort, of which there are many, should lead some authors to suppose that Palamas held the doctrine of the Immaculate Conception; Christ's humanity is a humanity without stain, and she who gave him this humanity 'resembled him in all things,' as Palamas says, that is to say she possesses by special grace original purity. It is indeed probable that Palamas's very striking piety with regard to the Virgin would have led him to accept that doctrine, if he had *shared the Western conception* of original sin. However, as we have noticed before and shall see again in certain passages concerning the Virgin, Palamas's view of the sin of Adam and the way in which it was transmitted, cannot be reconciled with the doctrine of the Immaculate Conception as defined by Rome; to give a complete idea of Gregory's thought it is therefore essential to remember the context of all his expressions.

---

[31] ibid., p. 161.
[32] *Hom.* 14, col. 177A.
[33] *Hom.* 57, ed. Oikonomos, p. 214.
[34] *Hom.* 53, p. 142.
[35] *Hom.* 52, p. 123.

TWO PARTICULAR PROBLEMS

The inheritance from Adam

We have seen that Palamas had learnt from Greek Patristic thought the conception that original sin was above all a *hereditary mortality*, leading the individuals of the human race to commit sins, but not implying any guilt for the actual sin of the First Father. This mortality, the consequence of Adam's sin and linked—more as cause than as effect—to the individual sins of his descendants, was transmitted by natural generation. That was the essential reason why Christ *alone* had no human father: 'He alone,' Palamas writes in his *Treatise on the Economy of the Word*, in which there are also many passages apparently favourable to the Immaculate Conception, 'was not conceived in iniquity nor engendered in sin (Psalm 51 : 7). . . . For the urge of the flesh . . . brings the original condemnation; it is corruption and, as such, must engender corruption.' [36] It is worth nothing that this quotation, which is part of a lengthy passage about original sin, is repeated word for word in the *Homily* on the Presentation, as if to prevent any incorrect interpretation of certain passages concerning the Virgin.[37] 'If he had come from a sperm,' he says elsewhere speaking of Christ, 'he would not have been a new man; belonging to the old race and heir to the error of Adam, he could not have received within himself the plenitude of the divinity.' [38] Again, it is characteristic that the sojourn of Mary in the temple, described by Palamas in terms that make Mary the model of the hesychast life, led her, according to Gregory, not to come to an understanding of the grace which she had received from the time of her conception, but to learn the nature of the sin of Adam, and to realize that 'no one could stop the murderous rush which was bearing away the human race.' [39] And when the Angel appeared to her to announce that she was to be the Mother of God, she spoke to him of her faith in the coming of the Spirit 'to further purify her nature, and give her the strength to receive the Child of salvation.' [40] In his sermon on the Dormition, Palamas asserts very plainly that it was at the Annunciation that God pronounced 'the words that made the counterpart to the condemnation of Eve and of Adam . . . and turned it into a benediction.' [41]

These few quotations make it clear that what Palamas says about the

---

[36] *Hom.* 16, col. 192C.
[37] *Hom.* 52, ed. Oikonomos, p. 124. An English translation of this homily has been published in the *Eastern Churches Quarterly*, X, 1954–5, No. 8, pp. 378–84, with the surprising omission of these important passages on original sin.
[38] *Hom.* 58, ed. Oikonomos, p. 230.
[39] *Hom.* 53, ed. Oikonomos, p. 169.
[40] *Hom.* 14, col. 176D.
[41] *Hom.* 37, col. 461D.

resemblance of the Virgin to her Son, or about her purity before the Annunciation, or again about the particular grace which she had received, should be taken in a sense which is after all relative, and does not assert that the future Mother of God was, before her Childbearing, free from the framework of the old law. Was she not the daughter of Joachim, and not of Anne only? Was she not destined to die like other humans subject to the inheritance of Adam, even though, after her death, God glorified her in her very body? This bodily glorification, specifically recognized by Palamas, is not connected with an Immaculate Conception which must have preceded the Childbearing, but is a consequence of Divine Maternity : 'If a soul in which grace dwells,' Gregory preaches, 'rises to the sky when it has separated itself from things here below . . . how could the body which received in itself the eternal and unique Son of God, the inexhaustible Source of grace, and which even gave birth thereto, fail to be lifted up from earth to heaven?' [42] Nonetheless the Virgin did indeed die, and Palamas shows that that death was the result of 'corruption' after Adam when he puts forward the original and unexpected hypothesis of the immaculate conception of St. John the Baptist; was not such a hypothesis possible, for John, like Jesus, died a violent death? Could one prove that 'the greatest among the children of women' would have suffered a natural death? 'He had no need,' says Palamas, 'to suffer a natural death; such death is a punishment for the fault of Adam; he who performed the commandments and who obeyed God in his mother's womb, was not subject thereto; the Saints must always give their life for virtue and religion according to our Lord's command, and for that reason a violent death for the sake of the Good suits them best; that is why the Lord himself tasted death in this fashion. It was necessary that the death of John should be the forerunner of the death of Christ . . .' [43] The interest of this passage, in which Palamas is certainly inconsistent with his own central and essentially Christocentric thought, lies not so much in the idea expressed, as in the conception of original sin which it assumes. For that conception eliminates any possibility of interpreting Palamas's thought in the sense of the Western doctrine of the Immaculate Conception. The manifold graces which God lavished on the Virgin Mary, before and after her Child-bearing, did not alter the fact that death, which came from Adam, could not be vanquished except in the deified Body put on by the hypostasis of the Son of God; therefore he alone was blessed by an immaculate conception in the womb of Mary.

---

[42] *Hom.* 37, col. 465C.
[43] *Hom.* 40, col. 513C.

CONCLUSION

As this work has no pretensions to be more than an 'introduction' to the study of Palamas, we will be very careful not to draw final conclusions about his character or his work. But some points seem established and could be taken as the point of departure for further study.

Historically speaking, it cannot be denied that the great majority of the Byzantines regarded Gregory as a representative of traditional Orthodoxy. His victory over Barlaam between 1338 and 1341 was complete and relatively easy; in Barlaam's person the Eastern Church condemned a system of thought making God a transcendent and unknowable essence; that essence, though it was the Prime Mover in the creation of the universe, remained inactive in the actual existence of the latter and left it a complete autonomy; the Incarnation, the sacraments, the Church, and the spiritual experience of the Saints were relegated to the domain of symbols, or considered as extraordinary miracles having no intrinsic connection with the permanent reality of created existence. The human intelligence, provided it did not pretend to knowledge of God, remained sovereign in its own domain, and could alone decide, independently of all revelation and all grace, human destiny here below. In fact the thought of the ancient philosophers—especially the Platonic dualism of spirit and matter—were the supreme authorities for Barlaam and his school; in this way the intellectual movement which they set on foot was leading the Christian East towards the fundamental principles of the Renaissance.

In the West at the same time a nominalist philosophy, comparable in its effects to that of Barlaam, prepared the way for the secularism of the Modern Age, and established the doctrinal foundations of the Protestant Reformation. At present we have not enough evidence to trace any direct influence of William of Ockham on Barlaam, but they certainly grew in the same intellectual atmosphere. If Barlaamism had triumphed, it might have led the Eastern Church along the paths down which William of Ockham's nominalism did lead the West, and it might have entailed, perhaps even more quickly, the same consequences. A comparative study of philosophical tendencies in the fourteenth century in the East and in the West might lead to unexpected parallelism, and perhaps soften the categorical judgments of some westerners concerning Palamas; can one, and should one, condemn the reaction of the Eastern Church faced with Barlaamism, unless one believes that the Christian Mystery can be adequately expressed in terms of Ockhamite nominalism?

It was only political circumstances which prevented the Palamite triumph of 1341 from being final. The proceedings against Palamas and his arrest were basically due to the desire of the Patriarch John Calecas to be rid of a political opponent; that Prelate's attempt to buy Palamas's support with honours in 1342, his long delay in turning to Akindynos, and his betrayal of the latter in 1346 show that he lacked any real doctrinal conviction. In 1344 the accusation of heresy and the condemnation of Palamas by the Synod were intended to compromise an eminent partisan of Cantacuzene, these generally unpopular measures only had the support of the Court of Anne of Savoy for a very short time, and their main effect was to prepare the way for Calecas's fall.

However this brief triumph of the anti-Palamites would not have been possible without the presence in Constantinople of a certain number of *doctrinal* adversaries of Palamas. This very heterogeneous body was represented by three main groups:

1. Some bishops who were by tradition anxious both to preserve the authority of their function in face of the Charismatism of the monasteries, and to keep the material advantages which a strict control of the monasteries provided.

2. Some representatives of those who favoured what one might call 'the theology of repetition,' for whom the decisions of ancient Councils constituted verbally final formulas which could not be developed in any way, not even in a way conforming to Tradition; they opposed every 'innovation' and, being fiercely anti-Latin, would not allow any one to adopt a creative attitude towards the West. In the thirteenth century such people opposed Gregory of Cyprus, and in the fourteenth Palamas.

3. The Humanists who, more or less openly, shared Barlaam's agnosticism.

In the first group the doctrinal element was reduced to a minimum, as is shown by the opportunist shifts of a Matthew of Ephesus, James Koukounares and many others. As for the two other groups, in spite of their apparently distinct doctrinal attitudes, they had in common the absence of a living theology, rooted in spiritual life and capable of responding to the challenge of the Modern Age. It was indeed possible to go on repeating the decisions of the Oecumenical Councils, while consecrating their spiritual and intellectual powers to the study of profane philosophy and seeking therein the definitive answer to the crucial problems of existence. While this way of thought was incapable of engaging in any true dialogue with Western thought, it could nonetheless result in a religious compromise on the basis of relativism. The original anti-Latin feeling of the anti-Palamite party actually tended to get blurred in the second half of the fourteenth century. More than that, the most brilliant adversaries of the monastic theology set out resolutely on the path of union with Rome; some of them did this in Barlaam's fashion, that is to say without real doctrinal conviction, since their philosophy prevented them from having any. Others were seduced by the masterly Thomist synthesis—it had been translated into Greek in the middle of the fourteenth century by Demetrius Cydones— which seemed to them to conform with their philosophical aspirations and to be much more 'Greek' than the theology of the monks. However one may judge the questions of conscience involved in these conversions, there is no doubt that they involve the abandonment of the living spiritual tradition of the Christian East.

All these tendencies only affected the lot of a few isolated individuals. What the Byzantine Church approved in Palamism was not an exhaustive 'compendium' of doctrine, nor a philosophy, but rather a way of thinking able to safeguard the presence of God in history, his real fidelity to his Church, and his mysterious union—sacramental and mystical—with the community, the Body of Christ, manifest in the spiritual life of each Christian. In this study we have tried to make clear the true meaning of Palamas's formulations and their traditional character. It is however obvious that Palamas used tradition in a living way; in response to the concrete situation with which he was faced, he extended and defined the distinction between essence and energy, and the Council of 1351 allowed that his thought was a 'development' of the decisions of the Councils. Though he refused to be called an 'innovator,' Gregory broke away from the formal and set conservatism characteristic of a part at least of Byzantine mediaeval theology. Moreover, he adopted the same living and realist attitude towards his own formulations, which he never defended for themselves, but only in so far as they seemed to him to be adequate expressions of the truth; 'Our religion is not a question of words, but of realities,' he was fond of repeating.

By approving Palamas's thought, the Byzantine Church resolutely turned its back on the spirit of the Renaissance. This break, which came about in the middle of the fourteenth century, can be seen in the art of the time too. The humanist tendencies so characteristic of what is called the 'Renaissance of the Palaeologi' noticeably diminished. It is this opposition to the Renaissance, rather than any objection to the West as such, which is characteristic of the Palamite victory. Palamas himself tried several times to get into touch with the Westerners, and his disciples did the same afterwards; but the ever closer links which became established between his adversaries and the West—on the basis of a common humanism, as much as or even more than on a common theology—and which led some Byzantines to capitulate unconditionally in face of the Latin theology of their time, drove back the immense majority of the Orthodox, who had recognized Gregory as a Doctor of the Church, into a systematically anti-Latin attitude. Only a few Palamite intellectuals, such as Gennadios Scholarios in the fifteenth century, kept an open attitude towards Latin thought.

In rejecting the secularism of the Modern Age, did Palamism provide an alternative? Was it not basically negative and obscurantist? We hope we have shown that it would not be right to say that. What Palamas attacked in 'profane philosophy' was not its worth in itself, but its pretension to be adequate for the Christian Mystery. In this respect, Palamism represented a new and decisive step forward in the Eastern Christian tradition towards liberation from the Neo-Platonic categories which always constituted the great temptation for Greek mysticism. This is true not only of his metaphysics, where Palamas's personalist and Christocentric thought shook free from the ambiguities of Dionysian apophatism, but also and above all of his doctrine concerning man. Palamas made a firm choice between biblical monism and Platonic dualism: man is not a spirit imprisoned in matter and longing to be free, but a being who, by the very nature of his composite character, is called upon to establish the Reign of God over matter and spirit inseparably joined. These essential Christian truths were proclaimed and approved by the Eastern Church at one of the most crucial moments in the history of Christianity, a time when Christian thought was threatened by internal disintegration. There is a permanent importance in Palamas's victory. He did not provide an exhaustive system able to give an answer to all problems, but he did give a sense of direction by which others were to be guided later.

The brutal end imposed by events on the development of Eastern Christian theology in the fifteenth century, did not allow the decisions of the fourteenth to bear all their fruits. Westerners were either completely ignorant of these decisions, or judged the little they did know in terms of philosophic assumptions which Palamas would not have recognized. Let us hope that our age, by objective study of the documents and by not giving absolute value to philosophic principles foreign to Revelation, will appreciate the great theologian of hesychasm better. Without shutting our eyes to the lack of completeness in his conclusions, and without being constrained by formulations to which their author himself attached no absolute value, we do find in his thought, taken as a whole, a constructive answer to the challenge to Christianity of the Modern Age: a personalist and existential theology and a spirituality which, freed from Platonic spiritualizing, integrates the whole man in the new life.

SELECT BIBLIOGRAPHY

Texts

Gregoriou tou Palama Syggrammata, ed. P. Christou, 5 vols. (Thessalonika, 1962, 1966, 1970, 1988, 1992).

Saint Gregory Palamas: The One Hundred and Fifty Chapters. A Critical Edition, Translation and Study, ed. R. E. Sinkewicz (Toronto, 1988).

Translations

Gregory Palamas: The Triads [selections], trans. N. Gendle, Classics of Western Spirituality, (Mahwah, NJ,1983).

Saint Gregory Palamas: Treatise on the Spiritual Life, trans. D. Rogich (Minneapolis, 1995).

Douze homélies pour les fêtes, trans. J. Cler (Paris, 1987).

"Saint Gregory Palamas' *The Decalogue of the Law according to Christ, that is, the New Covenant*," trans. & intro. S. A. Mouselimas, *Greek Orthodox Theological Review*, 25:3 (1980), 297-305.

"Homily 34 of Saint Gregory Palamas," trans. & intro. D. Rogich, *Greek Orthodox Theological Review*, 33:2 (1988), 135-166.

"Saint Gregory Palamas' Homily for Palm Sunday," trans. & intro. N. S. Weber, *Greek Orthodox Theological Review*, 34:3 (1989), 263-282.

"The Answer to Paul Asen of Gregory Palamas: A Fourteenth Century Apology for the One, Grand and Angelic Schema," trans. [with Greek text] and intro. P. Hatlie, *St Vladimir's Theological Quarterly*, 33:1 (1989), 35-51.

"To the Most Reverend Nun Xenia," "A New Testament Decalogue," "In Defence of Those who Practise a Life of Stillness" [=*Triad* 1:2], "Three Texts on Prayer and Purity of Heart," "Topics of Natural and Theological Science and on the Moral and Ascetic Life: One Hundred and Fifty Texts," "The Declaration of the Holy Mountain in Defence of Those who Devoutly Practice a Life of Stillness," in *The Philokalia*, vol. 4, trans. G. E. H. Palmer, P. Sherrard and K. Ware (London, 1995).

Secondary Material

Allchin, A. M.: "The Appeal to Experience in the *Triads* of St Gregory Palamas," *Studia Patristica*, 8:2 (TU 93; 1966), 323-328.

Ammann, A. M.: *Die Gottesschau im palamitischen Hesychasmus: Ein Handbuch der spätbyzantinischen Mystik*, 3rd ed. (Würzburg, 1986).

Barrois, G.: "Palamism Revisited," *St Vladimir's Theological Quarterly*, 19:4 (1975), 211-231.

Beck, H.-G.: "Humanismus und Palamismus," *Actes du XIIe Congrès International d'Études Byzantines*, I (Belgrad, 1963), 63-82.

Coffey, D.: "The Palamite Doctrine of God: A New Perspective," *St Vladimir's Theological Quarterly*, 32:4 (1988), 329-358.

Flogaus, R.: *Theosis bei Palamas und Luther: Ein Beitrag zum ökumenischen Gespräch* (Göttingen, 1997).

_____ "Palamas and Barlaam Revisited: A Reassessment of East and West in the Hesychast Controversy of 14th Century Byzantium," *St Vladimir's Theological Quarterly*, 42:1 (1998), 1-32.

Florovsky, G.: "Saint Gregory Palamas and the Tradition of the Fathers," *Greek Orthodox Theological Review* 5:2 (1959-60), 119-131 [=*Bible, Church, Tradition*, Collected Works vol.1, 105-120]

Grondijs, L. H.: "The Patristic Origins of Gregory Palamas' Doctrine of God," *Studia Patristica*, 5:3 (TU 80; 1962), 323-328.

Habra, G.: "The Source of the Doctrine of Gregory Palamas on the Divine Energies," *Eastern Churches Quarterly* 12:6 (1958), 244-52; 12:7 (1958), 294-303; 12:8 (1958), 338-347.

Halleux, A. de: "Palamisme et Scolastique: Exclusivisme dogmatique ou pluriformité théologique?" *Revue théologique de Louvain*, 4 (1973), 409-442.

_____ "Palamisme et Tradition," *Irénikon*, 48:4 (1975), 479-493.

Houdret, J.-P.: "Palamas et les Cappadociens," *Istina*, 19:3 (1974), 260-71.

Hussey, M. E.: "The Palamite Trinitarian Models," *St Vladimir's Theological Quarterly*, 16:2 (1972), 83-89.

_____ "The Persons-Energy Structure in the Theology of St Gregory Palamas," *St Vladimir's Theological Quarterly*, 18:1 (1974), 22-43.

Jugie, M.: "Palamas," *Dictionnaire de Théologie Catholique*, 11, 1735-1776.

Jugie, M.: "Palamite (controverse)," *Dictionnaire de Théologie Catholique*, 11, 1777-1818.

Kern, C.: "Les éléments de la théologie de Grégoire Palamas," *Irénikon*, 20:1 (1947), 6-33; 20:2 (1947), 164-93.

_____ *Antropologia sv. Grigoriia Palamy* (Paris, 1950).

Krivoshein, B.: "The Ascetic and Theological Teaching of Gregory Palamas," *Eastern Churches Quarterly*, 3 (1938), 26-33, 71-84, 138-156, 193-214.

Le Guillou, M. J.: "Lumière et charité dans la doctrine palamite de la divinisation," *Istina*, 19:3 (1974), 329-338.

Lison, J.: *L'Esprit répandu: La pneumatologie de Grégoire Palamas* (Paris, 1994).

Mantzarides, G.: *Palamika* (Thessalonika, 1973).

_____ "Tradition and Renewal in the Theology of Saint Gregory Palamas," *Eastern Churches Review*, 9:1-2 (1977), 1-18.

_____ *The Deification of Man: St Gregory Palamas and the Orthodox Tradition* (New York, 1984).

Meyendorff, John: *Byzantine Hesychasm: Historical, Theological and Social Problems: Collected Studies* (London, 1974).

_____ "Les débuts de la controverse hésychaste," *Byzantion*, 23 (1953), 87-120 [=*Byzantine Hesychasm* I].

SELECT BIBLIOGRAPHY

——— "Une lettre inédite de Grégoire Palamas à Akindynos," *Theologia*, 24 (1953), 557-582 [=*Byzantine Hesychasm*, III]

——— "L'origine de la controverse palamite. La première lettre de Palamas à Akindynos," *Theologia*, 25 (1954), 602-613; 26 (1955) 77-90 [=*Byzantine Hesychasm* II].

——— "Humanisme nominaliste et mystique chrétienne à Byzance au XIVe siècle," *Nouvelle Revue Théologique*, 79:9 (1957), 905-914 [=*Byzantine Hesychasm* VI].

——— "Society and Culture in the Fourteenth Century: Religious Problems," *Actes du XIVe Congrès International d'Études Byzantines*, I (Bucharest, 1974), 111-124 [=*Byzantine Hesychasm* VIII].

——— "*The Defense of the Holy Hesychasts* by St Gregory Palamas," in J. Meyendorff *The Byzantine Legacy in the Orthodox Church* (New York, 1982), 167-194.

——— "The Holy Trinity in Palamite Theology," in M. A. Fahey & J. Meyendorff, *Trinitarian Theology East and West: St Thomas Aquinas-St Gregory Palamas* (Brookline MA, 1977), 25-43.

——— "Mount Athos in the Fourteenth Century: A Spiritual and Intellectual Legacy," *Dumbarton Oaks Papers* 42 (1988), 157-165.

Miquel, P.: "Grégoire Palamas, Docteur de l'Expérience," *Irénikon*, 37:2 (1964), 227-237.

Nadal, J. S.: "La critique par Akindynos de l'herméneutique patristique de Palamas," *Istina*, 19:3 (1974), 297-328.

——— "La rédaction première de la Troisième lettre de Palamas à Akindynos," *Orientalia Christiana Periodica*, 40:2 (1974), 233-285.

Papademetriou, G.: "The Human Body according to Saint Gregory Palamas," *Greek Orthodox Theological Review*, 34:1 (1989), 1-9.

Patacsi, G.: "Palamism before Palamas," *Eastern Churches Review*, 9:1-2 (1977), 64-71.

Podskalsky, G.: "Gottesschau und Inkarnation. Zur Bedeutung der Heilsgeschichte bei Gregorios Palamas," *Orientalia Christiana Periodica*, 35:1 (1969), 5-44.

Rantovits, A.: *Mysterion tes Hagias Triados kata ton hagion Gregorion Palaman* (Thessalonika, 1973).

Richter, G.: "Ansätze und Motive für die Lehre des Gregorios Palamas von den göttlichen Energien," *Ostkirchliche Studien*, 31:4 (1982), 281-296.

Romanides, J.: "Notes on the Palamite Controversy and Related Topics," *Greek Orthodox Theological Review*, 6:2 (1960-61), 186-205; 9:2 (1963-64), 225-270.

Sahas, D.: "Gregory Palamas (1296-1360) on Islam," *The Muslim World*, 73.1 (1983), 1-21.

Savvidis, K.: *Die Lehre von der Vergöttlichung des Menschen bei Maximos dem Bekenner und ihre Rezeption durch Gregor Palamas* (St Ottilien, 1997).

Scazzoso, P.: *La teologia di S. Gregorio Palamas* (1296-1359) (Milan, 1970).

Schultze, B.: "Die Bedeutung des Palamismus in der russischen Theologie der Gegenwart," *Scholastik*, 26 (1951), 390-412.

——— "Grundfragen des theologischen Palamismus," *Ostkirchliche Studien*, 24 (1975), 105-135.

Sinkewicz, R. E.: "A New Interpretation for the First Episode in the Controversy between Barlaam the Calabrian and Gregory Palamas," *Journal of Theological Studies*, 31:2 (1980), 489-500.

―――― "The Doctrine of the Knowledge of God in the Early Writings of Barlaam the Calabrian," *Medieval Studies*, 44 (1982), 181-242.

Stiernon, D.: "Bulletin sur le Palamisme," *Revue des études byzantines*, 30 (1972), 231-341.

Theokletos Dionysiates (monachos): *Hagios Gregorios ho Palamas: ho vios kai he theologia tou* (Thessalonika, 1984).

Trethowan, I.: "Irrationality in Theology and the Palamite Distinction," *Eastern Churches Review*, 9:1-2 (1977), 19-26.

Ware, K.: "God Hidden and Revealed: The Apophatic Way and the Essence-Energy Distinction," *Eastern Churches Review*, 7:2 (1975), 125-136.

―――― "The Debate about Palamism," *Eastern Churches Review*, 9:1-2 (1977), 45-63.

Wendebourg, D.: *Geist oder Energie: Zur Frage der innergöttlichen Verankerung des christlichen Lebens in der byzantinischen Theologie* (Munich, 1980).

Williams, R.: "The Philosophical Structures of Palamism," *Eastern Churches Review*, 9:1-2 (1977), 27-44.

Yangazoglou, S.: "Philosophy and Theology: The Demonstrative Method in the Theology of Saint Gregory Palamas," *Greek Orthodox Theological Review* 41.1 (1996), 1-18.

Yannaras, C.: "The Distinction Between Essence and Energies and Its Importance for Theology," *St Vladimir's Theological Quarterly*, 19:4 (1975), 232-246.

INDEX

Adramyttium, conferences of: 26
Adrianople: 78, 79, 86
Alexiakon: 98
Alexis I Comnenus: 22, 32, 99
Alexis of Russia: 100
Amparis: 97, 98
Andronicus II Palaeologus: 15, 17, 21, 22, 24, 26, 27, 28, 29, 32
Andronicus III Palaeologus: 28, 40, 50, 52-5, 57-60, 62, 63-4, 75, 78, 89, 96, 101, 108
Anne of Savoy: 50, 58, 63-85, 93, 102-3, 108, 112, 113, 238
Anthony, St.: 39, 200
Anthony, hegoumenos: 49
Anthony, protos: 92
Apocaucos, Alexis: 23, 63-5, 69, 72, 75, 82, 85, 90, 113
Apophatic theology: 205-8
Aristotle: 29-31, 42, 43, 44, 116, 117, 131, 210
Arius, arians: 218, 219, 222, 228, 231
Arsenius, patr., Arsenites: 19, 21, 26, 63
Arsenius of Tyre: 17, 53, 94, 96-8,
Asen, Andronicus: 80, 94, 102
Asen, Manuel: 94
Asen, Michael: 94
Asen, Paul: 39, 201
Athanasius of Alexandria: 136, 200
Athanasius of Cyzicus: 60-1, 79, 87
Athanasius, hieromonk: 94
Athanasius Lepentrinos: 25-6
Athanasius I, patr.: 20-2, 24, 25, 26, 37(45), 64, 89
Athanasius, monastery of: 57
Atouemis, Theodore: 94
Augustine, St.: 118, 122, 228, 232
Avignon: 47, 55
Baptism: 152-5, 159-62
Basil St.: 57, 96, 110, 228
Benedict XII, Pope: 47
Beroea: 37-8, 40
Bitolj: *see* Pelagonia
Blakhernae, council of: 13, 230
Blakhemae, palace: 94
Blakhernite: *see* Theodore
Bogomils: *see* Messalians
Boukharis: *see* Isidore, patr.
Brotinos: 132

Brussa: 105-6
Bryennios: 40
Bulgaker, S.: 226
Bulgaria, Bulgarians: 24, 25, 26, 228

Cabasilas, Nicholas: 20, 23, 27, 80, 82, 83, 85, 140
Calamares, Constant: 103
Calecas, John, patr.: 21, 23, 46-88, 101, 112, 238
Callistos, patr.: 34, 36, 40, 41, 49, 66, 82, 93-4, 97, 99, 103, 108, 112
Calothetos, Joseph: 20(29), 51, 57(55), 60, 81
Cantacuzene, Helen: 109
Cantacuzene, Irene: 93
Cantacuzene, John VI: 20, 23, 35, 42, 47, 55, 57-60, 63-104, 107-8, 113, 227
Cantactizene, Matthew: 100, 103
Chalcedon: 25, 212
Chariton of Apro: 89
Charlemagne: 228
Charmida: 132
Chilas, John: 14-15
Chiones: 105-7
Chios: 76
Chora, monastery: 71
Choumnos, Irene-Eulogie: 17, 19, 67, 72, 83-4
Choumnos, Nicephorus: 17, 26, 83
Christ-Incomprehensible, monastery: 69, 112
Christ-Philanthropos,, monastery: 84
Christology: 180-4, 211-13
Church, doctrine of the: 179-80
Cinamos, mystikos: 72
Constantius, hieromonk: 111
Cos: 73
Creation, doctrine of: 221-4
Cullmann, O.: 185, 189
Cydones, daughter of: 35
Cydones, Demetrios: 35, 57, 83, 85, 87, 101, 239
Cydones, Prochoros: 20, 112
Cyparissiotes: 101

Cyprian of Kiev: 25, 26
Cyprus: 101, 105
Cyril of Alexandria: 181-2, 230

Daniel of Cyzicus: 15
David, bogomil: 36
Deification: 175-8
Demonstration: 43-5
Dexios, Theodore: 57, 93, 94
Dhikz: 139-40
Diadochus of Photice: 140, 153
Didymotica: 65, 87
Diogenes Laertius: 3o
Dionysius the Areopagite, pseudo-: 42, 44, 61, 132-3, 151-2, 163, 169, 187-92, 199, 204-9, 218-19
Dishypatos, David: 51-2, 78, 81, 83
Dorotheos, monk: 51, 70
Dositheus of Jerusalem, 5
Duns Scotus: 202
Dushan, Stephen: 91-2, 94, 102, 112

Egypt: 140
Elias, hesychast: 25
Energies: 48, 55, 61, 96-8, 119, 167, 179, 202-27
Esphigmenou, monastery: 24, 41, 49
Eucharistic communion: 150-2, 159-61, 177
Euthymius of Trnovo: 26
Evagrius: 135-6, 139-41, 146-7, 152, 154, 156

Filioque: 13-17, 228-32

Gabriel, monk: 25
Galesiotes, George: 99
Gallipoli: 103
Gemisthos Plethon: 27
Genoa, Genoese: 81, 99, 229
George: 112
George, bogomil: 36
Gerace: 55
Gerasimos, hieromonk: 103
Gerasimus of Jerusalem: 74
Germanos II, patr.: 14
Glabas: 49
Glossia, hermitage: 33-4
Grace, doctrine of: 121-2, 162-7
Gregoras, Nicephorus: 20, 29, 30, 34, 36, 37, 39, 43, 53, 55, 57, 62, 78, 81, 84-5, 88, 93-101, 104, 108-11, 127, 188, 203, 204
Gregory, hesychast: 34
Gregory of Cyprus, patr.: 13-17, 19, 20, 25, 44, 229-30, 238
Gregory of Dyrrhachium: 60
Gregory of Nazianzus: 130, 230
Gregory of Nyssa: 30, 96, 133, 134, 135, 137-8, 146-9, 151, 157, 169, 172, 200
Gregory of Sardis: 60
Gregory of Sinai: 34, 35, 41, 46, 49, 51, 76, 78, 100, 139(16)

Harmenopoulos, Constantine: 82
Hausherr, I: 136
Heart: 147-8
Heraclea: 68-9, 77, 94
Hesiod: 130
Hierarchy, celestial: 189-91
Hierissos, bishop of: 49
Hodighitria ou Hodegoi, monastery: 77
Holy-Apostles, Church, 89
Homer: 30, 130
Hospitallers: 81, 229
Humanism: 27, 55, 238
Hyacinth of Corinth: 73
Hyacinth of Thessalonica: 71, 77, 78, 83, 84, 90

Ignatius, monk: 94
Ignatius of Antioch, patr.: 74, 94, 96-7
Incarnation: 149-56, 191-6, 208-10
Innocent VI, pope: 108
Irene, nun: 36
Isaac, bogomil: 36
Isaac, protos: 49, 68, 79
Isaac of Madyta: 6o, 82
Isaac of Nineveh: 143
Isaias, hesychast: 49
Isaris, George: 82
Isidore, Patr.: 34-7, 41, 46, 51 69-71, 73-4, 81, 82, 87-90, 93
Ismael, Orkhan's grandson: 105
Italos, John: 30
Ivanka, E. von: 226
Iviron, monastery: 40

Jaeger, W.: 136
Jews: 106-7
Job, bogomil: 36
Job, monk: 38
John XIII, patr.: 19(25)
John XIV Calecas, patr.: *see* Calecas
John Chrysostom, St.: 111
John of Damascus, St., 96
John of the Ladder, St.: 18, 140-1, 143, 143, 146, 150-1

INDEX

John V Palaeologus, emperor: 23-4 65, 76, 79-80, 86, 99, 102-3, 107-10
John Tzimisces, emperor: 32
Joseph, bogomil: 36
Joseph, hieromonk: 103
Joseph of Adrianople: 82
Joseph of Ganos: 88, 93, 94, 97, 101
Jugie, M.: 53, 226-7, 241
Julian the Apostate: 130
Justin, St. : 119
Justinian, emperor: 135

Karyes: 49
Kastoria: 112
Kern, K.: 142, 241
Khilandari, monastery, 49
Knowledge of God: 117ff., 127, 167-71, 185-6
Kokkinos: see Philothee, patr.
Koukounares, James: 36, 76, 82, 238
Krivocheine, V.: 241
Kurtos: see Mark
Kutlumus, monastery: 49

Lampsacus: 105
Lapithos, George: 43, 58, 72, 84-5
Lavra, monastery: 33, 38-41, 49, 90, 112
Lazarus, hegoumenos: 66, 68
Lazarus of Jerusalem, patr.: 74(48), 78, 86, 89
Leontius of Byzantium: 18l, 212
Lepentrinos: see Athanasius
Light, uncreated: 55, 173-5
Logoi of beings: 119
Lossky, V.: 202(l), 241
Lusignan: 101
Lyons, council of: 13, 228

Macarius, pseudo-: 136-40, 143, 145-8, 153, 171, 176, 217
Macarius of Philadelphia: 82
Macarius of Serres: 101
Macarius of Thessalonica: 66, 71, 77, 90
Macarius of Vidin: 60
Magistros: see Thomas
Magoula, hermitage: 34, 49
Malachy of Methymna: 60
Man, doctrine of: 137-45
Marica: 24
Mariology: 232-6
Mark, monk: 14, 16, 41
Mark Kurtos: 49, 51, 76, 81
Matarangos, Nicholas: 81
Matthew of Ephesus: 79, 88, 93, 94, 97, 101, 104, 238
Maurozumes: 105
Maxime Lascaris Calopheros (?): 99
Maximus, St.: 96, 121, 133, 135-6, 138-9, 148, 173-5, 178, 181, 189, 196-8, 211-13, 221
Melchisedek: 178
Messalians (Bogomils): 32-3, 35-7, 48, 56, 92, 136-7, 143, 152, 153, 161, 165-6, 173, 176, 183, 207
Metochites, Theodore: 27, 29-30
Metrophanes of Patras: 88
Michael VIII Palaeologus: 13, 63
Monasticism: 31-2, 33-5, 38, 198-201
Monemcasia: 59, 69-70, 73, 76, 82
Moses: 30, 106-7, 128, 134, 149, 174, 195-6, 200, 213
Moses, bogomil: 36

Neophytus of Philippi: 80, 88, 101
Nicaea: 105-6, 219
Nicephorus, the Hesychast: 18, 46, 139-40, 146-7
Nicholas, the Mystikos, patr.: 63
Nicodemus, hesychast: 26, 33
Nikodemus the Hagiorite, 5
Nilus, St.: 135-6, 147
Nilus, the Italian, 25-6
Nilus of Lacedemove: 60
Nilus of the Sora: 26
Niphon I, patr.: 19(25)
Niphon, protos: 92
Nymphaion: 14

Oikonomos, S.: 24,
Okham: 116, 117, 198, 237
Origen: 1135, 138, 149, 151, 156, 172, 223
Original sin: 122-6
Orkhan : 105, 108

Pachomius of Antioch: 97
Pachymeres: 17, 22, 26
Palaeologues: see Andronic II, Andronic III, John V, Michael VIII
Palaeologus, Constantine: 28
Palaeologus, John, despot: 17, 26, 67, 83
Palaeologus, a Great Domestic: 111
Palamas, Constantine: 28
Palamas, Epicharis: 32, 38
Palamas, Kale: 32, 38
Palamas, Macarius: 32, 33
Palamas, Theodosius: 32, 33
Palamas, Theodote: 32
Palestine: 21, 104, 140
Pantaenetos: 132
Papikion, mount: 32
Paroria, hermitage: 51-2, 78
Paul of Xanthia: 82
Paul, legate: 81, 108-10, 227
Pegae: 105
Pelagonia: 40

Petra, monastery: 40
Petrarch : 55
Phacrases, George: 109
Philolaos: 132
Philosophy, Greek: 29-31, 45, 116ff., 126, 128-33
Philotheou, monastery: 40
Philotheus, patr.:15, 17, 21, 23, 24, 28, 30, 32, 33, 34, 37, 38, 39, 41, 49, 67, 711, 78, 81, 89, 90, 91, 94 99-100, 103-5, 108, 109, 110, 111, 112, 153, 227
Philotheus of Selymbria: 43
Philoxenos: 132
Photius: 13, 27, 228-9
Plato: 29-30, 42, 43, 45, 116, 130, 132
Plotinus: 130, 133, 216
Porine: 36
Porphry: 30, 130
Poverty, monastic: 21-4, 26, 102
Prayer, hesychast method of: 18, 45-7, 55, 134, 139-48
Prilep: 40
Procession of the Holy Spirit: 13-17, 43
Provata, hermitage: 33
Psellos, Michael: 27

Redemption, doctrine of: 158ff.
Resurrection of the soul: 154-5
Rhodes: 81
Roger de Flor: 21
Romanides, J.: 116
Rumanians: 5
Russia, Russians: 5, 24, 26

Sabbas of Vatopedi: 66, 71, 87, 90, 104
Saint-Auxentius, Mount: 25-6, 33
Saint-Basil, monastery: 101
Saint-Hyacinth, monastery: 107
Saint-John-the-Baptist of Petra, monastery: 68
Saint-Michael of Sosthenion, monastery: 66-7
Saint-Sabbas, hermitage: 38-41, 43-5
Saint-Stephen, monastery: 89
Scholarios, Gennadios: 14, 240
Scot Erigena: 204
Scoutariotes : 69
Seliotes: 25
Seminaria: 42

Serbia, Serbs: 27, 38, 71, 91-2, 108
Sevcenko, I: 23
Skoplje: 91
Slavs: 5
Socrates: 130
Soul, immortality of: :123
Stanlioe, D.: 63(2), 241
Stiglmayr, J.: 136
Stoics: 118-19
Stoudios, monastery: 18
Syllogisms: 117
Symbolism: 185-91, 195-8
Symeon, nomophylax: 68
Symeon of Mesopotamia: 136
Symeon of Metaphrastes: 217
Symeon the New Theologian: 18, 155, 162
Symeon, pseudo-: 46, 139(16), 190, 147
Synergy: 164-6
Syria: 104

Tafrali, O.: 64
Taronites: 105-6
Tenedos: 103
Theoctistos Studite: 20(29)
Theodore the Blakhernite: 49
Theodore Studite: 18
Theodosius of Trnovo: 36, 200
Theognostos of Russia: 100
Theoleptus of Philadelphia: 15, 15 20, 25, 26, 32, 35, 39, 64, 83, 140
Thomas Aquinas: 6, 204
Thomas Magistros: 40, 82
Thrace: 32, 78
Trnovo: 100
Turks: 5, 22, 24, 26, 34, 36, 88, 91, 103-8, 113
Tzyrakes, daughter of: 35
Union of the churches: 47, 116
Urban V, pope: 81, 110, 229
Uspenskii, Th.: 53

Vatopedi, monastery: 26, 33, 49, 71
Venice: 99
Villecourt, Dom: 136
Virgin, monastery of the: 101

Western church: 110, 113

Zealots: 23, 77, 85, 89-93, 102-13